Development Connections

Development Connections

Unveiling the Impact of New Information Technologies

Alberto Chong, Editor

Inter-American Development Bank

palgrave
macmillan

DEVELOPMENT CONNECTIONS

First published in 2011 by
PALGRAVE MACMILLAN®
in the United States—a division of St. Martin's Press LLC,
175 Fifth Avenue, New York, NY 10010.

Where this book is distributed in the UK, Europe and the rest of the
world, this is by Palgrave Macmillan, a division of Macmillan Publishers
Limited, registered in England, company number 785998, of Houndmills,
Basingstoke, Hampshire RG21 6XS.

Palgrave Macmillan is the global academic imprint of the above companies
and has companies and representatives throughout the world.

Palgrave® and Macmillan® are registered trademarks in the United States,
the United Kingdom, Europe and other countries.

ISBN: 978-0-230-11194-3 (paperback)
ISBN: 978-0-230-11193-6 (hardback)

Library of Congress Cataloging-in-Publication Data is available from the
Library of Congress.

A catalogue record of the book is available from the British Library.

Design by Newgen Imaging Systems (P) Ltd., Chennai, India.

First edition: April 2011

10 9 8 7 6 5 4 3 2 1

Printed in the United States of America.

Contents

Contents

Boxes

Figures

Tables

Tables

Acknowledgments

Development in the Americas (DIA) is the flagship publication of the Inter-American Development Bank. This issue was produced under the direction of Alberto Chong, principal research economist of the Research Department. The general editor of the volume was Rita Funaro, publications coordinator of the Research Department, who was assisted by Nancy Morrison. The technical editor was Carlos Andrés Gómez-Peña, economics associate. Eduardo Lora, the chief economist (a.i.) and general manager of the Research Department, provided extremely valuable guidance and advice throughout the life of this project. Santiago Levy, the Vice-President for Sectors, provided overall support for the project.

The principal authors of each individual chapter are as follows:

Chapter 1	Alberto Chong
Chapter 2	Alison Cathles, Gustavo Crespi, and Matteo Grazzi
Chapter 3	Alberto Chong, Arturo Galindo, and Mauricio Pinzón
Chapter 4	Alberto Chong, Cecilia de Mendoza, and Gianmarco León
Chapter 5	Viviane Azevedo, César Bouillón, and Amanda Glassman
Chapter 6	Samuel Berlinski, Matías Busso, Julian Cristiá, and Eugenio Severín
Chapter 7	Beniamino Savonitto and Jeremy Shapiro
Chapter 8	Alberto Chong and Cecilia de Mendoza

xviii ACKNOWLEDGMENTS

Many researchers were involved in the preparation of the background papers employed as the basis for this report. In particular, Nava Ashraf (Harvard University), Ana Balsa (University of Miami), Samuel Berlinski (Inter-American Development Bank), Mariana Blanco (Universidad del Rosario), Matías Busso (Inter-American Development Bank), Adriana Camacho (Universidad de Los Andes), Paul Carrillo (George Washington University), Eric Chyn (University of Michigan, Ann Arbor), Emily Conover (Hamilton College), Julián Cristia (Inter-American Development Bank), Santiago Cueto (Grupo Análisis para el Desarrollo), Ana Dammert (Carleton University), Ana de la O (Yale University), Taryn Dinkelman (Princeton University), Erica Field (Harvard University), Jose Galdo (Carleton University), Virgilio Galdo (Syracuse University), Sebastián Galiani (Washington University), Dean Karlan (Yale University), Molly Lipscomb (University of Colorado, Boulder), Claudia Martínez (Universidad de Chile), Margaret McConnell (California Institute of Technology), Néstor Gandelman (Universidad ORT), Marco González-Navarro (University of California, Berkeley), Justine Hastings (Yale University), Laura Jaitman (University College, London), Rafael La Porta (Dartmouth College), Gianmarco León (University of California, Berkeley), Florencia López-Boo (Inter-American Development Bank), Florencio López-de-Silanes (EDHEC), Olivia Mitchell (University of Pennsylvania), Mushfiq Mobarak (Yale University), Ricardo Monge (Comisión Asesora de Alta Tecnología, Costa Rica), Santiago Montenegro (Asofondos), Sendhil Mullainathan (Harvard University), Alvaro Pedraza (University of Maryland, College Park), Allan Pineda (Alimentos Preferidos), Martín Rossi (Universidad Torcuato di Tella), Ana Santiago (Inter-American Development Bank), Andrei Shleifer (Harvard University), Máximo Torero (International Food Policy Research Institute), Sergio Urzúa (Northwestern University),

Martín Valdivia (Grupo Análisis para el Desarrollo), Juan Vargas (Universidad del Rosario), Mónica Yáñez (University of Illinois, Urbana Champaign), Patricia Yáñez (University of Wisconsin, Madison), Leonard Wantchekron (New York University), and Jonathan Zinman (Dartmouth College).

Several research assistants contributed to the preparation of the background papers, including Kartik Akileswaran, Tania Alfonso, Nicolás Bottan, David Bullon-Patton, Gisela Davico, Cesar del Pozo, Maribel Elías, Angela García-Vargas, Kareem Haggag, Tomoko Harigaya, Juan Manuel Hernández, Jocelyn Hospital, Daniel Kahn, Adam Kemmis Betty, Jordan Kyle, Kyla Levin-Russell, Steven Li, Laura Litvine, Fernando Martel García, Niccoló Meriggi, Mark Miller, Cesar Mora, Francisca Muller, Sara Nadel, Sarah Nutman, Alejandro Ortiz, Miguel Paredes, Doug Parkerson, Sebastian Pireto La Noire, Dylan Ramshaw, Martin Rotemberg, Daniel Tello, Hannah Trachtman, Rosa Vidarte, Talya Wyzanski, and Anna York,

The following individuals gave useful input to specific studies and earlier drafts of this volume: Rafael Anta, Edna Armendáriz, Manuel Armas Reaño, Eduardo Borensztein, Juan Borga, Ramón Casilda, Francesca Castellani, Elsa Chong, César Cristancho, José Cuesta, Suzanne Duryea, Oscar Farfán, Maria Lourdes Gallardo, Jaime García, Adrián Gerlati, Raquel Gómez, Sonia Goncalves, Carlos Guaipatín, Jorge Guillén, Fidel Jaramillo, Ernesto López-Córdova, Mila Huby, Sarah Humpage, Eirin Kallestad, Eliana La Ferrara, Alfonso Lostanau, Carlos Ludeña, Marlene Macedo, Elton Mancilla, Judith Mariscal, Luis Daniel Martínez, Eduardo Nakasone, Romina Nicaretta, Frank Nieder, Hugo Ñopo, Jose Joaquín Ocampo, Doris Olaya, Carmen Pagés, Flora Painter, Aminta Pérez-Gold, Claudia Piras, Olivier Poupaert, Andrew Powell, Patricia Rojas, Mario Sánchez, Mario Sanginés, Carlos Scartascini, Laura Schechter, Mariela Semidey, Claudia Suaznábar,

Gabriela Vega, Federico Volpino, Gustavo Villouta, Gustavo Yamada, and Luisa Zanforlin.

This book could not have been produced without the immense effort and dedication of the administrative team of the Research Department and, in particular, Patricia Aráuz, Carla Carpio, and Myriam Escobar.

The comments and opinions expressed in this publication are those of the coordinator of the project and the authors of the corresponding chapters and do not reflect the views of the Inter-American Development Bank or its executive directors in any form.

Contributors

Viviane Azevedo, a national of Brazil, received a Ph.D. in Economics from the University of Illinois at Urbana-Champaign and is a consultant in the Research Department of the Inter-American Development Bank.

Samuel Berlinski, a citizen of Argentina, received a Ph.D. in Economics at Oxford University and is a senior research economist in the Research Department of the Inter-American Development Bank.

Cesar Bouillón, a Peruvian citizen, received a Ph.D. in Economics from Georgetown University and is a research economist in the Research Department of the Inter-American Development Bank.

Matías Busso, a citizen of Argentina, received a Ph.D. in Economics from the University of Michigan at Ann Arbor. He is currently a research economist in the Research Department of the Inter-American Development Bank.

Alison Cathles, a citizen of the United States, received an MPA from Cornell University. She is a consultant in the Science and Technology Division of the Inter-American Development Bank.

Alberto Chong, a Canadian and Peruvian citizen, received a Ph.D. in Economics from Cornell University. He is principal research economist in the Research Department of the Inter-American Development Bank.

Gustavo Crespi, an Argentinean and Italian citizen, received a Ph.D. in Science and Technology Policy Studies from Sussex

University. He is lead specialist in the Science and Technology Division of the Inter-American Development Bank.

Julian Cristiá, a citizen of Argentina, received a Ph.D. in Economics from the University of Maryland at College Park. He is a research economist in the Research Department of the Inter-American Development Bank.

Arturo José Galindo, a citizen of Colombia, received a Ph.D. in Economics from the University of Illinois at Urbana-Champaign. He is currently the regional economic advisor (a.i.) for the Andean Country Group at the Inter-American Development Bank.

Amanda Glassman, a citizen of the United States, is director of the Global Health Policy Program at the Center for Global Development and holds an M.Sc. from the Harvard School of Public Health.

Matteo Grazzi, an Italian citizen, received a Ph.D. in International Law and Economics from Universitá Bocconi. He is an economist in the Science and Technology Division of the Inter-American Development Bank.

Gianmarco León, a Peruvian national, is a Ph.D. candidate in the department of agricultural and resource economics at the University of California, Berkeley.

Cecilia de Mendoza, a citizen of the United States and Argentina, received an M.A. in Economics from Universidad Torcuato di Tella and is a consultant in the Research Department of the Inter-American Development Bank.

Mauricio Pinzón, a Colombian citizen, received an M.A. in Economics from Universidad de los Andes. He is a research assistant for the Financial and Private Sector Development Vice-Presidency of The World Bank Group.

Beniamino Savonitto, an Italian national, received an M.A. degree from Johns Hopkins University and is currently project director at Innovations for Poverty Action.

Eugenio Severín, a Chilean citizen, holds an M.B.A. from Loyola College and a diploma in public policies in education from Universidad de Chile. He is a senior specialist in the Social Sectors Department of the Inter-American Development Bank

Jeremy Shapiro, a citizen of the United States, received a Ph.D. in Economics from MIT and is currently a post-doctoral researcher in the department of economics at Yale University.

Preface

In my frequent trips to Latin America and the Caribbean, I have been amazed to find how information and telecommunications technologies (ICTs) are touching nearly every aspect of people's lives, every day. From female peasants in rural Bolivia, to fishermen in northern Mexico, to postal workers in Barbados, to taxi drivers in urban Chile, to office workers in Nicaragua: these technologies have become indispensable for societies to function. Cell phone use in developing countries has more than doubled in less than five years, and nearly three out of four people who own cell phones live in emerging countries. The growth in the use and application of ICTs in Latin America and elsewhere has been quite remarkable, with no end in sight.

Such explosive growth has sparked great optimism among many commentators who believe that ICTs hold the key to limitless rapid growth and development in Latin America and the rest of the developing world. Although the usefulness of ICTs is undeniable, it is also true that for every action, there is a reaction. The Internet can be a source of never-ending useful information, but there are also inherent dangers to it. Better-informed rural peasants, who use cell phones to learn the prices of their products in cities, can negotiate better with middlemen. But cell phones can also be distracting. Computers provide wonderful opportunities for children, but maintaining appropriate hardware and software requires substantial resources. While the promise is clearly there, virtually no systematic or solid empirical assessments exist on the mechanisms and impact of ICTs on the welfare of people in such basic areas as education, health, institution building, finance, and the environment. Are all these technologies equally useful? Should countries in our region prioritize some specific use or approach? What are the conditions under which ICTs can have a positive impact in Latin America and the Caribbean? How can the private and public sectors team up to optimize the impact of ICTs?

To help answer these questions, and to ascertain the impacts of ICTs for better or worse on the societies in our region, the Inter-American Development Bank dedicated this year's issue of its flagship publication, *Development in the Americas*, to study a number of specific initiatives related to ICTs. These initiatives illustrate a broad range of diverse applications in most countries of our region, and have been carried out with the collaboration of the private sector, nongovernmental agencies, and academia. The authors then painstakingly assembled detailed empirical information designed to evaluate each of these initiatives. The picture that emerges is one in which not all ICT tools are created equal. Some applications, such as finance and health-related tools, have had immediate and significant positive impact on the lives of people in our region. Others, such as those applied to environmental matters, have not had the same positive impact. The causes of this unevenness in the impact of ICTs on the welfare of the population can be traced to several reasons, but can probably be summarized by one idea: ICTs cannot do it all. ICTs are tools that help deliver solutions; they are not the solutions themselves. The promise is still there, and targeted and complementary investments can make the most of that promise. This book discusses some directions to be taken—and some to avoid.

It is with great pleasure that I present this book to policymakers, entrepreneurs, academics, and all those interested in our region. It is my hope that with the lessons provided in this volume, together we can tap the potential of ICT and forge *Development Connections* that help propel our region's economic and social progress.

Luis Alberto Moreno
President, Inter-American
Development Bank

A Field of Dreams or a Dream Come True?

If You Build It, He Will Come

In the well-known novel *Shoeless Joe* (Kinsella, 1982), inspiration for the movie *Field of Dreams*, the main character, Ray, is obsessed with a voice that tells him that if he builds a baseball field in the midst of a corn field in Iowa where he lives, his hero will appear. Ray steadfastly follows the voice, and eventually the field becomes a sort of conduit to the ghosts of legendary baseball greats, who show up in his field to play ball. At some level, the expansion of information and communication technologies (ICT) is analogous to the behavior of Kinsella's main character.[1] For developing countries in particular, the implicit view has been that as long as countries adopt these technologies, their societies will be quickly rewarded in terms of both higher productivity and improved welfare.

Not without reason, the expectations assigned to these new technologies have been sky-high. ICTs have brought truly new and innovative possibilities to developing countries. To cite just a few far-flung examples: in Argentina, the citizens of La Plata can directly participate in the public projects pursued by the local government; in Peru, poor peasants in Cajamarca can use the Internet to improve health treatment; in Colombia, coffee workers in rural areas can receive and make electronic payments; in

Paraguay, the transparency of national elections can be easily monitored using cell phones and the Internet; in Mexico, firms use web-based tools to encourage people to recycle; in Bolivia, individuals receive text messages to remind them to save money; in Haiti, following the 2010 earthquake, rescuers relied on ICTs to conduct help and recovery operations. In the last twenty years, the penetration of mobile phones has expanded more quickly in developing countries than in developed ones at a rate that is nothing short of remarkable. Similarly, the per capita growth rates of users of the Internet have been higher in developing countries than in developed ones. It took about 100 years for the telephone to reach a critical mass of people around the world, and about 50 years for the television to reach that point, but it has taken only 15 years for the mobile phone and the Internet to reach a critical mass of users (Kenny, 2006). However, for all the instant access to far-flung markets, political empowerment, virtual health diagnosis, and other enhancements, it is unclear whether ICTs have been able to deliver actual economic development to Latin America and elsewhere. The available evidence has been based mostly on anecdotal cases that describe success stories but provide very little solid empirical evidence on the link between ICT and purported related gains in productivity and welfare. While evidence of this link is minimal at both the macroeconomic and microeconomic levels, it is particularly scarce in the case of the latter.[2]

The Genie in Aladdin's Lamp?

There are compelling reasons to expect significant economic development from the adoption of ICTs. The most obvious way in which these technologies can help achieve economic improvements is by improving the quantity and quality of information available: or, more precisely, in economic terms, to reduce asymmetric and imperfect information in markets. This can help tasks related to search and coordination, which in turn may increase market efficiency. Individuals and firms can use ICTs to search for prices of products, look for jobs, find potential buyers of products, get ready for weather and natural disasters, connect with colleagues, and remain connected with friends and family (Aker and Mbiti, 2010).

Furthermore, some argue, the most recent ICTs enable a country to leapfrog development stages. They allow multiple agents to transmit and share information immediately, without the physical movement of information or individuals. Put more abstractly, ICTs enable information to be decoupled from other factors that were previously embedded together (Evans and Wurster, 1997). Unlike typical technological innovations in the past, ICT also increases the knowledge content of products and services and introduces previously unknown products, jobs, and livelihoods, among others (Torero and von Braun, 2006). As a result of these network externalities, ICTs have the ability to help create entirely new industries and, as a consequence, to create jobs that are directly and indirectly linked to these new industries. For instance, the mobile phone sector has spawned a wide variety of business and entrepreneurship opportunities, many in the informal sector. Several of these new jobs are directly linked to the mobile phone growth strategy of firms. Many mobile phone companies, for example, have partnered with formal and informal shops throughout Latin America and the Caribbean to sell prepaid phone cards in small denominations (Aker and Mbiti, 2010). Finally, ICTs play a role in the development of public policies by augmenting the range of possibilities and the manner in which policies can be implemented. For instance, policies to alleviate poverty can be much better targeted with ICT tools, producing less waste, more efficiency, and higher returns (see Chapter 8).

Similarly, policies that focus on women can be much more effective using these new technologies.

Although ICTs are promising, these technologies may not be the silver bullet that some policymakers believe them to be. First, it is difficult to provide networked services in areas where population densities are low, such as rural areas and small towns—where a considerable share of the Latin American population lives. Problems related to the cost and complexity of physical access to ICTs are not even the most significant barriers to their greater utilization (Kenny, 2006). Lack of human capital is an equal or more relevant problem. Illiteracy poses a major problem for ICT-related technologies, particularly the Internet.

Language barriers also pose a problem. A large share of the population in Latin America, and most of its poor, cannot read, much less write, in English, the language of the Internet.[3] (For many Latin Americans living in rural areas, their first language is a minority language such as Quechua or Aymara, not even Spanish, Portuguese, or French.)

Moreover, a large percentage of people in Latin America and the Caribbean eke out a subsistence living and hence are less reliant on market transactions; for them, it is doubtful that the utility of ICTs will be particularly significant. Finally, institutional barriers, such as laws and regulations, also play an important role in the development of ICT applications in the region and are difficult to adjust.

While it is crucial to keep in mind the limitations of ICT, it is equally important to understand that even within particular ICTs, not all applications and technologies are created equal. Some have proven more useful than others and have had a greater impact in the short run. Along with the "old" ICTs such as radio and television, "new" ICTs such as mobile technology have proven to be extremely valuable to societies in developing countries, regardless of the area of application.

Taking Everything into Account

This book takes an agnostic view of the possible link between ICTs and their economic impact, as seen from the point of view of individuals, and focuses instead on applying rigorous research methods to study the issue. In evaluating the impact of ICTs—in Latin America and the Caribbean and elsewhere—a critical problem has been the lack of reliable data that may allow the specific role of a particular ICT tool to be isolated. While some advances in data collection have been made in recent years, as illustrated in chapter 2, this central issue persists for the most part. A solid understanding of what ICTs are able to achieve cannot rely on unproven success stories that sometimes end up being not so successful after all, as they are quite costly and carelessly widespread (Kenny, 2006). Indeed, projects with ICT-related components have been widely supported by multilateral organizations, bilateral aid agencies, and nongovernmental organizations (NGOs)—without rigorous evaluation of their impact.

A simple way of illustrating a proper assessment of the extraordinary potential that ICT can have in contributing to economic development is by comparing new ICT tools and applications with the world's first two-way ICT: the postal service. Chong and others (2010) carried out a simple exercise by mailing 347 letters from the United States to nonexistent addresses in 107 countries around the world and measuring how long it took for the letters to be returned to the sender, as well as the percentage of the letters that were returned within 90 days of being mailed (see figures 1.1 and 1.2). They found that the success rate of sending three letters to any particular country in Latin America and the Caribbean was highest in countries such as Argentina, Belize, Bolivia, Chile, Colombia, Costa Rica, Ecuador, El Salvador, Mexico, and Paraguay, while it was lowest in countries such as Honduras, Nicaragua, and

Panama. On average, it took the postal service nearly 76 days to return the letters to the sender, ranging from 33 days in the case of Ecuador to 196 in the case of Venezuela, excluding the countries whose postal services did not return the letters to the sender. Somewhat unsurprisingly, the study found that there was a strong correlation between the level of development of the country and the efficiency of the postal service.

In this context, the potential of new ICT tools is clear. In the case of both mobile phones and e-mail, the equivalent success rate would be 100 percent. Similarly, the equivalent rate would be

Figure 1.1   Efficiency of the Postal Service: Percentage of Letters that Were Returned within 90 Days of Being Mailed

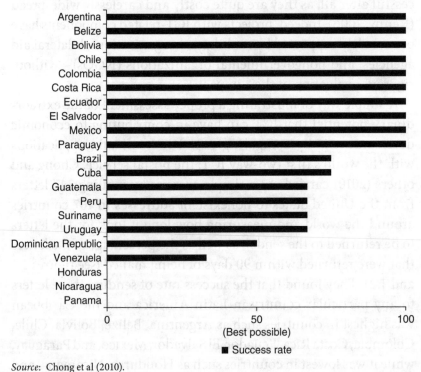

Source: Chong et al (2010).

Figure 1.2   The Case of Traditional ICT: Return to Sender Postal Service (in days)

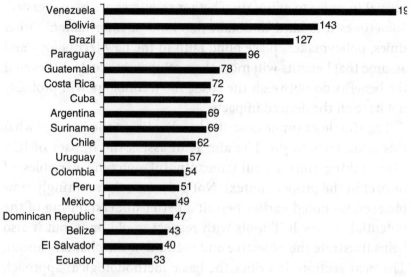

Source: Chong et al (2010).

measured not in days, but in minutes. More importantly, the level of development of the country is not associated with the efficiency of the ICT tool: that is, this technology is actually leapfrogging a development stage. The case for new ICTs is seemingly straightforward. Or is it?

To better assess the potential contribution of ICTs to development, two additional factors must be considered. The first is the institutional structure that makes it possible for the technology to work. The second is the costs and benefits of employing the new technology in relation to the old one. Thus, in the case of this simple example, one would have to consider the fixed costs of installing the new technology and related networks, as well as factor in the cost of first-class international mail delivery—US$0.98

in relation to the cost of the electronic transmission of information, including the cost of maintenance. Proper evaluations are crucial in order to ascertain whether resources are being wasted. Sometimes it is hard to obtain this kind of information. Other times, policymakers place blind faith in the new technology and assume that benefits will more than compensate costs. Yet even if the benefits do outweigh the costs, the technology will probably not have all the desired impacts.

The simple example described earlier lies at the heart of what this book tries to do. The aim is to assess the impact of ICT when taking into account meaningful outcome variables of impact in the proper context. Not only does the seemingly simple exercise noted earlier permit a better understanding of the potential of new ICT tools with respect to old ones, but it also helps illustrate the objective and method of the chapters ahead. The next section describes the basic methodological approach of this book.

The Cost of a Streetlight

A well-known joke in economics tells the tale of a drunk on his way home from a bar one night. He realizes that he has dropped his keys and gets down on his hands and knees and starts groping around beneath a streetlight. A policeman asks what he is doing. "I lost my keys a block ago," says the drunk. "Then why are you looking for them under the streetlight?" asks the policeman. "Because," the drunk says, "that is where the light is."

This joke illustrates the fact that data in economics are scarce: there are many dark patches where the light of investigation cannot shine. Data are even scarcer in the case of development economics. The lack of adequate data to better understand basic problems in development economics has been a recurring problem for decades.

This book avoids this problem by "installing a new streetlight." It relies on a large set of field experiments—actual projects that were tested in the field—in several countries in Latin America and the Caribbean. It focuses on randomized experiments: that is, experiments in which the members of treatment groups and control groups are randomly assigned to those groups. Pure random assignment guarantees that, similar to medical trials, the treatment and control groups will tend to have identical characteristics (Bruhn and McKenzie, 2009). Randomized experiments are increasingly used in formal empirical research in development economics. This relatively novel approach in empirical research in the social sciences helps shed light on topics that went previously unexamined, as data were inexistent. Randomized controlled trials (RCTs) allow researchers to uncover new data and thus provide new and novel approaches to study a broad array of applications. In short, randomized experiments allow researchers to avoid having to do empirical research only where there is light. The issue then becomes the cost of the streetlight. Some argue that RCTs are expensive. They are. However, the question is not how much a field experiment costs but, as argued earlier, the returns to the investment. Viewed this way—the correct way—there is no question that field experiments are worth their value. After all, the private sector has been using them extensively and today, perhaps, more than ever.

From Red Lobster to Field Experiments

It might be argued that randomized trials, as nice as they are, have little practical use in the real world. But the private sector is already using them widely—and with good results. Capital One has become the world's largest credit card issuer over the past twenty years, for example, largely because of the aggressive use of experimental methods (Pearlstein, 2010). The firm developed an elaborate system for constantly testing the success of new products and marketing pitches with customers in every region of the United States. ICTs have accelerated the spread of randomized testing to other industries and firms, such as Google, Amazon, and eBay, which frequently run real-time trials, and TD Bank from Canada, which insists that some kind of experiment be used in every major initiative.

Other firms use special software to run their own randomized tests (Pearlstein, 2010). By mining the wealth of data already in a company's computer, such software makes it possible to test the impact of a new product or tactic by comparing the outcomes against those of a "placebo" control group. Red Lobster, for example, used such software to test nine remodeling schemes for its restaurants, mixing and matching low-, medium-, and high-cost options for interior and exterior designs. The winning combination boosted sales by 8 percent, with an ICT investment that was worth $200 million. Similarly, Kraft can now predict what products will do well in what markets among which consumers, broken down by the size of the store, the time of the year, and the type of packaging and promotion. Family Dollar Stores used randomized trials before installing refrigeration units in its 6,800 outlets that, up to that point, had sold only dry goods. Based on a small test of only a few dozen stores, it found that the impact was far greater than the sales gains from milk, eggs, and frozen pizza. The bigger impact on profit came from increased volume in its traditional dry goods (Pearlstein, 2010).

The reason why the private sector is so keen on field experiments is the same reason why academics and policymakers have become so interested in them. Field experiments—and, in particular, RCTs—allow researchers to identify whether the change in one parameter has an impact on an outcome variable. That is, they are able to provide evidence on the direction of causation between two variables. As simple as this may sound, it has been a persistent problem in business and academic research for decades, as correlation is not equivalent to causation—a difference that may have deep strategic and policy implications.

Another reason why RCTs are becoming such a widespread method of testing is that they help identify the specific variable that may have caused the particular result under investigation. RCTs help to disentangle a particular outcome from the various factors that may have caused it. Thus, the method can have many uses in policy-relevant applications. For example, in education, RCTs can be focused to better understand computers in schools programs and, in particular, the impact on rural areas and the poor. With respect to health, relevant and serious impact evaluations can be conducted on e-diagnostics, health education, and electronic medical records. In finance—an area in which RCTs have been more broadly applied—efforts to use text messages to remind people to save can be tested, for instance. In the area of the environment, ICT-information-based campaigns to recycle can be evaluated. With respect to building institutions, steps to monitor voting can be tested, and the role of voting monitoring to sustain democracies and minimize corruption can be determined more precisely.

Why Bother with Lifeboats If Everyone Can't Fit In?

This book takes a microeconomic approach and focuses on a group of ICT-related projects in Latin America. Dozens of ICT-related initiatives are currently under way in the region. It is virtually impossible to evaluate them all. This, however, does not mean that an effort should not be made to assess the impact of some of them.

In this microeconomic exercise, this book tries to assess the impact of select ICT tools for specific policy-relevant cases. While the studies in this book review formal empirical evidence produced in recent years both in Latin America and elsewhere, they place a great deal of importance on producing new evidence on the role of ICT on development in the region. The reasons are straightforward.

First, there is almost no evidence on the role of ICTs on socio-economic outcomes in developing areas, and even less for Latin America and the Caribbean. Second, most of the existing evidence is biased toward finding positive results. As Ravallion (2008, p. 26) explains, "It is often difficult to publish an academic paper that reports unexpected, negative, or ambiguous impacts, when judged against current theories and/or past evidence. The prior belief is that the project will have positive impacts, for that is presumably the main reason why the project was funded in the first place. Then a bias toward confirming prior beliefs will mean that our knowledge is biased in favor of finding positive impacts." It is easy to confirm that negative impacts or no impacts will barely get reported in published papers in academic journals. Ravallion continues by arguing that "researchers will tend to work harder to obtain positive findings, or at least results consistent with received wisdom, so as to improve their chances of getting their work published. If one collects 20 indicators, then there is a good chance that at least one of them will show statistically significant impacts of the project even when it had no impact in reality. A researcher keen to get published might be tempted to report results solely for the significant indicator" (2008, p. 27).

In addition to a comprehensive review of the literature, this book tries to avoid the potential bias described by Ravallion by selecting ICT-related projects based on how frequently they have been cited in the main newspapers in most countries in Latin America. A list of the most common types of ICT-related initiatives in the region was compiled and ranked, taking into consideration geographic diversity, sectoral diversity, and to some extent, the innovativeness of the project. Forty-six were selected. Some of them are government-sponsored initiatives that were about to begin; others are projects designed and implemented specifically for this effort; others are the result of direct partnerships with NGOs in different countries; and still others result from partnerships with specialized not-for-profit institutions, academics, and universities. Most of the projects—forty-one of them—were initially conceived as experimental exercises (mostly RCTs) or quasi-experimental exercises. The rest employed traditional econometric methods.

Clearly, this is not a book about ICT innovations per se, but one about the application of innovations to development and whether they work. In a field in which there has been almost no serious research on the topic, this is the most sensible approach.

Figure 1.3 shows the distribution by sector of the RCTs selected for investigation. About 18 percent of the projects are on topics related to education. These projects range from evaluating national programs such as the well-known "one laptop per child" initiative in rural areas in Peru, to the use of special software to help educate handicapped children in Ecuador, to the use of webcams to monitor the performance of children in the classroom in Lima. Another 20 percent of the projects focus on institutions; they range from the use of text messages to help formally register people displaced by the war in Colombia, to a natural experiment[4] in Bolivia that measures the productivity increase in the public sector when ICT elements are introduced. Another 18 percent are health-related projects that contain an ICT element. They range from the use of web-based tools to educate teenagers on sexual education issues in Bogota, to the use of the Internet to give incentives to individuals so they can commit to making healthy choices in terms of smoking, weight, and exercise. About 14 percent of the

Figure 1.3   Distribution of Randomized Controlled Trials with ICT Components (Percent)

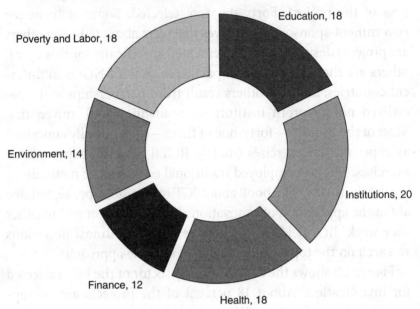

Source: Authors' calucations.

projects have an environmental component. These projects range from a comparison of old and new methods of ICT diffusion to teach people to recycle garbage and refuse materials in Mexico, to the use of ICT to study environmental degradation in Brazil. Another 18 percent of the initiatives are related to firms and labor. The projects range from the use of mobile phones to learn about prices in Honduras and Colombia, to using ICT methods in order to track the production cycle of cow herds in Argentina. Finally, the remaining 12 percent of projects are initiatives linked with finance. They include the use of text messages to encourage people to save, as well as the development of innovative devices to encourage electronic banking.

Although the forty-one studies represent the original universe of RCTs, some of the initiatives could not be fully pursued for reasons that went beyond the control of the corresponding researchers in charge. Five projects had to be discarded altogether. While this experience highlights the difficulty in designing and implementing field experiments, it only reaffirms the importance of doing them—as valuable lessons were learned from each of the failed trials. In one case, for example, despite the interest of all parties in pursuing the initiative, and after many attempts, it was not possible to include the desired number of participants because they lacked the minimum computer-related capabilities to benefit from the program. As this book illustrates repeatedly, complementarities between ICT tools and other forms of capital (in this case, human capital) are critical.

Nearly 90 percent of the studies were successfully completed. Table 1.1 presents a breakdown by sector of the success rate of the RCTs undertaken. Overall, nearly 39 percent of the field experiments that were conducted strongly benefitted from having an ICT component.

Nearly 60 percent of the field experiments that had a component related to finance, and 57 percent of those with a labor and poverty component strongly benefitted from ICT tools. Not so in the case of education and environment, where the strong positive impact of ICT tools is less clear. Furthermore, there was no significant link between ICT applications and sectoral economic outcomes in nearly 22 percent of the initiatives.

Sectoral Policies for ICT

A clear policy implication emerges from these findings. With adequate economic policies in place, governments can take great advantage of ICT tools for development. ICT helps address market failures caused by problems of coordination and asymmetric

Table 1.1   Randomized Controlled Trials (RCT) and Sectoral Impact

Percent

	Strong ICT Link	Partial ICT Link	Minimal Link
Finance	60	40	0
Institutions	50	38	13
Health	38	38	25
Education	14	57	29
Environment	17	33	50
Poverty and Labor	57	29	14
Overall	39	39	22

Source: Authors' calculations.

information. The great risk of ICT tools is expecting too much of them. While not exhaustive, this book focuses on the basic areas in which ICT applications have been most commonly applied or may be vitally important for the design of some public policy in the region. One of the key conclusions of this study is that ICT, while potentially very useful, is not a silver bullet. Policymakers may have set expectations too high—to the point that when ICTs fail to live up to these expectations they, either alone or pressured by disenchanted constituencies, may ignore the potential these tools have to change lives and eventually lose interest in them as a development tool.

A Way to Increase Financial Inclusion

As financial sectors develop, financial inclusion increases and income inequality diminishes. Despite the benefits of establishing links with the financial system, very few households in the developing world use such links. On average, only 35 percent of Latin American and Caribbean households have a bank account—a low percentage compared to advanced economies, where no less than 90 percent of the population has this type of link with the financial system. Expanding access to financial services to cover a larger population is costly. Most of the activities performed by financial institutions have traditionally been carried out though their branches. However, branching in places where the population is scant or where geographic or security conditions are difficult can be so costly that the benefit of including new people in the business of the institution is outweighed by its cost. Here is where technology can play a crucial role. ICTs can decisively reduce the cost of expanding financial services and spread the benefits of financial inclusion, particularly among the poorest.

Households can enjoy access to financial services through several types of technological improvements. The development of the Internet has allowed many households across the world to exploit the benefits of online banking, such as paying utilities or transferring money. The possibility of banking through cellular phones is a popular and expanding avenue in the financial world. It can help diminish financial exclusion by offering services to low-income groups that have access to mobile telephones but not to financial services. ICTs can also be a useful tool to provide information to help people make better financial decisions. For example, financial literacy campaigns can be delivered with the help of ICTs, as well as reminders to individuals to save more money and thus to achieve their savings goals. Governments can also take advantage of the improvements in technology by finding new ways to design subsidy schemes for the poor. Such government-backed efforts can help the poor overcome traditional barriers to access the financial system. Beyond national boundaries, ICTs allow relatives living abroad to remit money home in a faster and cheaper way, improving the well-being of recipient households.

In spite of the enormous benefits associated with these new financial technologies, up to now, Latin America and the Caribbean have lagged well behind the rest of the developing world. There still is a long way to go before the poorest households in Latin America will be able to afford a computer and Internet service of their own. In terms of regulation, even though nothing outright forbids the provision of these new types of financial services, there are regulatory barriers that affect the way mobile banking services are provided. One of the major issues associated with potential partners is the difficulty in defining a sustainable business model around small payments, uncertainties related to countries' regulatory frameworks, and the need for sufficiently reliable nonbank correspondents. Nonetheless, many pilot projects have taken off in the region with an eye on achieving what Asian and African countries accomplished some years ago in terms of electronic financial transactions. Latin America and the Caribbean have the advantage of being able to take stock of the lessons learned.

Benefits to Institutions

Countries with lower institutional quality are more likely to have slower economic growth, higher economic inequality, more social conflicts, and fewer and lower-quality government services. The level of institutional development in many Latin American and Caribbean countries is similar to the world average. However, compared to developed countries, the region lags far behind in terms of institutional and governance indicators. A large body of evidence points to the need for the countries of the region to adopt policies aimed at improving institutional development. Different experiences around the world have proved that ICTs can be useful in improving the quality of institutions. For the special case of Latin America, recent evidence shows that ICTs are becoming an effective instrument not only to improve the efficiency of the public sector, but also to help the population hold the government more accountable.

One of the main outcomes of the ICT revolution is the faster and more transparent diffusion of information. In the political sphere, information dissemination has the power to affect political behavior and voting decisions—no minor issue considering the fact that a more informed and politically active electorate increases the incentives of the government to be responsive. New channels of information can also affect the way people perceive their societies and adapt their own behavior. This has important policy implications, especially for developing countries. In societies where literacy is relatively low and newspaper circulation is limited, new forms of communication can play a crucial role in circulating ideas. Policymakers can use this channel to transmit important social and economic messages. Thus, ICTs may be employed as a public policy tool.

The Health Potential Is There

Individuals and government alike want their health services to provide care that is patient-centered, available, accessible, safe, reliable, effective, and equitable. The application of ICT tools in the area of health care shows high potential to improve health care provision, cost-effectiveness, and health outcomes in the region. In most countries, however, it is still in its infancy. Scaling up such tools will require significant increases in human resources, hardware and software, and infrastructure. It is probably neither cost-effective nor feasible at this stage for Latin America and other developing countries to replicate the solutions of developed countries. The region needs to adapt solutions according to each country's health priorities, the development of the health system, and existing national ICT infrastructure.

One of the priorities for the region at this stage is piloting and implementing more comprehensive ICT-related health interventions for chronic care. Telemedicine has been implemented with relative success and seems to be a promising intervention to reduce costs and improve care of patients in isolated areas.

The next stage in ICT innovation for many of the health systems in the region involves implementing electronic medical records. This will allow health systems to take advantage of the full benefits of other health innovations such as systems to monitor and track patients with chronic conditions, telemedicine, and ICT epidemiological surveillance systems. Carefully evaluating and disseminating the results of the pioneering experiences in the region is key for replicating the successful experiences and learning from mistakes.

Even though e-health, in general, is perceived to be a key cost-effective innovation to enhance the performance of the health system, its implementation has been slow even in developed countries. The limited adoption of ICT by health care providers, especially hospitals and insurers in the United States, can be explained by a confluence of factors: lack of demonstrated cost-effectiveness of ICT for specific providers because of the underlying fragmented structure of health provision and financing; the high financial risk of adopting new technologies; the costs and difficulty of the behavioral change needed for technology adoption; the temporary efficiency losses and potential medical errors during the transition; and the significant legal issues concerning adoption, such as licensure, liability, malpractice, confidentiality, and compliance with insurance. These concerns highlight the important role of the government to pilot and be an early implementer of many of these innovations, following strict evidence-based criteria.

Many countries of the region have not yet overcome basic problems in their health sectors. Even though a serious assessment of the costs and benefits of many health innovations must be undertaken, many of them may absorb too many resources compared to the current amount spent on health in the region. The risk is that these innovations—especially those that involve network effects—may be less effective when implemented in fragmented systems that already suffer from coverage, equity, provision, and financing problems. Thus, policymakers should balance gradual implementation of health innovations with continued reform of the overall sector in order to ensure that the full benefits of these innovations are realized.

An Educational Fad?

The last few years have witnessed a flurry of high-quality research on the impacts of ICT in education. Yet significant uncertainties still surround these interventions, especially in the case of highly visible initiatives, such as one laptop per child. ICT in education can be costly and may crowd out important alternative programs with significant returns. Given their irreversible nature due to the high initial costs, the unknowns regarding their impacts, and the limited capacity of governments to manage these complex interventions, it seems reasonable to proceed gradually with initiatives. Taking baby steps rather than leaps and bounds, planners can learn from experience, evaluate the impacts generated, and change decisions based on new information.

The studies in this book show that increasing access to computers in schools by itself has low returns, at best. Complementary inputs are critical, including the proper hardware, software, electricity, teacher training, and technical and pedagogical support. However, over and over, countries tend to put all their eggs in one single basket by simply providing computers. Budgeting for all the complementary inputs needed would minimize the waste of resources—and, crucially, provide a golden opportunity to improve the quality of education.

Furthermore, certain uses of ICT can yield large positive results. Hence, it seems reasonable for governments to channel limited computer access to these more promising uses. In particular, providing one or two hours a week of ICT training to students seems optimal, given the evidence regarding the large impacts of this training on ICT skills and the wage premium that workers with these skills may eventually receive in the labor market. Also, computer-assisted instruction has been shown to have significant potential to accelerate learning in math—a remarkable outcome, given the low level of achievement in this area within the region. In areas such as math and language, in programs where computers can be used to support teaching practices, teacher training plays a critical role, in addition to the use of computer-assisted instruction. Hence, carefully planning the component and allowing sufficient funds to support the needed complementarities, such as teacher training, should be prioritized.

While research has demonstrated mostly null effects of computer access at school on educational achievement, recent research has shown that increased computer access at home can have *negative* consequences. Studies have also shown that these negative effects are concentrated among students with weaker adult supervision. Interventions aimed at increasing access at home should take these considerations seriously into account to implement mechanisms to ensure proper use. In particular, computers could be loaded with interactive educational software and certain competitions can be launched to stimulate their use. Also, violent and sexual content should be blocked.

Love Is Not in the Air

ICTs can improve environmental behaviors, environmental policy, or the environment itself by influencing individuals to undertake environmentally friendly actions, aggregating information necessary for more intelligent policy (such as climate monitoring), or directly reducing resource consumption and environmental degradation. This book reviews each of these channels, with a focus on both the ways in which ICTs impact the environment and the existing evidence quantifying this impact.

A variety of studies seek to quantify the impact of environmentally friendly consumption made possible by ICT, such as replacing paper communication with e-mail. These benefits, however, must be weighed against the environmental costs of ICTs, in particular, electricity consumption and the disposal of electronic waste. Studies of isolated technologies help quantify the potential of ICTs to directly mitigate environmental concerns, but research is needed to understand these tradeoffs, particularly at an aggregate level.

Similarly, clear evidence is scarce concerning the impact of the creation and aggregation of ICT-enabled information on environmental policy, the actions of firms or other agents, or environmental outcomes. At a national and regional level, considerable resources have been invested in developing monitoring systems that use ICTs, primarily to track climate change, deforestation, and wildlife, and to assist in natural disasters. The task of rigorously evaluating the environmental consequences of this investment using statistical approaches is formidable. The task may be better met with careful documentation and analysis of the spread and uses of information generated by these systems.

At a micro level, ICT-generated information may also be useful in solving localized environmental challenges. Understanding whether these efforts result in the solution or mitigation of localized issues will be important to policymakers concerned with environmental issues and to officials tasked with the aggregation of local environmental information.

The results from several recent RCTs designed to test the effectiveness of ICT information campaigns in inspiring pro-environmental behaviors offer little evidence on the effectiveness of this strategy. Similarly, using the Internet to engage individuals in actions to reduce their environmental footprint does not appear to be a viable strategy, either because of the ineffectiveness of this medium or the still-limited extent of Internet access in many parts of Latin America.

Therefore, the use of ICTs to enable behavioral change must take a more direct role. Innovative uses of ICTs to influence individuals' choices, such as smart chip technology, which can make it easier to repay loans to buy natural gas vehicles, are emerging and represent a promising development.

National actors may be able to boost the environmental impact of ICTs by adopting policies that encourage individuals and firms to adopt technologies that have a proven net-positive environmental impact. In addition, governments should consider leveraging ICTs to create more efficient information aggregation and communication systems, which can facilitate more rapid and efficient responses to natural disasters and other environmental developments.

If Not a Silver Bullet, Then What to Do?

Be sensible and recognize that ICTs are not an end. Although Latin America and the Caribbean still lag in terms of overall ICT penetration, policymakers are tempted to "load up" on ICT-related hardware and software, with the stated objective of catching up to reduce the digital divide. This book shows that this is the wrong policy. ICTs are a means to an end—not the opposite. Policies must be sensible and consonant with the realities of the national landscape. Policymakers should beware of fads, internalize cost–benefit considerations, and, in particular, consider opportunity costs. Newer does not mean best.

Be aware that complementarities are essential. ICTs do not arise and spread in a vacuum. The quality of institutions and regulations, the skills of the population, and the physical infrastructure are all crucial to the success of ICT applications. In short, ICT technology does not replace the nuts and bolts of everyday life; it complements them.

Define policy goals in terms of use, not access. Policy goals are potent conduits for prioritizing and using resources. Hence, they should be defined so as to achieve certain milestones that are expected to generate positive impacts. The evidence reviewed in this book shows that access by itself does not generate impact, but that certain types of use do. Therefore, it seems reasonable that countries should aim to attain goals defined in terms of achieving certain measures (and types) of use rather than in extending mere access.

Foster cooperation to develop public goods. The interest in using ICT in different sectors is growing among countries in the region. There are important ways in which countries can cooperate to increase their chances of success. To do so, they should channel resources to activities that generate benefits for all (public goods), either through their own domestic spending or by pooling resources internationally. The first of such activities is the implementation of large-scale rigorous evaluations. These evaluations generate significant benefits for all countries in the region, as they produce evidence about what works and how to improve effectiveness. However, such evaluations are costly and can carry political risks, as some of their results may not be what was expected. Countries (and international donors) must be able to absorb bad news (negative or null results) and adjust programs or activities accordingly.

Explore private-public partnerships. Private firms, especially those producing mass-market goods, are striving to make the most of ICTs in the developing world in both urban and rural areas. They are exploring countless innovative ICT applications that range from product placement on Internet-based soap operas to Internet boats that bring web connectivity to one port a day. For different reasons, multilateral institutions and the public sector have the same interests. This perfect storm provides a unique opportunity for potentially fruitful collaboration.

Encourage large-scale projects to increase relative returns on investments. Producing computer software, say, to translate from Spanish to Quechua, requires significant fixed costs that are spread over the number of computers that will use it. In small programs, producing specialized software is economically unfeasible. But as programs expand, the returns to investing in software increase dramatically. For example, for a laptop program that has distributed 1 million computers in a country, it makes perfect sense to spend US$10 per computer in software (a tiny part of the total cost of ownership). This amounts to US$10 million, clearly a budget large enough to fund the development of sophisticated software.

This cost-benefit equation is similar to the development of a vaccine. Its production entails large fixed costs, and the ultimate outcome is unclear. Once developed, significant testing is needed to assure its effectiveness. But once produced and tested, the marginal costs of using the vaccine an additional time are negligible. Countries could pool resources for the development (and testing) of a variety of software and produce a free inventory of tested software. How can countries agree to fund these activities? Multilateral institutions may be the solution. They are mandated to fund activities to foster development in the entire region. What better allocation of funds than to produce certain public goods that will be enjoyed by most of their members?

Recognize that one seagull does not a summer make. The most important things to learn from any evaluation relate to its lessons for future policies, as Ravallion (2008) explains. It is natural to want research findings not to be too specific, but to be applicable to guide practice in other settings. However, this is seldom warranted. A special case of the general problem of external validity is scaling up. Much can change when a pilot program is scaled up: the inputs to the intervention can change, the outcomes can change, and the intervention can change. The actual impacts of scaling up can differ from the trial results, because the socioeconomic composition of program participation varies with scale. Trial results could over- or underestimate impacts on scaling up.

For all these reasons, policymakers should not be satisfied with limited ICT evaluations. Longer-term randomized trials repeated across varying contexts and scales should be used to decide what works and what does not. This is particularly important both from the perspective of assessing development effectiveness and for assuring the reliability of the policy applications. A common criticism of RCTs is that they have little validity beyond the specific exercise undertaken. Repetition in different contexts and scaling up go a long way toward improving their general applicability, as well as their development effectiveness.

2

The Region's Place in the Digital World: A Tale of Three Divides

The concept of "digital divide" has evolved over time. The term appeared in the 1990s in conjunction with the greater commercial availability of information and communication technologies (ICTs). The unequal diffusion of new technologies across and within countries raised concerns that the advantages of these technologies might be limited to those countries and individuals that were already privileged in terms of economic resources—and thus would worsen preexisting inequalities.

In the earliest stage of ICT diffusion, the main concern of researchers was simply access to such technologies. Therefore, most of the relevant literature at the time focused on the distinction between "haves" and "have-nots." However, as the level of ICT adoption increased, it became clear that people with access to ICTs varied widely in their ability to use the technology and thus in their capacity to take advantage of the benefits that technology can provide. In other words, it became obvious that it was not enough to have access to ICTs to exploit their full potential; people also had to be able to use these technologies.

Consequently, the concept of access was broadened in many studies to become synonymous with "use." But access is mainly driven by resources, while use is related to demand (Di Maggio,

Hargittai, Celeste, and Shafer, 2004). So, opportunity and choice were merged into the same analysis, and the results could be misleading. Therefore, new approaches to the issue appeared in the literature. The Organization for Economic Co-operation and Development (OECD) recognized this conceptual shift and in 2001 defined the digital divide as "the gap between individuals, households, business and geographic areas at different socioeconomic levels with regard both to their opportunities to access ICTs and to their use of the Internet for a wide variety of activities" (OECD, 2001, p. 5). Meanwhile, Di Maggio and Hargittai (2001) introduced the concept of "digital inequality," which refers not only to mere differences in access, but also to different ICT usage patterns. Something that was later on defined as first-order and second-order digital divides refers to two types of inequality: one in access to the technology and the other in the ability to use the technology (Riggins and Dewan, 2005). More recently, the definition of digital divide has further evolved to encompass the *results* of the use of such technologies. The International Telecommunications Union (ITU) has suggested that a country's transition toward an information society can be described in a three-stage model (ITU, 2009a, 2010). The first stage corresponds to what has been called the ICT readiness phase, reflecting the level of network infrastructure and access to ICTs. The second stage refers to ICT intensity, or the degree to which ICTs are being used by the society at large. The third stage relates to ICT impact: the capacity to obtain adequate benefits from the effective use of ICTs.

Depending on the definition of digital divide, the appropriate measurement unit varies. Moreover, to fully describe the scenario, it is necessary not only to define the digital divide (and how to measure it), but also to establish its scope. Differences in ICT diffusion can be assessed not only internationally, between continents and countries, but also internally between regions or groups of individuals in the same country.

The chapters in this volume relate to the different impacts of ICT use in Latin American and Caribbean societies. This chapter focuses only on the access and use dimensions of the digital divide for five different ICT technologies: fixed phones, mobile phones, computers, Internet connection, and broadband. This choice is driven mainly by data availability and international comparability. However, in assessing different technological gaps, it is important to take two caveats into account. First, the analysis does not make any adjustments for the quality of access and use, such as the information processing capacity of each technology. Second, as the pace of ICT innovation accelerates, new inventions—as well as radically improved versions of technologies that are already known—are being launched commercially, thus constantly changing the patterns of ICT access and use. For instance, the statistics used in this chapter on broadband Internet access refer to the number of total subscribers with fixed access, which includes dial-up, cable modem, digital subscriber line (DSL), and leased line subscribers (ITU, 2009b, 2009c). However, these figures do not capture the increasing importance of high-speed mobile Internet access, whose diffusion in the region started in 2007 with the launching of 3G licenses. Initial data suggest that this technology is spreading fast and could reshape the whole pattern of Internet and broadband access in Latin America.[1]

This chapter assesses the relative position of the region regarding these technologies at three different levels of analysis: the global divide, mostly between the OECD member-countries and Latin American and Caribbean countries; the intraregional divide between different countries in the region; and the internal divide within Latin American countries.

The Access Gap

The adoption of ICTs can be linked to a variety of factors, including differences in pricing, income, infrastructure, network externalities, and regulation (Madden, Coble-Neal, and Savage, 2004; Chinn and Fairlie 2006, 2010). Differences in these fundamentals across countries affect the evolution of the digital gap.

Figure 2.1 presents ICT trends in Latin America and the Caribbean since 1995. Penetration levels for telephone technologies are shown in panel a, while other ICTs with lower levels of penetration are plotted on a smaller scale in panel b. The diffusion of mobile telephony has skyrocketed from 1998 to 2008, while the trend for fixed telephony over the same time period has been relatively flat. Personal computer, Internet, fixed, and mobile broadband penetration are all trending upward, but the overall penetration levels remain low. Although ICTs have proliferated in the region since 1995, the global divide between the OECD and Latin American and Caribbean countries persists because, in most cases, while the region has made progress, so have the OECD countries (table 2.1).

The trends in terms of access gaps can be summarized as follows:

- The gap in the penetration rate for combined *mobile and fixed telephony* is shrinking, but the trends related to these two technologies are quite different. The gap in *fixed telephony* has declined constantly since 1995. There has been an absolute decrease in the number of fixed telephone lines per 100 inhabitants in OECD countries (from 51.1 in 1998 to 43.8 in 2008), while the number of fixed lines for Latin American and Caribbean countries has inched up slightly (from 18.1 in 1998 to 21.1 in 2008). Thus, the gap has narrowed because

Figure 2.1   ICT Trends for Latin America and the Caribbean, 1995–2008

a. Telephone technologies

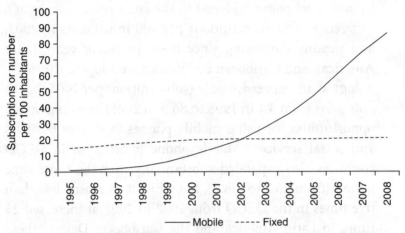

b. Computers and internet access technologies

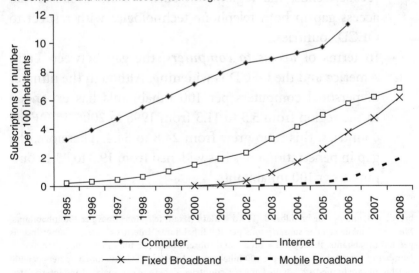

Source: ITU (2009b, 2009c).
Notes: For a list of Latin American and Caribbean countries covered, see table 2.1, note b. There are two scales, one for mobile and fixed telephony; the other for computers, the Internet, fixed

OECD users have switched from fixed to mobile phones, not because fixed-phone technology has become so widespread in Latin America and the Caribbean. By contrast, the gap in *mobile telephony* widened in the late 1990s, peaking at a difference of 53 subscriptions per 100 inhabitants in 2002, and steadily narrowing since then. In recent years, Latin American and Caribbean countries have adopted this technology at an impressive pace (subscriptions per 100 inhabitants grew from 3.4 in 1998 to 86.3 in 2008), opening up big opportunities for using mobile phones to deliver business and social services.[2] Mobile phone penetration in OECD countries also expanded substantially over the same time period (from 25.7 to 114.8), but while it increased less than five times in the OECD from 1998 to 2008, it increased 25 times in Latin America and the Caribbean. Despite these recent trends, the region still suffers from a substantial access gap in both telephone technologies with respect to OECD countries.

- In terms of ***access to computers***, the gap between Latin America and the OECD is widening. Although the number of personal computers per 100 inhabitants has expanded in the region from 5.5 to 11.3 from 1998 to 2006, in OECD countries, this ratio grew from 24.8 to 54.4. Therefore, the gap in penetration rates has widened from 19.3 to 43.1 computers per 100 inhabitants.[3]

broadband, and mobile broadband. Fixed = Main (fixed) telephone lines per 100 inhabitants. Mobile = Mobile cellular subscriptions per 100 inhabitants. Internet = Internet subscriptions per 100 inhabitants. Broadband = Broadband subscriptions per 100 inhabitants. Computer = Number of personal computers per 100 inhabitants. Available ITU data for computers per 100 inhabitants are limited after 2006. For a few countries, data were extrapolated and interpolated to create a uniform set of observations across time periods and countries. When data were available for Internet users and not for Internet subscribers, the trend of the ratio between the two was used to deduce Internet subscriber data.

Table 2.1   ICT Subscriptions and Number of Personal Computers

ICT	Latin America and the Caribbean[b]	OECD[a]	Gap	Latin America and the Caribbean	OECD	Gap
	(Subscriptions per 100 inhabitants)					
	1998			2008		
Telephony						
Mobile	3.4	25.7	22.3	86.3	114.8	28.5
Fixed phones	18.1	51.1	33.0	21.1	43.8	22.7
Internet	0.8	4.7	3.9	6.9	27.3	20.4
Fixed broadband	2000			2008		
	0.03	1.1	1.0	6.2	24.7	18.5
Mobile broadband	2002			2008		
	0.0	0.03	0.03	1.9	29.7	27.8
Computer	(Number of personal computers per 100 inhabitants)					
	1998			2006		
	5.5	24.8	19.3	11.3	54.4	43.1

Source: Author's calculations based on ITU (2009b, 2009c).

[a] OECD countries include: Australia, Austria, Belgium, Canada, Czech Republic, Denmark, Finland, France, Germany, Greece, Hungary, Iceland, Ireland, Italy, Japan, South Korea, Luxembourg, Netherlands, New Zealand, Norway, Poland, Portugal, Slovak Republic, Spain, Sweden, Switzerland, Turkey, United Kingdom, United States. Mexico is included in Latin America and the Caribbean and not in OECD.

[b] Latin America and the Caribbean includes: Antigua and Barbuda, Argentina, Bahamas, Belize, Bermuda, Bolivia, Brazil, Chile, Colombia, Costa Rica, Cuba, Dominica, Dominican Republic, Ecuador, El Salvador, Grenada, Guatemala, Guyana, Haiti, Honduras, Jamaica, Martinique, Mexico, Nicaragua, Panama, Paraguay, Peru, Saint Kitts and Nevis, Sao Tome and Principe, St. Vincent and the Grenadines, Suriname, Trinidad and Tobago, Uruguay, Venezuela.

- The digital gap in **Internet and broadband subscriptions** is increasing greatly. Although the number of Internet subscribers in the region increased from 0.8 to 6.9 (per 100 inhabitants) between 1998 and 2008, OECD subscription rates jumped from 4.7 to 27.3. As a result, the gap between the two regions reached a record 20.4 subscribers in 2008. The divide is expanding even faster in the case of fixed broadband, due to the faster diffusion of this technology in OECD countries: the penetration rate in Latin America and the Caribbean grew from 0.03 to 6.2 subscribers per 100 inhabitants from 2000 to 2008, while in the OECD, it jumped from 1.1 to 24.7 during the same period.[4] The digital gap in mobile broadband is growing even faster, mainly because Latin America and the Caribbean started so late in this race. Indeed, while mobile broadband technologies had only begun to diffuse in the region in 2007 reaching 1.9 subscribers per 100 inhabitants in 2008, by that time, the average penetration rate in the OECD had already reached 29.7 subscribers per 100 inhabitants—roughly the same level as fixed broadband in the region.

The Global Digital Divide

The literature on technology diffusion suggests that technologies tend to follow an S-shaped adoption path. After an initial period of rapid growth and beyond an inflection point, technology adoption reaches a plateau, or saturation point (Hall, 2006). This could actually be "good news" for Latin America and the Caribbean. Because they are in the early stages of the diffusion curve, they might be able to close the digital gap during the next few years. Unfortunately, a more thorough assessment of this hypothesis is not as optimistic, as the parameters that determine diffusion may not be the same for all countries (Chong and Micco, 2003). These parameters depend on innovation and absorptive capabilities, which are deeply rooted in the idiosyncratic characteristics of national innovation systems.[5] There is no guarantee that countries will ever catch up with one another, and even if they manage to, nothing guarantees that they can do so within a reasonable time frame.[6]

To explore the pace at which Latin America and the Caribbean is closing the global digital gap, it might be worth exploring how long it would take a typical country of the region to reach the *current* OECD diffusion levels given two parameters: the current penetration gap and the historical pace at which the typical Latin American and Caribbean country has managed to disseminate the technology from the moment it becomes commercially available.[7] Dividing the current penetration gap by the historical diffusion pace followed by each country gives an idea of how long it would take a given country to reach the current OECD level. This figure offers an indication of the magnitude of the time lags under two assumptions: business as usual (the country keeps diffusing in the future at the same pace it has in the past) and that the OECD countries will not make further progress (they have reached the saturation point). Although such assumptions can bias the estimated lags in both directions, this approach can still provide some insight on the dynamic implications of the digital divide.

The time-distance analysis highlights the persistence of the digital divide(s) and indicates that the region is unlikely to reach the *current* OECD levels within a reasonable time frame. Figure 2.2 summarizes the time-distance for the typical (median) country in 1998 and 2008. The only technology in which the region is gaining ground is mobile telephony. The region has shortened the time lag from approximately 180 years in 1998 to only about 9 years in 2008. The region is also converging in fixed telephony, albeit more slowly; the time to catch up to the OECD has been cut from

Figure 2.2   Time Needed for Latin America and the Caribbean to Reach Current ICT Levels in OECD Countries

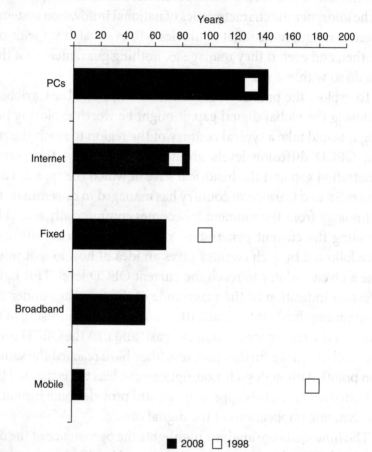

Sources: Authors' calculations based on ITU (2009b, 2009c)

Notes: Data for computers are from 2006 (or latest year available) and 1996 (or latest year available). Figures for Latin America and the Caribbean are the median of the region. Data for OECD countries are included only once the country has become a member of OECD. If new membership occurred from January-June, the data are included that same year. If new membership occurred from July—December, the data are included the following year. Data from the Slovak Republic were not included in the 1998 OECD penetration. The penetration lags of Latin America and the Caribbean are calculated by first deriving the annual pace of adoption using the earliest period that the technology was available in each country (Fixed: 1960; Mobile: 1980; Internet: 1988; Broadband: 1998; Computers: 1975). If a country did not report data for the earliest period, the earliest available data were used.

around 97 years in 1998 to around 70 years in 2008. The region is showing no sign of closing in on the OECD with other ICTs. In some cases, the gap has actually grown: for computers, the gap has increased from 130 to about 142 years, and for the Internet, it has grown from 75 to 80 years. The time lag of Latin America in (fixed) broadband is around 50 years, despite the fact that it is a relatively new technology.

What factors are delaying ICT diffusion in the region? A look at ICT prices provides some clues. The equilibrium diffusion model assumes that the main determinant of diffusion is the change over time in the cost of acquiring the new technology. As acquisition costs (adjusted for quality) decrease, the number of users increases. Comparable international data on ICT costs have not been readily available until recently. The latest ITU report (ITU, 2010) presents cross-sectional information on fixed, mobile, and broadband price baskets in dollars (PPP$). Information regarding Internet subscription prices was published in 2006 (ITU, 2006). There are no international price data on personal computers (PCs). In addition to absolute price differences, ICT affordability depends on prices relative to a country's income (ITU, 2010). Figure 2.3 plots ICT penetration rates against prices as a percentage of the monthly income per capita for the full sample of countries for which data are available.

The correlation is clear: as relative prices for the four ICTs decline, penetration rates increase. Moreover, the relationship between penetration rates and affordability seems to be strongly nonlinear. For most countries, ICT costs are within 10 percent or less of monthly per capita incomes. This applies to the front-runners in the region, such as Argentina, Brazil, Chile, and Costa Rica (in all the technologies). However, in several poor countries, ICT costs represent a substantial part of the monthly income per capita, and therefore, affordability is critically jeopardized. For

Figure 2.3   Relationship between ICT Price as a Percent of Monthly Income and Access to ICT

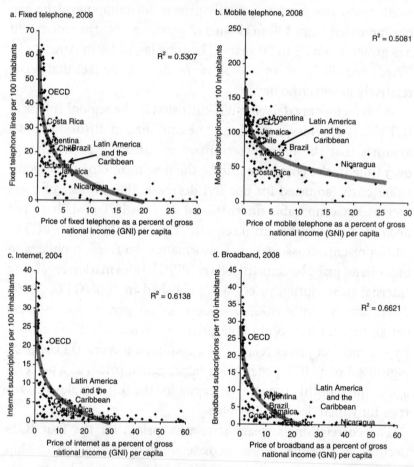

Source: ITU (2006, 2009b, and 2009c).
Notes: For graphing purposes, countries with price/monthly gross national income (GNI) per capita ratios higher than 30 percent for fixed telephony and mobile telephony and 60 percent for Internet and broadband were not included in the samples.

example, in the case of Nicaragua, fees for mobile telephones climb up to 17 percent, and for broadband, they reach almost 40 percent of the monthly income per capita. Overall, ICT costs represent around 4 percent of monthly income for the average Latin American and Caribbean country in the case of fixed and mobile telephony (1 percent and 0.8 percent, respectively, for the average OECD country). These figures jump to 15 percent and 27 percent of monthly income in the case of Internet and broadband (2.2 percent and 1.3 percent, respectively, for the average OECD country, noting that data on the Internet are for 2004).

This large gap in affordability implies that for many countries, particularly the poorest ones, marginal changes in ICT pricing will have a limited impact on penetration rates. Penetration rates for ICTs take off only when prices represent less than 5 percent of monthly per capita income (see figure 2.3). Radical changes in pricing policies (and associated regulations) might be needed in countries where prices are around or above 20 percent of country incomes.

ICT prices depend on the interaction between demand and supply. Demand tends to be a function of factors that capture the value of each ICT service for consumers, whether households or firms. Factors include the consumer's income, education, and age (Goolsbee and Klenow, 1999; Forman, Goldfarb, and Greenstein, 2003. The supply of ICT services, on the other hand, might be affected by a number of factors, including investments in ICT infrastructure and profit margins, which in turn depend on the level of competition, market size, and the quality of regulatory interventions (ITU, 2010).[8]

Based on these considerations, ICT diffusion levels can be modelled as a function of a set of variables that capture shifts in demand and supply. The penetration rate of each ICT in a given country is assumed to be related to five factors: (i) the level of income per capita; (ii) the stock of human capital, measured by average years of schooling; (iii) the population density; (iv) the regulatory quality; and (v) the degree of trade openness.[9]

Most of these identified factors are relevant determinants of technology diffusion across countries. Unsurprisingly, income per capita and human capital have a strong positive influence on the diffusion of all technologies.[10] Second, population density has a positive—albeit small—effect on all technologies, except for mobile phones, where the effect is slightly negative. On the supply side, the lower costs of providing telecommunication infrastructure in a more densely populated country explain this result. On the demand side, greater consumer utility from network effects provides an explanation. The regulatory quality of a country is found to be a relevant driver of diffusion for all the technologies. However, trade openness presents unexpectedly unclear results; fixed phone, computer, and broadband diffusion actually decline with trade openness. This finding is also consistent with some previous studies (Daude, 2010).

These results suggest the main factors that may contribute to the global digital divide, but do not identify the relative importance of each factor. A complementary analysis provides some insight in this regard. Table 2.2 summarizes the contribution of each explanatory variable to the penetration rate gaps between the average OCED country and the average Latin American and Caribbean country. For all the technologies, the most important factor is the difference in per capita income, which explains 44.6 percent of the gap for mobile phones and up to 78.7 percent for computers. The lower contribution of income to the mobile phone divide can be explained by the relatively cheaper cost of accessing that technology.

Differences in human capital and regulatory quality contribute significantly to the technology gap. Differences in education explain from 7.9 percent of the gap in the case of computers to 30 percent in the case of mobile phones. Differences in regulatory quality account for from 12.2 percent for computers to

30 percent for mobile phones. Regulatory quality contributes 2.7 percentage points (about 16 percent) of the gap in Internet penetration and 2.9 percentage points (about 25 percent) of the digital divide in broadband between the two regions. This finding

Table 2.2   ICT Penetration Rates and Decomposition of the Gap between Latin American and Caribbean and OECD Countries

	Fixed (1)	*Mobile* (2)	*Computer* (3)	*Internet* (4)	*Broadband* (5)
Total penetration rate gap	30.4	43.1	37.7	19.7	14.1
Explained component[a]	28.9	48.8	33.7	16.7	11.7
Contribution from:					
GDP per capita	19.1 (66.0%)	21.8 (44.6%)	26.6 (78.7%)	12.6 (75.6%)	7.9 (67.1%)
Years of schooling	6.2 (21.4%)	14.7 (30.0%)	2.7 (7.9%)	1.4 (8.4%)	1.4 (12.1%)
Population density	0.1 (0.3%)	−0.1 (−0.1%)	0.1 (0.3%)	0.1 (0.7%)	0.1 (0.6%)
Regulatory quality	3.9 (13.4%)	14.7 (30.0%)	4.1 (12.2%)	2.7 (16.1%)	2.9 (25.0%)
Trade openness	−0.4 (−1.5%)	0.6 (1.3%)	−0.2 (−0.4%)	0.0 (−0.2%)	−0.2 (−2.0%)
Unexplained component	1.5	−5.8	4.0	2.9	2.4

Sources: Authors' calculations based on ITU (2009b, 2009c); Barro and Lee (2000); World Bank (2010a, 2010b).

[a] The total explained component does not equal the sum of the contributions from the variables because of the presence of unreported time effects.

Note: Gap as of 2008 for all technologies except computers, which is calculated as of 2006.

seems to confirm the relevance of regulation as a determinant of Internet diffusion (Estache, Manacorda, and Valleti, 2002). Finally, population density and trade openness contribute little to the gaps.

In summary, the global digital divide between Latin America and the Caribbean and the OECD countries is a persistent phenomenon that differs greatly from one technology to another. Even for those technologies where the gap in penetration rates is narrowing between the two regions, a business-as-usual scenario indicates that Latin America and the Caribbean is unlikely to catch up within a reasonable time frame (with the possible exception of mobile telephony). Slow-moving variables, such as income and education, are largely to blame for this persistent lag. Does this mean that nothing can be done to close the digital divide in the short run? The answer is no. The importance of regulation for adoption rates suggests that significant short-run gains can be achieved by applying the correct set of regulatory reforms, especially in the case of new vintage technologies such as mobile phones and broadband.

The Regional Digital Divide

The relevance of income, education, and regulatory quality as determinants of cross-country ICT diffusion suggests that strong differences in ICT penetration rates may also be expected across countries in the same region. The available data confirm this suspicion (figure 2.4). Argentina, Uruguay, Chile, and Mexico are regional leaders in Internet and broadband subscriptions, while low-income countries such as Honduras, Nicaragua, and Guatemala rank among the countries with the lowest diffusion. Costa Rica, Uruguay, and Argentina are the front-runners for fixed telephone lines, while Bolivia, Nicaragua, and Haiti have the lowest penetration rates. Argentina, Panama, and El Salvador lead the region in mobile subscriptions, while Costa Rica, Guyana, and Haiti are at the bottom.

Mobile telephony is the only ICT in which Central American countries have kept pace with the average of the rest of Latin America and the Caribbean. For this technology, lack of infrastructure, cost, and income may be less binding for low-income countries. Provided that network infrastructure exists and is affordable, access to mobile phone technologies requires little initial investment (phone sets can be cheap) and does not necessarily require subscription (prepaid cards are widely available in the region).

A substantial disparity across countries also exists in access to computers (figure 2.4). Costa Rica leads the region, with more than twenty computers at home per 100 inhabitants, followed by Brazil, Chile, Mexico, Trinidad and Tobago, and Uruguay. At the opposite end, the Dominican Republic, Bolivia, Guatemala, and Honduras have fewer than five PCs per 100 inhabitants. Overall, countries are adopting ICTs at different speeds. The within-region spread (as measured by the interquartile range of penetration rates) has increased for all technologies, except for fixed telephony. This rise in heterogeneity is especially important for the newest technologies, particularly mobile phone and broadband.

The Digital Divide within Countries of the Region

The third dimension of the digital divide occurs within countries—the internal divide. Penetration of ICT differs substantially across income and education levels, between rural and urban areas, and across ethnic groups. This chapter examines the ICT internal divide only by income. ICT access is highly sensitive

Figure 2.4 Differences in ICT Subscriptions within Latin America and the Caribbean

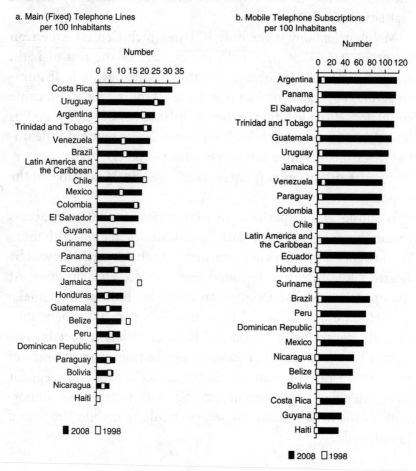

a. Main (Fixed) Telephone Lines
per 100 Inhabitants

b. Mobile Telephone Subscriptions
per 100 Inhabitants

c. Internet and Broadband Subscriptions
per 100 Inhabitants

d. Number of Personal Computers
per 100 Inhabitants

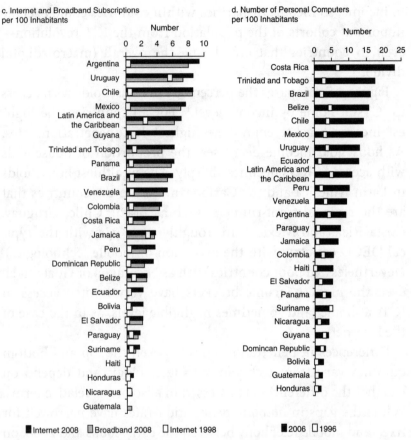

■ Internet 2008 ▨ Broadband 2008 ☐ Internet 1998   ■ 2006 ☐ 1996

Source: ITU (2009b, 2009c).

Notes: For graphing purposes, the following countries were not included: Antigua and Barbuda, the Bahamas, Cuba, Dominica, Grenada, Martinique Saint Kitts and Nevis, Sao Tome and Principe and St. Vincent and the Grenadines. Data for these countries were included in regional averages for Latin America and the Caribbean. Mobile: Earliest available data for Sao Tome and Principe that are not zero are 2002. Internet: Earliest available data for Ecuador and Guyana are 1999; for Colombia, Dominica, Haiti, Martinique, Nicaragua and Paraguay are 2000; for Saint Kitts and Nevis are 2002; for Cuba are 2003; for Antigua and Barbuda and Bermuda are 2004; for Uruguay are 2005; for Jamaica are 2006. Latest available data for Saint Kitts and Nevis are 2006 and for Martinique are 2007. Computers: Earliest available data for Costa Rica, Cuba and Honduras are1997; for Grenada, Guyana, Martinique, Panama, Paraguay, St. Kitts and Nevis and St. Vincent and the Grenadines are 1998; for Dominica and El Salvador are 1999; for Antigua and Barbuda, Dominican Rep., Haiti, Sao Tome and Principe and Suriname are 2001; for Bahamas are 2002. Latest available data for Bermuda, Dominica, Grenada, Martinique and St. Kitts and Nevis are 2004; for Argentina, Bahamas, Bolivia, Brazil, Chile, Costa Rica, El Salvador, Guatemala, Guyana, Jamaica, Nicaragua, Panama, Paraguay, Peru, Sao Tome and Principe, St. Vincent and the Grenadines, Suriname, Uruguay, and Venezuela are 2005.

to income, so income disparities within countries could exclude important cohorts of the population from the ICT revolution—even in countries that are closing the overall (macro) digital divide.

Figure 2.5 compares the percentage of households with access to ICTs at home by income level.[11] For all countries, the highest income bracket enjoys the highest ICT penetration rates. As household income decreases, the proportion of households with access to ICTs declines sharply. The wealthiest households in Latin America and the Caribbean (and in the countries that are the regional front-runners, such as Brazil, Chile, Uruguay, Costa Rica, and Mexico) are roughly on a par with the typical OECD country (with the exception of mobile technologies). Nevertheless, in poor countries such as Nicaragua or Guatemala, even the highest income brackets have very limited access to ICTs at home (and sometimes negligible levels, as in the case of the Internet).

Differences in penetration rates between the top and bottom quintiles vary from technology to technology, and depend on whether the differences are assessed in absolute or relative terms. While the gaps in *absolute* penetration rates have narrowed for fixed and mobile telephony between the early 2000s and 2008, on average, the divide has widened for computers and the Internet. Given these trends, absolute measures of inequality can be misleading. For example, the most recent data show that Paraguay, Honduras, and Guatemala have some of the smallest internal Internet divides in the region. However, the magnitude of these gaps can be attributed to the low levels of Internet adoption across *all* income brackets in these countries. In other words, it is not safe to conclude that internal Internet access is less income-sensitive in these countries than in other countries of Latin America and the Caribbean.

Another way of assessing the issue is by looking at relative penetration rates, which indicate whether rich households are more likely to gain access than poor households. Using relative measures of inequality, households in the highest-income quintile in Ecuador report about 100 times more Internet access than households in the poorest quintile. The same is true for PCs in Bolivia. Within-country adoption rates vary much more in the region than in OECD countries.[12] The relative penetration gaps suggest that for the average country in the region, the internal divide is narrowing for mobile telephony, computers, and, to a lesser extent, fixed telephony. By contrast, the internal divide is clearly widening for Internet access.

The Usage Gap

Reaping the benefits of the ICT revolution requires not only the possibility of accessing ICTs, but also the capacity to use them in effective and productive ways. Today, the majority of developing countries are still stuck in the access stage (ITU, 2010). As ICT penetration increases, the usage divide with the developed world will become more relevant. However, when assessing the actual dimension of such a gap—between Latin America and the Caribbean and the OCED countries, as well as within the region— problems arise because of limitations in the data. The only effective way to measure the real intensity of ICT use in a country is by gathering information from household surveys. However, especially in developing countries, national surveys have only recently started to include questions about ICT use, and most questions are restricted to the Internet. Moreover, the degree of international comparability of surveys is low.

Available international data on Internet users are often estimated based on the number of Internet subscriptions,[13] rather

Figure 2.5   Percent of Households with Access to ICTs in the Home by Income Quintile

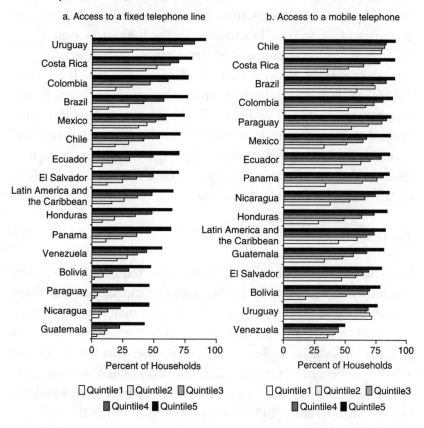

a. Access to a fixed telephone line

b. Access to a mobile telephone

☐ Quintile1 ☐ Quintile2 ▨ Quintile3
■ Quintile4 ■ Quintile5

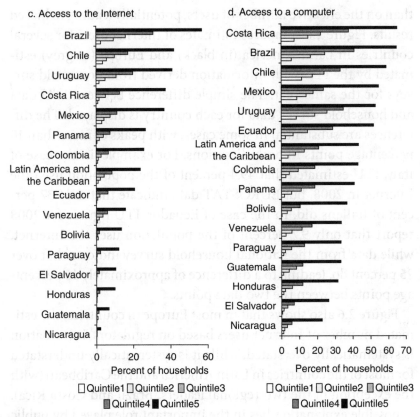

c. Access to the Internet

d. Access to a computer

Source: OSILAC (2010).

Note: Data are for 2008 or the latest year available.

Fixed telephone lines: Data for Bolivia, El Salvador, Honduras, Mexico, Panama, Paraguay, Uruguay and Venezuela are for 2007, and for Chile, Guatemala, and Nicaragua are for 2006.

Mobile: Data for Bolivia, El Salvador, Honduras, Mexico, Panama, Paraguay, Uruguay and Venezuela are for 2007, and for Chile, Guatemala, and Nicaragua are for 2006.

Internet: Data for Bolivia, El Salvador, Honduras, Mexico, Panama, Paraguay, Uruguay, and Venezuela are for 2007, and for Chile, Guatemala, and Nicaragua are for 2006.

Computers: Data for El Salvador, Honduras, Mexico, Panama, Paraguay, Uruguay, and Venezuela are for 2007, for Chile, Guatemala, and Nicaragua 2006 and for Bolivia are for 2005.

than on the effective number of users, potentially leading to biased results. Figure 2.6 compares estimates of Internet users for several countries in Latin America (in black) and Europe (in grey) estimated by the ITU with information derived from household surveys for the same year. The simple difference between ITU data and household survey data for each country is displayed. The differences are substantial in some cases, with peaks of more than 10 percentage points in both directions. For example, in the case of Italy, ITU estimated that 49.4 percent of the population used the Internet in 2008, but EUROSTAT data indicate that only 37 percent of Italians did. In the case of Ecuador, ITU figures for 2008 report that only 9.7 percent of the population uses the Internet, while data from the national household survey indicate that over 25 percent do, leading to a difference of approximately 16 percentage points between the two data points.

Figure 2.6 also shows that in most European countries, the estimated number of Internet users based on regulators' information is systematically overstated, while it is systematically understated for most of the countries in Latin America and the Caribbean (with the exception of the two regional leaders, Brazil and Costa Rica). A possible explanation lies in the important role played by public access points in providing Internet access to a much larger part of the population in Latin America and the Caribbean, compared to Europe, where access is essentially private. Clearly, assessing the dimension of the Internet digital divide on the basis of the ITU data or on the basis of household survey data leads to different conclusions. In particular, the usage divide between OECD and Latin American and Caribbean countries, if computed with ITU data, may be overestimated. The computation of the intraregional divide in Internet use may also be too high. If ITU underestimates usage rates in countries with lower technology diffusion, the effective intraregional spread will be smaller.

Figure 2.6   Estimates of Internet Users: ITU Data versus Household Surveys, 2006–08

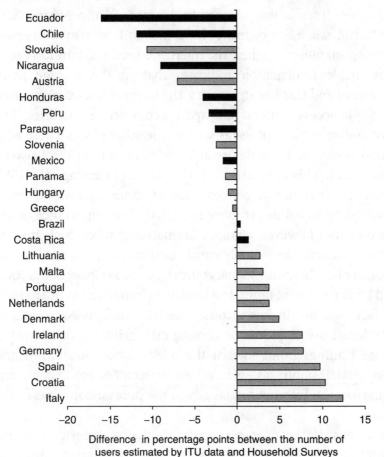

Difference in percentage points between the number of
users estimated by ITU data and Household Surveys

Sources: Authors' calculations based on ITU (2009b and 2009c), OSILAC (2010), EUROSTAT (2009).

Notes: Units for household surveys are percent of individuals. Data refer to 2008, except for Chile (2006); and Honduras, Mexico, Panama and Paraguay (2007). In the case of Brazil and Costa Rica, ITU data are for 2007, while OSILAC (2010) data are for 2008.

In addition to allowing a correct evaluation of the usage divide across countries, microdata from household surveys permit the analysis of Internet use *patterns*. In the case of Latin America and the Caribbean, a few countries have enough information to assess two important issues: where the Internet is used and how it is used.

Available information indicates that in the average Latin American and Caribbean country, the Internet is used most often in public access centers, followed by commercial facilities. The least common place of use is schools (or other places where education is provided), while use at home or at work fall in between (figure 2.7). This contrasts with the pattern in Europe (EU15),[14] where Internet use is concentrated at home and work, while community-based use is more marginal. The importance of the place of use, however, changes dramatically when high-income Latin American and Caribbean countries are compared to the poorest ones. In high-income countries such as Chile, Costa Rica, and Uruguay, use at home and work is as important as use in public facilities. But in low-income countries such as Nicaragua or Honduras, use at public or commercial facilities predominates. These findings point toward the relevance of (subsidized and commercial) public access solutions (telecenters and cyber-cafes) to narrow the Internet digital gap in the poorest countries of the region.

Citizens of the average country in Latin America and the Caribbean use the Internet mostly for information gathering and communication. The two least frequent types of use are for e-commerce (purchasing or ordering goods and services online) and for e-government. Using the Internet for leisure and educational/training fall in between (figure 2.8). Internet use is concentrated on the most basic applications, confirming that its potential contribution to an information society is still not being fully exploited. In contrast, in Europe, although use for communication and information is also dominant, the Internet is also

Figure 2.7   Location of Internet Use (Percent of Individuals)

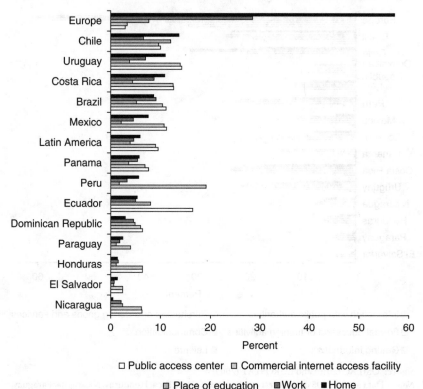

□ Public access center □ Commercial internet access facility

□ Place of education   ■ Work   ■ Home

Source: OSILAC (2010) and EUROSTAT (2009).

Notes: Data are for 2008 or the latest available year. The average for Latin America and the Caribbean is computed using the countries in the figure that report data. Ecuador does not report data for "commercial Internet access facility," and Peru and Paraguay do not report data for "public access center." The variables used from EUROSTAT for Europe were: Home = In the last 3 months, I have accessed the Internet at home (2008). Work = In the last 3 months, I have accessed the Internet at place of work (other than home) (2008). Place of Education = In the last 3 months, I have accessed the Internet at place of education (2008). Public access center = In the last 3 months, I have accessed the Internet at the public library (2008). Commercial access facility = In the last 3 months, I have accessed the Internet in an Internet café (2008).

used for more advanced purposes, in particular, for educational purposes and interaction with public authorities.[15]

While Latin American and Caribbean countries vary in terms of the intensity of use by type, the relative importance of the

Figure 2.8   Type of Internet Use (Percent of Individuals)

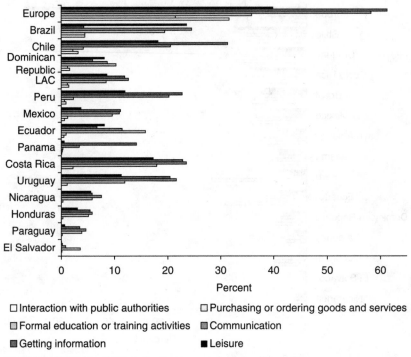

Interaction with public authorities   Purchasing or ordering goods and services
Formal education or training activities   Communication
Getting information   Leisure

Source: OSILAC (2010) and EUROSTAT (2009).
Notes: Data are for 2008 or the latest available year. Costa Rica, Honduras, Nicaragua, Paraguay, and Uruguay do not report data for "interaction with public authorities," and El Salvador reports that 0 percent of individuals use the Internet for "interaction with public authorities." The variables used from EUROSTAT for Europe were: Leisure = I have used the Internet in the last 3 months for leisure activities related to obtaining and sharing audiovisual content (2008). Getting information = I have used a search engine to find information (2007). Communication = I have used the Internet in the last 3 months for communication (2008). Formal education or training activities = I have used the Internet in the last 3 months for training and education (2008). Purchasing or ordering goods and services = I have used the Internet in the last 3 months for purchasing/ordering goods or services (excluding shares/financial services) (2005). Interaction with public authorities = I have used the Internet in the last 3 months for interaction with public authorities (2008).

different applications is remarkably similar across countries. The Internet is used mostly for information gathering and communication in almost all the countries in the region. In several countries, including Brazil, Ecuador, Costa Rica, and Uruguay, the use

Figure 2.9   Location of Individual Internet Use by Household per Capita Income Quintile, Latin America and the Caribbean

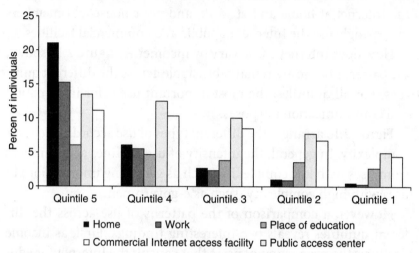

Source: OSILAC (2010).
Notes: Data are for 2008 or the latest year available. Data from the following countries and years were averaged: Brazil, 2008; Chile, 2006; Costa Rica, 2008; Ecuador, 2008; El Salvador, 2007; Honduras, 2007; Mexico, 2007; Nicaragua, 2006; Panama, 2007; and Paraguay, 2008. There are several exceptions: Home: Data for Brazil are from 2005; Work and place of education: Data for Paraguay are from 2007; Public access: No Paraguay data were used; Commercial access facility: No Ecuador data were used.

of the Internet for educational purposes reaches some degree of importance.

Do the place and type of Internet use vary with income levels within countries (the internal divide)? Figure 2.9 shows how the usage location pattern for the average Latin American and Caribbean country changes by household income quintile. The data mirror the situation at the international level: the wealthiest households use the Internet mainly at home and at work, while these two places are almost irrelevant for the poorest households. Yet, the Internet usage rate of people in the highest and lowest income brackets varies little for shared access points such as schools, public access centers, and commercial Internet facilities. This reflects two concurrent tendencies: high-income household members use the Internet less and less in those locations since they already use the Internet at home and at work, and poor household members increasingly use the Internet in public and commercial facilities.

How does Internet usage vary by income? As figure 2.10 shows, the patterns of use are remarkably stable across the different quintiles. For all quintiles, the most important use is for information and communication purposes.

Figure 2.10 arranges the different types of use according to their complexity. In general, the intensity of use declines as one moves from uses with low complexity (such as gathering information) to uses with high complexity (such as e-government).

However, a comparison of the patterns of use across the different quintiles reveals two interesting findings. First, as income declines, the proportion of users that consult the Internet for educational or training activities increases. One explanation may be that the Internet complements education, particularly for those people with less access to education. If this is true, the potential of the Internet for closing educational divides could be huge. An alternative explanation could be that individuals in poor households often have free access to the Internet only in connected educational establishments. In this case, usage would clearly correlate with the educational application.

A second noteworthy finding is that as income declines, advanced types of Internet use also decline. Sophisticated uses, such as e-commerce and e-government, are far more relevant in the top quintile. This decline may be related to other inequalities such as lack of human capital, liquidity constraints (users need a credit card to participate in e-commerce), or informal employment status (which might hinder interaction with public authorities).

The patterns of Internet usage in the region also differ greatly by the age of the user. In general, the highest proportion of

Figure 2.10   Patterns of Individual Internet Use by Household per Capita Income Quintile, Latin America and the Caribbean

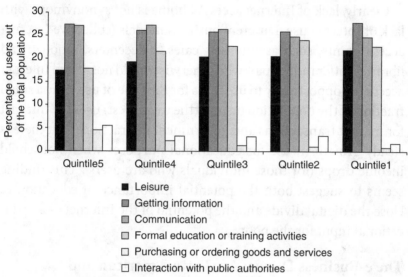

- ■ Leisure
- ■ Getting information
- ◫ Communication
- ☐ Formal education or training activities
- ☐ Purchasing or ordering goods and services
- ☐ Interaction with public authorities

Source: OSILAC (2010).
Notes: Data are for 2008 or the latest year available. Data are normalized by dividing each particular type of use by the sum proportion of uses in the quintile. Data from the following countries and years were averaged: Brazil, 2008; Chile, 2006; Costa Rica, 2008; Ecuador, 2008; El Salvador, 2007; Honduras, 2007; Mexico, 2007; Nicaragua, 2006; Panama, 2007; and Paraguay, 2008. There were several exceptions getting information: Brazil, 2005; Paraguay, 2006; El Salvador, no data. Purchasing or ordering goods and services: No data were available for Panama and Paraguay for the first quintile and for El Salvador for the first and second quintile. Interaction with public authorities: The following countries and years were averaged: Brazil, 2008; Chile, 2006; El Salvador, 2007; Mexico, 2007; and Panama, 2007. No data are available for Panama for the first and second quintile and for El Salvador for the first, second, and third quintile.

Internet users ranges from fifteen to twenty-four years of age, while Internet use is lowest among those in the oldest age bracket (sixty-five and older). The location of Internet use for these different age groups also varies. The youngest groups tend to use the Internet frequently at school and at public and commercial access centers. But, as users age, use at work and at home becomes relatively more important. Finally, individuals who are 65 or older use the Internet almost exclusively at home.

Clearly, lack of Internet access at home is not synonymous with lack of Internet use. Different business models (collective Internet access points, such as Internet "cafés," telecenters, schools, and libraries) offer individuals who otherwise could not afford Internet access the opportunity to use it. As for the type of use, only a small fraction of the population (usually the wealthiest) uses the Internet for market transactions and government interactions. But there is steady growth in use for educational purposes when household income drops (for those individuals who are users). This finding seems to suggest both the potential importance of education to close the digital divide and the potential of the Internet as an educational input for the poor.

The e-Business Divide: Are Latin American and Caribbean Firms Missing the ICT Revolution?

The ICT revolution has not only changed the lives and habits of individuals and households, but has also radically revolutionized how modern business is conducted. ICTs can benefit enterprises through two main channels: by increasing the efficiency of internal processes, which can enhance firms' productivity, and by broadening market reach, both domestically and internationally through new marketing and commercialization approaches, such as e-commerce.

In 1987, Robert Solow, winner of the Nobel Prize in economics, wrote that "You can see the computer age everywhere but in the productivity statistics."[16] Times have changed, and today there is general consensus that ICT adoption improves productivity in the long run,[17] at both the general economy (macro) and firm (micro) level. In the context of growth accounting, a large body of research has clearly shown the link between the acceleration of productivity growth and ICTs (see, for example, Oliner and Sichel,

Figure 2.11   Internet Users and Location of Internet Use by Age Bracket

a. Internet users

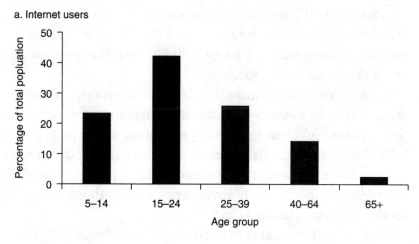

b. Locations of Internet use

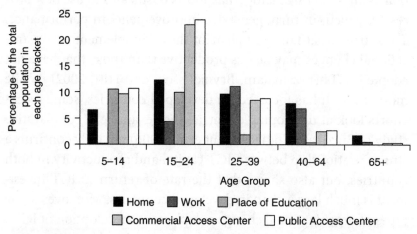

Source: OSILAC (2010).

Notes: Data are for the latest year available. The latest available data for Ecuador, Mexico, Peru, and Uruguay are for 2009; for Brazil, Costa Rica, El Salvador, and Paraguay are for 2008 (with the exception of Internet use at home, where the latest available data for Brazil are for 2005); for Honduras and Panama are for 2007; for Chile and Nicaragua are for 2006; and for the Dominican Republic are for 2005. Data were not available for Internet use at a commercial access center for Ecuador; and for Internet use at a public access center for Paraguay or Peru. The data correspond to the percentage of total population in each age bracket; since it is possible for an individual to use the Internet in multiple locations, these will not necessarily sum to 100 percent.

1994, 2002). In particular, Jorgenson (2001) has argued that the sharp decline in the relative prices of ICT equipment is the key to understanding the resurgence of economic growth in the United States since 1995. Later, Jorgenson and Vu (2005) broadened the analysis, arguing that ICT investment has been the engine of the world's economy since 1995.

Nevertheless, the contribution of ICTs to productivity gains varies widely by country and industry, suggesting that adoption per se is not sufficient to take full advantage of the potential of ICTs. Furthermore, this variation in the relationship between ICTs and gains in productivity supports the hypothesis that ICTs complement other forms of investment, such as those in human capital and organizational change.

Looking at firms seems to confirm this hypothesis; ICTs function as an "enabling factor" that allows businesses to use new processes, which, in turn, generates improvements in performance. Thus, firms that fail to implement these complementary organizational changes may be less productive than those that have not adopted ICTs (Bresnaham, Brynjolfsson, and Hitt, 2002). While most research has focussed on developed countries, some recent efforts look at developing countries. For example, a comparative study of Brazil and India (Basant et al., 2006) not only confirms a strong relationship between ICT capital and productivity in both countries, but also shows that the rate of return to ICT investment is much larger than in developed countries. Moreover, some types of organizational change complement the adoption of ICTs. In particular, firms with flatter, less hierarchical organizational structures tend to reap greater returns from ICTs.

Even if the benefits of ICT are clear, firms might face several constraints in the process of adoption, especially small and medium enterprises (SMEs) and particularly in developing countries. First, many enterprises cannot afford to purchase and maintain expensive hardware and software and adapt to new procedures (Crespi, Criscuolo, and Haskel, 2007). Second, connectivity costs tend to be higher in areas with poor telecommunication infrastructure and inadequate regulatory frameworks. Third, limited ICT literacy—lack of knowledge about and trust in ICTs—prevents firms from adopting the technologies and fully realizing their potential benefits. Fourth, content that is suitable for the needs of SMEs is limited, decreasing the potential advantages of adopting ICTs.[18] Finally, in comparison to developed countries, services provided online are still limited and their regulation is embryonic, thus reducing the attractiveness of ICTs.

These elements seem to have inhibited enterprises in Latin America and the Caribbean from adopting ICTs. But, when assessing regional performance with regard to e-business, the lack of internationally comparable objective data becomes a serious problem. Only a handful of countries have carried out official surveys based on business registers. And, even in these cases, questionnaires have been so ad hoc that data are not strictly comparable across countries. In addition, confidentiality issues make accessibility to the surveys quite restricted. The only countries where information on Internet access by firms is relatively reliable and comparable are Argentina, Chile, and Uruguay. Data on these three countries can be compared with similar data from developed countries.

The magnitude of the Internet divide in the business sector strongly depends on the size of the firm. While in the developed world, the differences between small and large firms in terms of Internet penetration rates are quite marginal (fewer than 10 percentage points), in Argentina, Chile, and Uruguay, the gaps vary significantly by firm size. While the adoption rates of large firms in Uruguay and Chile are similar to those of large firms in developed countries, the gap between large and small firms in these countries is more than 30 percentage points. A large digital divide affects small firms in the region, not only with respect to European enterprises of the same size, but also in comparison to larger firms in Latin America and the Caribbean (see figure 2.12).

Clearly, data on access do not capture data on use. However, using the "extent of business Internet use" variable of the World Economic Forum's Executive Opinion Survey compensates somewhat for this shortcoming. This survey collects subjective information from a sample of businesses leaders from 133 countries.[19] Responses are combined and aggregated at a country level to produce country scores. On one hand, these responses are perceptions, introducing an unknown degree of error that could affect comparability. On the other hand, the survey covers a large sample of countries, allowing for benchmarking of relative performances.

Figure 2.13 shows that the business sector in Latin America and the Caribbean clearly lags behind the OECD average (at least in terms of business perceptions). However, the figure also points to great variation in the region. For example, while scores for Brazil and Chile are close to the OECD average, scores for Paraguay and Bolivia lag far behind.

Although the relative position of Latin America remains stagnant in comparison with the OECD, the question is whether e-business in the region is underperforming according to structural parameters such as productivity, human capital, and regulatory quality and infrastructure. Figure 2.14 summarizes the answers to this question.[20] While greater e-business intensity might be expected based on the region's prevailing levels of productivity and human capital, Latin America and the Caribbean seems to have the right level of e-business intensity given its ICT infrastructure and regulatory quality. Thus, these last two factors may be binding constraints that limit the intensity of e-business in the region. Although Latin America and the Caribbean have

Figure 2.12   Percentage of Businesses with Access to the Internet, by Firm Size, 2002–04

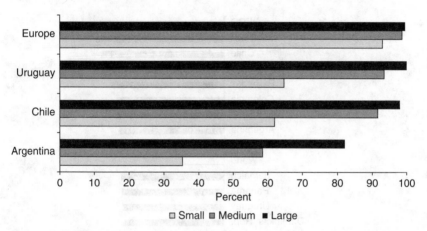

Sources: EUROSTAT (2006), INDEC and SECYT (2006), Ministerio de Economía, Chile (2006), MINEC et al (2006).
Notes: The classification of business size varies by data source. For Europe (EU15): Small enterprises (10–49 persons employed); medium (50–249 persons employed); large (250 or more persons employed). For Europe, the data for businesses do not include the financial sector. For Uruguay: Small business (5–19 persons employed); medium (20–99 persons employed); large (100 persons employed or more). Argentina's classification is based on company revenue: Small (less than 50 million pesos); medium (200 million pesos–50 million pesos); large (more than 200 million pesos). Chile's classification is based on annual sales in unidad de fomento (UF): Small (2,401–25,000 UF); medium (50,001–100,000 UF); medium–small (25,001–50,000 UF); large (100,001 and more UF). Data for medium and medium–small were averaged to create the medium category used for comparative purposes.

enough human capital and productivity to support greater diffusion of e-business, the infrastructure and regulatory quality may be holding firms back.

A Digital Snapshot of the Region

Three digital divides are present in the region. The first is a large global gap in the adoption and use of ICTs between OECD countries and Latin American and Caribbean countries. Even more

Figure 2.13 Extent of Business Internet Use: An International Comparison

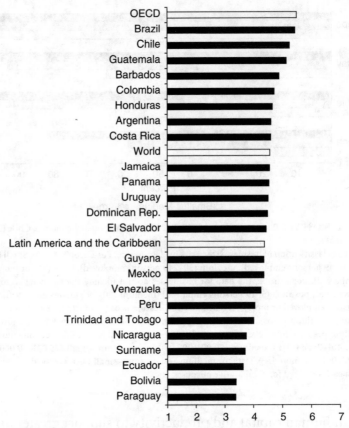

Source: WEF (2010).
Notes: Scores (1=Not at All; 7=Extremely) reflect the weighted average of 2008 and 2009 calculated by WEF (2010). Some 133 countries participated in the survey.
World = The average of the 133 participating countries.

worrisome, the adoption trends suggest that—with the exception of telephone technologies—the divide is widening in the remaining, more advanced technologies (Internet, broadband, and PCs).

Figure 2.14   The Relationship between Productivity, Regulation, Human Capital, and Infrastructure and the Extent of Business Internet Use, 2008

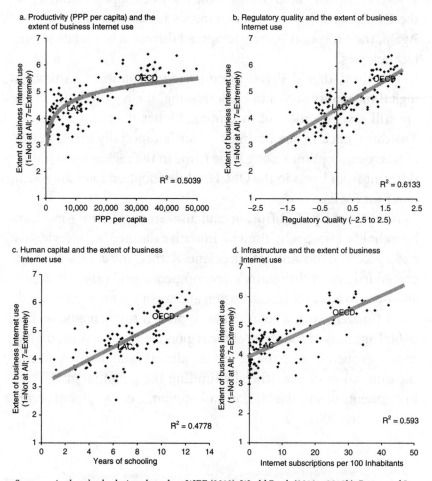

Sources: Authors' calculations based on WEF (2010); World Bank (2010a, 2010b); Barro and Lee (2000) and data set; ITU (2009b and 2009c).

Notes: For productivity (GDP per capita and business Internet use): For graphing purposes, the scale for purchasing power parity was cut off at 50,000 and data from Luxembourg (70,980.88) were suppressed.

The second digital divide is the gap *between* the countries of Latin America and the Caribbean. A handful of countries are at levels not very different from the least developed countries of the OECD, and a large set of countries lag considerably behind. Again, the exception is the widespread diffusion of mobile phone technologies.

The third digital divide occurs *within* countries. Although digital inequality seems to be decreasing, the regional indicators are still several orders of magnitude higher than in the OECD. The divergence in the business sector is especially great. Levels of Internet adoption among large firms in the region are not very different from levels in the OECD, while adoption rates are much lower for SMEs.

To promote ICT diffusion and use among Latin American households effectively, limited initiatives aimed at individuals and specific firms are not sufficient. Rather, initiatives must be embedded into each country's development agenda and a systemic approach to advance ICT diffusion and use must be implemented. Unfortunately, such a coordinated approach rarely happens. The digital agendas of countries of the region tend to assess the digital divide as merely an issue of access, almost completely ignoring the dimension of use—thereby limiting the potential of ICTs as instruments of social inclusion and economic development (Peres and Hilbert, 2009).

3

Banking on Technology for Financial Inclusion

Almost everyone in advanced economies has a bank account—90 percent of households to be more precise. But it isn't that way everywhere in the world. In the average Latin American and Caribbean country, only 35 percent of households have a bank account.[1] Meanwhile, firms in the region consistently point to problems accessing credit as a major obstacle to their development. According to the World Bank Enterprise Surveys (World Bank, 2010b), Latin American enterprises rank access to credit third on a list of constraints to their growth, behind high informal employment and political instability.

Why is access to financial services important? At the aggregate level, financial access has a positive impact on total factor productivity, which feeds into overall gross domestic product (GDP) growth. At the same time, financial development reduces income inequality and helps alleviate poverty (Beck, Levine, and Loayza, 2000; Beck, Demirgüç-Kunt, and Levine, 2007). But beyond the favorable macroeconomic effects, very simply, access to finance benefits individuals. It helps tide people over tough economic times, ensures them against risks, broadens their investment opportunities, reduces their vulnerability, mobilizes their savings, and facilitates the everyday buying and selling of goods and services.[2]

Financial development is especially beneficial for the poor. Figures 3.1 and 3.2 highlight a well-known fact in the finance

Figure 3.1   Financial Development and Access to Financial Services

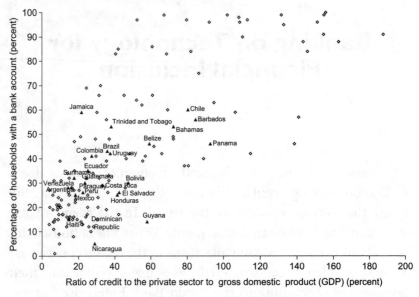

Source: World Bank (2010a).

literature. As financial sectors develop, financial inclusion increases and income inequality diminishes. The overall development of financial systems leads to a pro-poor outcome. This should come as no surprise; the poorest population is the most likely to face strong liquidity and credit constraints, and thus is more vulnerable to sudden changes in income. Deeper credit markets allow the poor to borrow more in order to grow their businesses, cover health costs, pay school fees, and simply make ends meet when their incomes slump.

Credit is not the only benefit that stems from gaining access to financial systems. Financial systems also provide valuable payment services that can help improve people's lifestyles, reduce poverty, and enhance the productivity of firms. Households and

Figure 3.2   Income Inequality and Access to Financial Services

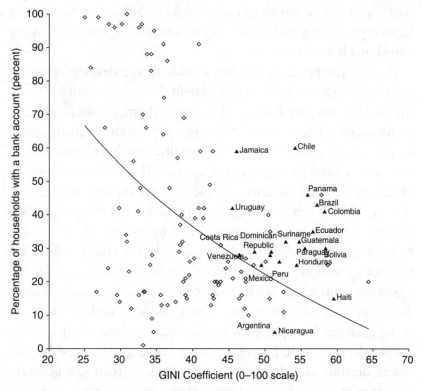

▲ Latin America and the Caribbean   ◇ Rest of the World

Source: World Bank (2010b).

firms can reduce transaction costs significantly by accessing financial services through different mechanisms, ranging from visiting bank offices to using cell phones. These alternatives can save time and free up a precious economic resource—labor—so it can be used in the most efficient way possible. For example, a small firm that can use the financial system to pay its utility bills rather than sending someone to pay for them in person is freeing up the time of workers, who can focus their energy on producing more goods and services. Similarly, a household that owns a home-based microenterprise can put the time that it spends waiting in line in banks to cash checks to better use purchasing inputs, producing and increasing its income, or simply enjoying additional leisure time.

Despite the benefits, few households in the developing world establish links to the financial system. There are many reasons for this; this chapter dwells on just one of them. Expanding access to financial services to cover a large population is costly. Most activities performed by financial institutions have traditionally been carried out through their branches. However, branching in places where there are fewer people, that are difficult to reach, or that are unsafe can be so costly that the benefit of opening and maintaining the branch is outweighed by its cost. Here is where technology—the focus of this book— plays a crucial role. New technologies allow service providers to obtain economies of scale. Costs per transaction can be reduced dramatically as transactions are completed outside of the branch network, and transactions using cash can be replaced with transactions done electronically. As physical access improves, opening accounts becomes simpler, prices decline, and demand grows, which in turn can generate the large volume of small transactions that can make this segment profitable. In summary, information and communication technologies (ICTs) can play a crucial role in reducing the cost of expanding financial services and spreading the benefits of financial inclusion, particularly for the poorest.

Empirical research and project case studies have analyzed the main barriers to improved financial access. Beck, Demirguc-Kunt, and Martínez Peria (2006) find big differences in the degree of physical access to formal financial institutions, the documentation required to open an account and effect banking transactions, and the fees and costs to access financial services in a sample of 193 countries. These differences are explained in part by high transaction costs associated with processing, monitoring, and enforcing small loans, particularly in geographically remote areas. People in rural areas must spend as much as a day walking or travelling by bus to the closest bank in order to complete a financial transaction, sometimes in extremely hazardous conditions. To address these problems, new kinds of mobile financial services were introduced years ago in parts of Africa and Asia. Unconventional ways to supply financial services through the use of mobile branches, cell phone technology, and deposit collectors (such as post offices, Internet kiosks, and retailers' point of sale) have emerged. All these mechanisms use technological advances to reduce transaction costs and increase access to people in remote areas.

Hooked Up at Home

Households can access financial services through several types of technological improvements. The development of the Internet has allowed many families around the world to pay utilities, transfer money, or send remittances from the comfort of their homes, for example. However, it will be a long time before the poorest households in the developing world will be able to afford a computer and Internet service of their own. Moreover, the cost of accessing Internet services in rural areas, where many of the poor reside, is still high. In the meantime, other solutions have been developed to provide banking services to poorer populations. Through mobile banking, the use of cellular phones, and other technologies, many of the underbanked in the world are gaining access to financial payments systems.

These initiatives have usually been driven by the private sector; the role of governments has been to provide an adequate regulatory framework. To complement such efforts and foster financial inclusion, governments recently have been channeling subsidies to the poor through new technologies. Important conditional cash transfer programs in the region, including the "Oportunidades" program in Mexico and "Familias en Acción" in Colombia, have been paying subsidies either through individual banking accounts with an electronic payment card or with electronic payment cards linked to a group account.

Another growing trend is the use of point of sale (POS) devices in commercial establishments to make credit and debit payments.[3] POS devices are especially on the rise in Brazil, Colombia, Mexico, and Peru. They help households reduce their transportation costs and, by limiting the cash they must carry on them, lower their risk of being robbed when going to the bank.

Technology may be used not only to overcome traditional barriers to access the financial system, but also to help people take full advantage of the financial system. For example, cell phone reminders can help people save money regularly so they can meet their savings goals. Regular reminders can help people increase their self-control and remind them of the value of saving now so they have money to pay for things they need or desire later. The use of cell phone reminders to save can effectively increase saving rates among the poorest. More generally, technology can be used as a tool to communicate with clients, helping them make better-informed financial decisions about their retirement plans, or increasing financial literacy in general.

The new technologies can also extend beyond national boundaries, allowing relatives living abroad to remit money to their home countries, and effectively increasing financial inclusion across countries and generations. A large literature has explored the benefits of international remittances for recipient households (Yang, 2008; Yang and Choi, 2007; Yang and Martínez, 2005). Households that receive remittances are more likely to save and to make investments in durable assets, education, or health than households that do not receive remittances. Recipient communities and countries also benefit as inequality is reduced and economic growth is spurred. Mobile banking (discussed below) could potentially be applied to the remittances market to reduce transaction and opportunity costs, and thus increase the amounts remitted to home countries.

M-banking: Banking within Everyone's Reach

Branchless banking, as m-banking is more widely known, uses a third-party outlet and available technology to offer basic deposit, transactional, and payment services. Operations are usually backed by a government-recognized, deposit-taking institution. The customers can choose between using bank offices or accessing services through payment cards or mobile phones (Ivatury and Mas, 2008). The evolution of branchless banking has its roots in automated teller machines (ATMs) and banking vans. The growing coverage of the Internet and the more developed wireless technology have allowed the creation of Internet banking, banking agents that operate under contractual relationships with established retail outlets, and mobile phone transactions (Mas, 2008a).

Mobile banking as a mechanism for financial inclusion has been growing at a fast pace around the world. Unfortunately, no hard data are available that allow meaningful cross-country comparisons, but banking through cellular telephones has been a promising avenue in many Asian and African countries, including Bangladesh, the Philippines, and South Africa.

Mobile finance has been boosted by the strong growth of mobile phones throughout developed and developing countries.[4] Worldwide, people have more phones than bank accounts. Figure 3.3 shows the relationship between the growth in mobile

Figure 3.3   Access to Financial Services and Access to Cell Phones

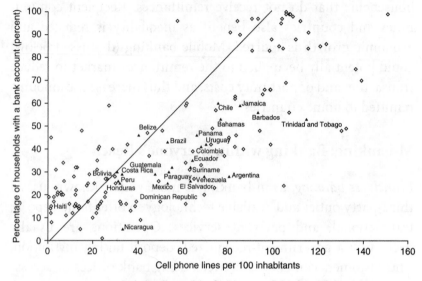

Source: World Bank (2010b).

finance and cell phone penetration for a variety of countries, including many in Latin America and the Caribbean. The 45-degree line indicates the points in which the penetration of cell phones is equal to that of bank accounts. The fact that so many countries, especially Latin American ones, fall below this line indicates that cell phones are far more popular than bank accounts.

There are many reasons why people do not have bank accounts. Having a telephone will not change important underlying factors determining that decision—but having a cellular phone can solve one issue that limits financial inclusion: limitations in the brick-and-mortar infrastructure of a financial institution. In many places, reaching the poorest is a geographic challenge. Imagine a coffee farmer who lives in the mountains in Colombia, hundreds of kilometers away from the nearest town. Despite producing one of the most valued commodities in the world, this farmer would find it difficult to be linked to the financial system, since there is not likely to be a bank office or an ATM nearby. There is little incentive for the coffee grower to have a bank account, and there is even less incentive for a bank to open an office in a remote area for a handful of coffee farmers. Technology can break this constraint and align the interests of both parties.

Until recently, the coffee grower would need go to the nearest town—possibly many hours away from his farm—sell his coffee, most likely receive cash, stuff it into his pockets, and save it until the time arrived to sell his next crop. Once in a while the farmer would grab some of that cash and travel back to town to buy fertilizer or some other production input, along with other basic supplies for his family. The cash could get stolen, lost, ruined by rain, or spent in a buying impulse.

Using mobile banking services could vastly improve this farmer's lifestyle. He probably has a cell phone, since Colombia's coffee industry has joined the growing trend of merging cell phones with financial services. In 2009, a pilot to provide financial services to the coffee- growing community was promoted by the National Federation of Coffee Growers of Colombia, the Inter-American Development Bank, cell-phone provider Telefónica, and the Banco de Bogotá, a large Colombian bank. The mechanism used is a straightforward one in the mobile banking community.

The coffee growers sell their coffee at the nearest cooperative. The proceeds of the sale are deposited in a bank account that each coffee grower has opened at the bank—an account that they can fully manage through their cell phones. Coffee growers can purchase supplies and production inputs at local facilities by accessing their bank account with their cell phones. This not only eliminates the risks of managing cash, but also significantly reduces transaction costs by saving coffee growers a trip to the nearest town to purchase goods and services.

According to the Consultative Group to Assist the Poor (CGAP), branchless banking helps cut transaction costs by at least 50 percent, compared to traditional banking channels. A regular transaction using branchless banking could cost about US$0.50, almost US$2.00 less than the traditional system in the Philippines, and US$0.53 less in Peru (Ivatury and Mas, 2008).[5]

For coffee growers in Colombia, and for millions of other people in the developing world, mobile phones can provide banking services in several ways. Most banking institutions enable clients to use their cell phones or a phone line to manage their accounts. People can check their balances, transfer money between accounts, or pay utilities, for example, following voice-driven menus. But the truly innovative mobile banking approaches go beyond these "additive" services and offer ways to transform the use of mobile phones to increase financial inclusion. The coffee growers program is just one example. The main idea is that the cell phone can work as a payments mechanism (in stores or as a means to receive remittances) and eventually could replace other means of payments, such as cash and check cards. The main difference is allowing the cell phone to act as a reserve of value. This can be done by linking the phone to a banking account or an electronic wallet. With an electronic wallet, users can "charge" their phones with a certain amount of money that they can use to make purchases at a store or some other participating location. The funds can be used until they are exhausted, like a debit card.

Bank accounts and electronic wallets are subject to different types of regulation. Bank accounts are regulated by banking oversight offices or central banks. Electronic wallets, on the other hand, do not require a bank account and thus are not necessarily regulated by banking regulators or supervised by the proper authorities. They are usually subject to different regulations aimed at limiting the amount of funds that can be assigned to the phone.

Another way to implement cell phone technology for financial transactions is mobile money service. Customers can transfer money to commercial establishments or to people just by sending a text message. Effectively, small retailers serve as bank branches. Their phones are linked to a mobile money account.

In Kenya, this system has been growing rapidly. The system, called M-PESA, is operated by Safaricom, Kenya's largest mobile operator, and is used by 9.5 million people (23 percent of the population). Transfers through the system are equivalent to 11 percent of the country's GDP each year. Considering that only 4 million people in Kenya have a bank account, this is a huge step toward financial inclusion. The growth of the system has been outstanding, attracting 1 million customers in its first ten months of operation and attesting to the fact that m-banking addresses a direct need of the population. Before M-PESA was in place, 77 percent of Kenyans kept their money "under the mattress" at home, and about 11 percent of them said their savings had been lost or stolen (Jack and Suri, 2010). According to Morawczynski and Pickens (2009), household users of M-PESA not only can transfer money more safely, more quickly, and more cheaply, but also they have been able to increase their incomes by between 5 and 30 percent. In addition, there is evidence that M-PESA not only facilitates individual transactions, but also permits intergenerational transfers of money that help compensate for the lack of a well-functioning social security system: 41 percent of M-PESA money transfers are sent to parents, and 8 percent to children.

South Africa, another well-known example, has implemented an m-finance service called WIZZIT, promoted as "a bank in your pocket." It works as a virtual bank (it has no branches) and offers a payment mechanism to the unbanked and under-banked that allows customers to make person-to-person pay-ments, transfers, and prepaid purchases through a cell phone. The service also provides customers with a *Maestro* debit card to make payments in retail outlets. WIZZIT does not require a minimum balance. It charges a subscription fee and transac-tional fee, depending on the type of transaction. A study con-ducted by CGAP surveyed 515 low-income South Africans—214 of them customers of WIZZIT—to inquire about how they used and viewed m-banking (Ivatury and Pickens, 2006). The people surveyed used WIZZIT because of its convenience, cheapness, and safety.[6]

The Asian case par excellence is the Philippines. Services there are supplied by two companies: SMART Communications and GLOBE Telecom. SMART Money links the user's phone to a cash account. Through SMART, cell phone users can access their account in the Banco de Oro, the business partner of the product. Customers can make cash deposits and withdrawals, transfer credit and cash, carry out cashless purchases, pay bills, enroll in direct deposit services through their employer payroll, and accept international remittances. The competing company, GLOBE Telecom, offers a service called G-Cash. It has the same business scheme as SMART Money, including services such as payment of income taxes and annual business registration fees; transfers from bank accounts to G-Cash via ATMs; and payment by Internet for cinema tickets, online stores, and games. A big dif-ference between the companies is the availability of debit card ser-vices; while SMART Money couples service to a MasterCard debit card, G-Cash currently does not.[7]

In the case of Rwanda, the service known as Me2U allows peo-ple to transfer cell phone airtime. Given the fungibility of airtime, this has been used as a quasi-money transfer in the country, and has become a prominent risk-sharing device. For example, in February 2008, a magnitude 6 earthquake hit some areas of the country, leaving a toll of 43 dead and more than 1,090 injured, destroying 2,288 houses, and causing regional school closures and electrical outages. The availability of the Me2U service allowed the population to respond quickly. Even before official aid arrived to the affected regions, people living elsewhere were able to transfer airtime to the affected regions. Blumenstock, Eagle, and Fafchamps (2010) estimate that following the quake, the additional aggregate value of incoming airtime sent to people in affected regions reached roughly 13,500 RWF (US$27). Though modest in absolute terms, this represents a large increase, compared to the affected region's average of 8,480 RWF (US$17). It is also large relative to Rwanda's average annual income of roughly US$1,000.

Even in the most studied case (Kenya's M-PESA), questions remain about the effects of mobile banking (M-PESA) on aggregate economic growth. In theory, it could spur growth by allowing routine transactions to be processed more quickly and reliably. Moreover, by making lending easier, it could allow capital to move more efficiently, facilitating economic activity that might not otherwise occur. The lack of formal evaluations of the aggregate effects of branchless banking precludes an overall assessment of the effects of these innovative uses of technology to expand the reach of the financial sector.

No Latin American country outright forbids the provision of financial services through cell phones. However, three regulatory blocks affect the way mobile banking services are provided: the regulation of nonbank correspondents, money-laundering regulations, and regulations regarding the issuance of electronic money.

Non-bank correspondents are nonbank commercial institutions, such as shops or convenience stores, that provide certain
banking services. This innovative arrangement has emerged in
many countries, including Brazil, Colombia, Mexico, and Peru.
For example, a local convenience store could collect deposits and
transfer them to a bank, or withdraw money from a bank account
and hand the money to the main holder of the deposit account.
In practice, this requires only a POS device that links the commercial establishment to a banking network. It also requires an
adjustment in financial regulation to allow a third party that is
not a bank to handle deposits.

This is not a trivial feature, since deposits are one of the most
protected assets in modern societies. The whole system of prudential regulation and supervision is designed to safeguard them.
Regulations tend to be strict as to who can handle deposits, how
they should be managed, and how they should be insured to reduce
risk, especially for the most uninformed households. Despite the
importance of these regulations, most countries have been able to
accommodate nonbank correspondents, subject to certain safety
provisions.

Brazil boasts a decade-long experience with nonbank correspondents. The scheme, initially developed around the year
2000, allows financial institutions to offer many financial services through lottery kiosks, post offices, pharmacies, and similar
establishments through a POS device installed on site. Currently,
the correspondent banking outlets can provide transaction and
payment services to people without bank accounts. Some can also
take deposits, allow withdrawals from savings accounts, and complete other financial transactions, such as managing investment
funds. The system has developed so deeply that some institutions have been authorized to use correspondents to receive loan
and credit card applications. A World Bank study suggests that

nonbank correspondents have been a successful strategy to boost financial services to poorer, remote social segments in Brazil. The system has been effective in reducing the high variable costs of small transactions and the fixed costs of having bank branches in low-density areas (Kumar, Nair, Parsons, and Urdapilleta, 2006).

The fourth country in the emerging world with the most non-banking correspondents is Peru. The nonbanking agents, or *"los cajeros corresponsales,"* were established in 2005. Four big banks dominate the agent network, located mainly in the Lima metropolitan area (51 percent of the total agents). The banks do not charge customers a fee to use the nonbanking agents. According to Mas (2008b), the Peruvian experience has also been successful, since banking penetration has reached an additional 16 percent of Peru's population in just over two years.

In an attempt to look at m-banking opportunities in Latin America, the Multilateral Investment Fund (MIF) of the Inter-American Development Bank surveyed financial institutions and mobile telecommunication operators in seven countries of the region (Bolivia, Brazil, Ecuador, the Dominican Republic, Mexico, Peru, and Brazil). The survey included questions regarding the provision of mobile services, regulatory and legislative barriers, and business strategies. According to MIF, the major issues associated with potential partners (such as banks, telephone companies, microfinance institutions, retailer networks, and other potential nonbank correspondents) is the difficulty in defining a sustainable business model in the context of numerous small payments, uncertainties related to the countries' regulatory framework, and the need for sufficiently reliable nonbank correspondents.

Money-laundering regulations impose another important constraint on how mobile banking may develop in the region. Money laundering is a huge concern worldwide and, thanks to its association with drug trafficking, in Latin America and the Caribbean in particular. Regulations usually impose limits on the value of transactions that need not be supervised by a local authority. Without regulations, the risk is high that drug lords and terrorists could use mobile banking to transfer funds to their local operations. This problem becomes even more serious in countries where most of the cell phone lines are prepaid and line holders need not be fully identified. This highlights the need to develop the mobile banking industry solely though the promotion of fully identifiable and personally owned cell phones.

Finally, regulations setting limits on electronic money creation are extremely important. They mostly affect the possibility of developing m-banking through electronic wallet systems. When linked to a bank account, mobile bank services are ruled by the norms and regulations that affect any deposit in a financial institution. To protect deposits, financial institutions must take several steps—which amount to costs of doing business—for taking deposits, such as knowing the client before opening an account, or paying a deposit insurance fee, or keeping a fraction of the deposits "frozen" in what is known as a reserve requirement. Nonbanks do not have to pay these costs since they are not regulated. This can create a distortion: two entities offering a similar service must follow different regulations that may affect the costs they incur in providing the service, as well as the use of funds.

In some countries, regulations on the creation of electronic money have sparked strict prohibitions on the type of instruments upon which mobile banking can grow. In Colombia, only banks are allowed to intermediate anything that looks like a deposit. This has limited the expansion of the use of cell phones as electronic wallets or similar instruments.

There is no unique regulatory model guiding the development of m-banking. What matters is that regulators know and understand the risks they are facing and find an adequate way of dealing with them. Strengthening mobile banking benefits several parties. Households and commercial establishments gain through increases in savings, better management of cash, and higher sales. Banks gain by recruiting new customers into their customer base through a low-cost conduit, increasing the productivity of banking workers, and lowering transaction costs with a small investment in technology and infrastructure. Mobile phone operators also gain by boosting demand for and loyalty to their services and brands. Regulators need to put in place the right regulatory network so that the rest of society enjoys the benefit of the mobile banking net.

Paying Subsidies with Debit Cards

Possibly the most cost-effective public policy with great potential to include the traditionally unbanked is the payment of cash transfers through bank accounts. Several Latin American countries, notably Argentina, Brazil, Colombia, Mexico, and Peru, have large cash transfer programs that use their financial systems to make payments. Governments can deposit payments in beneficiaries' bank accounts, and beneficiaries can draw on these funds using either debit cards issued by their banks or mobile devices. The use of electronic payments reduces transaction costs for beneficiaries, including the time spent in lines to receive payments, the time to convert the payments into cash, the risk of having cash on hand that either can be stolen or spent too easily in day-to-day activities, or the risk of dealing with a corrupt public official who may demand a bribe for giving the subsidy to the beneficiary.

Linking cash transfers directly to bank accounts reduces costs associated with corruption and crime, and can cut down the time that beneficiaries must spend at a public office to receive the transfer. However, only the use of an electronic means of payment such as a debit card or a mobile device can help people eliminate the transaction costs of converting subsidies into cash. While the use of bank accounts to receive cash transfers still needs to be evaluated rigorously, many conclusions have already been reached.

The few available studies focus on Argentina and Mexico. A recent study by Duryea and Schargrodsky (2008) about the *Plan Jefas y Jefes de Hogar* program in Argentina sheds some light on the benefits to households of receiving transfers through accounts linked to a debit card. Besides saving time, this mechanism has helped households to smooth consumption over time and shift their purchases away from informal establishments to stores in the formal economy. This is a cash transfer program that benefits nearly 1.5 million people, who receive the equivalent of approximately US$50 a month. The program switched from cash payments to payments in ATMs through a debit card in 2004 and 2005. Beneficiaries receive a debit card from *Banco Nación*, a local, state-owned bank that opens a free deposit account for that purpose for them. Through the debit card, the recipients of the transfer can withdraw their money from an ATM or make transactions in any store that has a POS device. In addition, purchases made with these cards are exempt from paying 15 points of the 21 percent value-added tax (VAT) prevailing in Argentina.

The study shows that over 90 percent of the people sampled prefer to be paid through the debit card mechanism than with direct cash payments. Most feel it is more efficient and more secure, and estimate that they save a great deal of time using the ATM payment instead of cash. On average, it takes more than four hours to receive the cash payment, while it takes only forty minutes to find an ATM and withdraw money. The time saved is used to work more, mostly in every household member's main job, and thus increase the household's income. This payment mechanism has also significantly reduced the number of kick-backs and increased purchases in formal-sector stores where debit cards are accepted.

In Mexico, a wide variety of programs transfer subsidies through the financial system. The best known is *Oportunidades*, Mexico's leading cash transfer program, which currently benefits more than 5 million families. The switch from cash payments to bank accounts in the *Oportunidades* program has been gradual and started in 2001. To date, about 20 percent of the beneficiaries—about 1.1 million families, mostly in urban areas—are paid through bank accounts. The accounts have been opened in *Bansefi*, a government-owned microsavings institution. As of December 2009, about 250,000 families had received an ATM card linked to the account where the subsidy is paid; that number is rapidly expanding and will reach several thousand more by the end of 2011. When comparing 20,000 randomly selected beneficiaries who received their subsidy in an account with 20,000 randomly selected *Bansefi* account holders, and after taking into account differences in income, Seira (2010) found that the *Oportunidades* bank account holders were more likely to save money than those who did not receive the benefit. The median savings of an *Oportunidades-Bansefi* client was more than twice that of a traditional bank account client (246 peso vs. 101 pesos on a monthly basis). The *Oportunidades* account holders also performed twice as many transactions as *Bansefi* clients who did not participate in the *Oportunidades* program, suggesting that the increased savings rate was voluntary among households.

In Brazil, the *Bolsa de Familia* program uses electronic cards to pay subsidies. The recipients of the subsidy receive an ATM card that can be used in the extensive network of the largest public bank in the country, *Caixa Econômica Federal*. Similarly,

Colombia's *Familias en Accion*, a large program currently transferring nearly US$50 dollars on a bimonthly basis to more than 2.5 million families across the country, pays the subsidy through bank accounts in the *Banco Agrario*, the country's only first-tier, state-owned bank. There have been no evaluations of the impacts on households of receiving subsidies through bank accounts and debit cards in Brazil and Colombia, but evidence on the use of electronic payments to distribute subsidies is positive. If the experience of Argentina and Mexico is any indication, poor households could be expected to save more, reduce their exposure to corruption and theft, and, most importantly, enjoy more time to work and thus to buoy their income. All of these constitute important elements in the quest to defeat poverty.

Dial "S" for Savings

Credit is an important avenue to financial inclusion, but it is not the only one. The poor are also able to save for future investments. Unfortunately, even in places where financial services are available and people are ready and willing to save, savings rates are low. Only recently, research on psychology and economics has started to look at nontraditional ways to provide commitment devices and reminders that allow individuals to achieve their savings goals.

Cell phones can be used not only to provide financial services, but also to encourage certain types of behavior, particularly to help people exercise greater financial discipline and self-control. An example is saving. People usually promise themselves that they will set aside money until they achieve a certain goal. However, these promises are often broken because people postpone savings to the future, turn a blind eye to future needs, or choose current over future consumption.

A recent study by Karlan et al (2010) explores the impact of reminding deposit holders about commitments on how much money they want to save and how often they should make deposits. An experiment was carried out in Bolivia, Peru, and the Philippines in which specific banks sent messages to their clients to remind them about their savings commitments. Banks sent the message before the expected deposit date and a reminder after the date. The reminders have a positive and significant impact on savings, compared to clients who also made saving commitments but did not receive the reminders. On average, the people who received the reminders achieved their deposit goals 3 percent more often and were able to save 6 percent more.

The growing literature on behavioral economics has focused considerably on the study of time-inconsistent preferences and how some mechanisms can help people overcome their bias for immediate gratification (O'Donoghue, and Rabin, 2001; Bryan, Karlan, and Nelson, 2010, Giné, Karlan, and Zinman, 2010). The standard economic model assumes a person's relative preference for well-being at an earlier date and a later date is the same: that is, that intertemporal preferences are time-consistent. But evidence suggests that people's preference for gratification sooner rather than later becomes stronger as the earlier date nears. In particular, consumption, savings, and borrowing behavior is sometimes difficult to reconcile with traditional models of intertemporal choice (Karlan et al, 2010).

Karlan et al show that reminders change intertemporal allocations and improve consumer welfare by linking future expenditure opportunities to today's choices. In the authors' words, they mitigate "attentional failure": that is, inattention to future consumption opportunities.

The experiment conducted by Karlan and his team varied slightly from country to country. Field experiments were run with three different banks in Bolivia, Peru, and the Philippines. In each experiment, individuals opened a savings account that included varying degrees of incentives or commitment features designed to encourage them to reach a savings goal. Some individuals were randomly assigned to receive a monthly reminder via text message or letter, while a control group received no reminder.

In the Philippines, a bank offered an account in which clients committed to save a certain amount of money in a certain period (US$50 or more, from three months to two years). The bank randomly chose a fraction of clients with cell phones and sent them a reminder to save via a text message once a month. For different clients, the text varied in the way that it emphasized either a gain or a loss from saving. For example, the reminder emphasizing the gain from saving read: "Frequent deposits into the Ghandom Savings account will make your dream come true. A reminder from First Valley Bank." The message emphasizing a loss stated: "If you don't frequently deposit into the Ghandom Savings account, your dream will not come true. A reminder from First Valley Bank." Some clients were also chosen randomly to receive a "late" message if they did not deposit money that month. Some of the "late" messages emphasized the gains of savings, and others the loss.

In Peru, the researchers worked with a state-owned bank, *Caja de Ica*, and offered a new product called *Plan Ahorro* to clients. The clients selected a time frame to achieve a certain savings goal (six or twelve months) and a minimum deposit to make each month. If the client reached a goal, he or she was rewarded with an 8 percent interest rate, twice the regular interest rate of the savings product offered. A fraction of clients were selected to receive reminders. Some reminders included the goal, and others did not. As in the Philippines, the wording changed in some reminders to emphasize a gain from savings or a loss from failing to save. Late reminders were also sent. Cell phone coverage in the area was low, so the bank sent the reminders by mail. Two additional treatments were tested. One randomly sent a letter to some people in the reminder group that focused on their particular goal (in addition to containing the boilerplate reminder). Another treatment independently and randomly offered clients a gift upon opening the account: a jigsaw puzzle of their goal, a photo of their goal, or a pen. Those in the jigsaw puzzle group received a piece of the puzzle after each deposit.

In Bolivia, the researchers worked with a private bank, *Ecofuturo*, and sent text messages to clients of the *Ecoaguinaldo* program. This savings strategy aims to encourage people to deposit a certain amount of money every month; by the end of the year, they would have saved the equivalent of one month's wage, the amount formal workers receive at the end of the year by law. When signing up for the program, clients determined how much they would save every month. If clients made all their deposits within the first ten months, they would be rewarded with a 6 percent interest rate (twice as high as they would receive otherwise) and a free life and accident insurance policy. Clients were randomly assigned to receive a text message. Some messages included reminders about the benefits, while others did not. Table 3.1 summarizes the messages sent to the Bolivia and Peru clients.

Using reminders proved useful not only in increasing savings, but also in increasing the likelihood that clients in Bolivia would meet their target amount (3 percent). Not only did the reminders have an effect, but the way in which the message was phrased mattered as well. Reminders that highlighted the client's particular goal, such as school fees, were twice as effective as reminders that did not mention the goal. These findings are novel empirical evidence about the importance of reminders in household finance.

Table 3.1   Messages and Reminders Sent to Clients in Bolivia and Peru

Peru

Regular reminder	**Standard**	**Gain**	We would like to remind you that your next Plan Ahorro deposit should be made on [X]. If you make all of your deposits, you will receive a total of [Y] in additional interest rate incentive!
		Loss	We would like to remind you that your next Plan Ahorro deposit should be made on [X]. If you miss a payment, you will lose a total of [Y] in additional interest rate incentive!
	Specific	**Gain**	We would like to remind you that your next Plan Ahorro deposit should be made on [X]. If you make all of your deposits, you will receive a total of [Y] in additional interest rate incentive that you will be able to use to reach your savings goal of [Z]!
		Loss	We would like to remind you that your next Plan Ahorro deposit should be made on [X]. If you miss a payment, you will lose a total of [Y] in additional interest rate incentive that you will be able to use to reach your savings goal of [Z]!
Late Message	**Standard**	**Gain**	We would like to remind you that your Plan Ahorro deposit should have been made by [W]. If you wish to continue in Plan Ahorro, you should make your deposit as soon as possible. If you make all of your deposits, you will receive a total of [Y] in additional interest rate incentive!
		Loss	We would like to remind you that your Plan Ahorro deposit should have been made by [W]. If you wish to continue in Plan Ahorro, you should make your deposit as soon as possible. If you miss a payment, you will lose a total of [Y] in additional interest rate incentive!

Table 3.1   (Continued)

Late Message	**Specific**	Gain	We would like to remind you that your Plan Ahorro deposit should have been made by [W]. If you wish to continue in Plan Ahorro, you should make your deposit as soon as possible. If you make all of your deposits, you will receive a total of [Y] in additional interest rate incentive that you will be able to use to reach your savings goal of [Z]!
		Loss	We would like to remind you that your Plan Ahorro deposit should have been made by [W]. If you wish to continue in Plan Ahorro, you should make your deposit as soon as possible. If you miss a payment, you will lose a total of [Y] in additional interest rate incentive that you will be able to use to reach your savings goal of [Z]!

Bolivia

Regular Reminder	**Standard**	Gain	Ecofuturo reminds you: Your Ecoaguinaldo is within reach! Don't forget your deposits this month! You will be one step closer to your savings goal.
		Loss	Ecofuturo reminds you: Don't fail to reach your Ecoaguinaldo! Don't forget your deposits this month! If you don't make your deposit you increase the chance of not reaching your savings goal.
	Specific	Gain	Ecofuturo reminds you: Maintain your Ecoaguinaldo life insurance! Don't forget your deposits this month! You will keep your insurance by making all of your deposits on time.
		Loss	Ecofuturo reminds you: Don"t lose your Ecoaguinaldo life insurance! Don't forget your deposits this month! You will lose your insurance if you don't make all of your deposits on time.

Source: Karlan, McConnell, Mullainathain and Zinman (2010)

This innovative use of modern technology to influence savings decisions proved effective, particularly given the low cost of cellular phone texting. The advantage of using text message reminders over mailings lies mainly in its cost advantage in terms of both money and labor. Comparing the results of the experiments in Bolivia and Peru, the researchers found that the bank receives a profit of about US$0.20 per client with text messages, compared to a loss of US$2.32 per client with mailings.

Another tool to provide useful information to help clients make better financial decisions is information technologies. Hastings, Mitchell, and Chyn (2010) conducted a randomized experiment in Chile to determine if providing workers with information on the variations in fees charged for pension funds made a difference in which fund workers finally chose.

Chile has been a world leader in advancing privately managed pension funds. In the current market, there are significant differences in the fees different companies charge. The Chilean government implemented an information policy that presents the returns and fees of each fund, as compared to the cheapest one. However, some people still choose the higher-priced funds. Thus, there is substantial interest in finding ways to enhance participants' awareness and understanding of how fees and charges influence the growth and value of their pensions. One way to accomplish this is to determine whether people become more price-sensitive to fees when they are depicted in alternative formats.

In the experiment, the researchers used an on-site spreadsheet that computed the expected balance of each respondent's pension fund based on past returns and fund commissions, and each individual's wage, balance, and age. The balances were computed for each pension fund and shown to the interviewees in different ways. For one group, the returns were shown in comparison to the highest-cost fund (highlighting the relative loss). For the second group, the returns were compared to the cheapest fund (highlighting the relative benefit).

The experiment found that people with lower levels of education, income, and financial literacy rely more on the advice of employers, friends, and coworkers than on fundamentals in choosing a fund. Furthermore, the researchers found that such individuals are more responsive to the way the information is presented (information framing) when interpreting the relative benefits of different investment choices.

The Chilean experiment shows that financial literacy campaigns can be delivered with the help of information technology. However, the possibility of extrapolating these results to other contexts is limited. The use of information technology as a tool of financial education must take into account local market conditions and the likelihood that the ICT can be adequately adopted.

In the southern Andes of Peru, Arariwa, a microfinance nongovernmental organization (NGO), tested whether information technology could be used to improve the impact of a financial literacy program. They randomly assigned different radio and video aids to forty-nine credit officers working in 666 communal banks in thirteen provinces of the departments of Cusco and Puno, Peru.

The program evaluated consisted of nine monthly 45-minute training sessions that use a 5-to-7-minute video, nine 25-minute radio programs that reinforce the material in the training sessions, and nine homework assignments that encourage households to commit to behavioral changes. Valdivia, Karlan, and Chong (2010) report that too few ICTs were adopted to be able to detect any benefits in savings, retention, or repayment rates.

The main reason why video aids were not used was because of the lack of DVD and TV sets. Even though clients offered to lend their equipment to other clients for the training sessions, it quickly became an inconvenience. On the other hand, clients rarely heard the radio messages. It was hard to convince local radio stations to replace their prime-time programming with another type of content, and when the desired content was aired, clients reported not being close to a radio or not listening to it. In addition, electricity was spotty, making it harder for both treatments to reach the desired population.

More rigorous evaluation remains to be done concerning the use of information technology to increase financial literacy. Those evaluations will be the only way to learn what works and what doesn't work in different contexts.

Rewriting the Bottom Line for Firms

The benefits of technology and banking can be reaped by the corporate sector, as well as households. In particular, the use of the Internet for financial transactions has the potential to significantly increase the productivity of businesses around the globe.

Figure 3.4 shows a strong correlation between Internet coverage and average firm total factor productivity, a measure of the efficiency with which a firm uses its production inputs. Although it is difficult to establish a causal relationship from this figure, it is interesting to note how strong the relationship is. To understand more about the relationship between productivity and Internet use, it is useful to explore the conduits through which the relationship takes place.[8]

One hypothesis is that the Internet can facilitate several types of transactions and thereby free up valuable resources for more productive purposes. An example of a time-saving activity is Internet banking. In many places in the world, firms assign people the job of standing in line in banks for hours to do routine tasks like

Figure 3.4   Total Factor Productivity and Internet Users

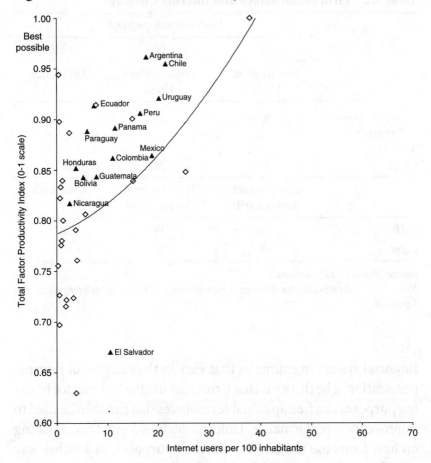

▲ Latin America and the Caribbean   ◇ Rest of the World

Source: Author's calculations based on World Bank (2010a and 2010b).

paying utilities, transferring money, and signing acceptance slips for funds transferred into their accounts.

Internet banking makes these dreadful days a thing of the past—at least in countries where the Internet is widespread. Table 3.2 compares the performance of firms with access to the

Table 3.2   Firm Performance and Internet Coverage

	Sales Growth (percent)		
	(1)	(2)	(3)
	Low Internet Users	High Internet Users	Difference
Small/Medium Enterprises (SME)	9	20	11***
Large	6	22	16***
	Low Internet Access Tariff	High Internet Access Tariff	Difference
SME	15	19	4***
Large	19	21	2***

Source: Authors' calculations.
Note: "***" indicates that the difference between means are statistically significant at 1 percent.

financial system in countries that vary in their degree of Internet penetration. The theory is that firms that use the Internet for banking purposes can free up valuable resources that can then be used to improve their performance. Unfortunately, information is lacking on how firms use the Internet for such purposes, so another way must be used to measure the use of such services. The Enterprise Surveys (ES) conducted by the World Bank of firms around the world for the past decade or so identifies whether firms have a bank account. The usage of Internet-provided banking services is then approximated by the product of having a bank account and being in a country with high Internet usage. If the Internet is widespread, it is assumed that firms with a bank account are more likely to use Internet financial services.

Despite shortcomings in the data and assumptions, some interesting results confirm the hypothesis. Table 3.2 reports the average growth rate of sales of firms of different sizes with access to bank accounts in countries with different levels of penetration of the Internet. On average, the growth rate of firms with access to the financial system through a bank account is much larger in countries with high Internet penetration than in countries where Internet usage is low. This difference is statistically significant for small- and medium-sized enterprises (SMEs) (see column three).

Figures 3.5 and 3.6 go one step further by exploring how the impact of accessing the financial system affects a firm's growth, and how that relationship depends on the development of the Internet. The figures plot the change in firms' growth associated with having a bank account for different levels of Internet usage (figure 3.5) and different costs of accessing the Internet (figure 3.6). There is a strong positive relationship between the share of the population that uses the Internet and the impact of having a bank account on a firm's sales growth.[9] Higher Internet penetration leads to higher impacts of having a bank account on a firm's growth rate.

Figure 3.6 presents exactly the same analysis using another measure of Internet penetration: the cost of accessing the Internet, rather than the population coverage of the Internet. The results are qualitatively similar. Higher costs are associated with lower usage. In countries with lower costs, the impact on a firm's growth rate of accessing the financial system is greater than in countries with higher costs. This impact is more notable for SMEs than for large firms.

Using the Internet for banking activities cuts transaction costs, which firms can use to enhance their performance. This is mostly the case for SMEs. The savings from using technology can have a positive economic impact, reducing poverty and growing employment.

Figure 3.5   Marginal Effect of Checking or Savings Accounts on Sales Growth and Internet Users

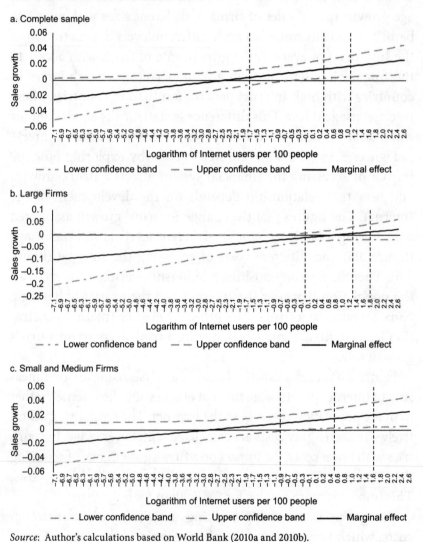

Source: Author's calculations based on World Bank (2010a and 2010b).

Figure 3.6   Marginal Effect of Checking or Savings Accounts on Sales Growth and Broadband Internet Access

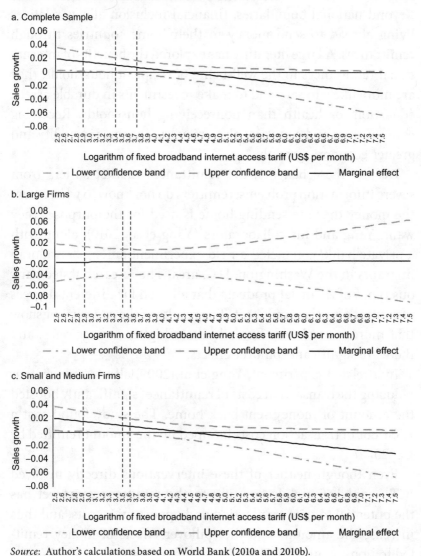

Source: Author's calculations based on World Bank (2010a and 2010b).

It's a Small World After All

Beyond national boundaries, financial inclusion allows relatives living abroad to send money to their home countries through remittances. A large literature has explored the benefits of international remittances to the well-being of recipient households: they are more likely to save and to make investments in durable assets, education, or health than nonreceiving households. Receiving communities and countries also enjoy less income inequality and greater economic growth.

Despite these benefits, the remittances market suffers from severe information problems; remitters do not know to what extent the money they are sending home is used for the purposes they want. Yang and his collaborators (Yang et al, 2010), along with a private bank, conducted a field experiment among Salvadoran migrants in the Washington, D.C. area. The research tested various types of financial products that allowed for different degrees of control over the funds sent. The results of the experiment show that more control over funds leads to higher savings rates, and there are significant spillover effects.

In a related experiment, Yang et al (2009) also tested whether reducing the transaction costs of remittances significantly boosted the amount of money sent back home. The study found that a US$1 cut in transaction costs bumped up the amount remitted by US$25.

Even though neither of these interventions directly involved ICTs, applying mobile banking to the remittances market has the potential to trim transaction and opportunity costs, and thus increase the amounts and the spillover effects of money remitted to home countries. Since Latin America and the Caribbean is one of the world's largest remittance receivers, the development potential of these interventions is enormous.

The Internet is slowly changing another branch of international transactions: global giving and international aid. Traditionally, official bilateral and multilateral aid has been allocated based on country-wide indicators, as well as political economy considerations. Internet-based contributions by private individuals have amounted to a revolution in cross-boundary philanthropy, allowing individuals to choose individual projects, rather than countries, as beneficiaries of their giving. Flows of global aid are now going to projects in countries that are unlikely to receive large amounts of official international aid, such as Iran and the Democratic Republic of Congo.

The revolution in Internet-based giving, introduced by organizations like Kiva and Global Giving, has facilitated the development of a global giving system that complements current official aid. Desai and Kharas (2009) compared the allocation of funds from these organizations to official development assistance and found that private aid is less oriented toward country-specific factors and more toward frontline projects and individuals in developing nations. These findings mean that private and official aid are not competing with each other; rather, they are complementary. While official aid supports countries, private aid helps individuals complete their projects.

The Hitch

Information technology can lessen the transaction costs that households and firms face on a daily basis. The use of cellular phones and the Internet for financial purposes can help many throughout the world combat poverty, improve their standard of living, and become more productive. Projects around the world are now using different methods to increase the likelihood that the poorest people and the smallest firms can gain access to the financial sector through technological devices. Yet consumers' ignorance of the uses and benefits of these services represents an enormous barrier to disseminating these services to different sectors of the population. Reaching consumers with financial education is costly. Various schemes have emerged in the region, from incentives to the private sector, as through *Banca de las Oportunidades* in Colombia, to initiatives of the public sector, as through *BanRural* in Guatemala.

To date, Latin America and the Caribbean has been moving relatively slowly to exploit technology to foster financial inclusion. Nonetheless, many pilot projects have taken off, with the aim of achieving what Asian and African countries accomplished years ago—with the advantage of being able to take stock of the lessons learned.

Latin America and the Caribbean has learned the hard way, through crises, how to design prudential systems of financial regulation and supervision. The prudential regulation of electronic payments devices is crucial to maintain financial soundness. Despite the region's advances in regulating the financial system, authorities must be aware of new types of fraudulent activities that base their Ponzi-type schemes on the use of electronic payments systems. As noted by Carvajal et al (2009) and by the widely covered scandal of D.M.G. Grupo Holding (DMG) in Colombia, criminals are using prepaid cards, cell phones, and other apparently legal devices to scam people into participating in pyramid schemes. Cooperation between authorities, including financial regulators, state prosecutors, and police forces, is of great importance to prevent many valuable instruments for promoting financial inclusion from losing their credibility in the eyes of the general public because they are occasionally used illegally. In some countries, this may be more difficult to accomplish than accommodating the regulatory environment to the high tech future of banking.

4

Rewiring Institutions

Institutions shape economic and social behavior. Countries with lower institutional quality are more likely to have slower economic growth, higher economic inequality, more social conflicts, and fewer and lower-quality public services.

While the institutional development of countries in Latin America and the Caribbean is similar to the world average, the region lags far behind developed countries in governance indicators (see figure 4.1). Consider these measures. In an index devised by Acemoglu, Johnson, and Robinson (2001) that looks at differences in institutions resulting from different types of states and policies,[1] Latin America and the Caribbean scores 89 out of 100, close to the world average of 85, but well behind the average of 99 for the countries of the Organization for Economic Co-operation and Development (OECD). In a World Bank measure of democratic accountability, the region scores well compared to the world average (59 versus 48 out of 100), but trails the average of 89 for OECD countries. The pattern is similar for corruption, which many consider to be an important determinant of economic performance. Although the region's average exceeds the world average (57 versus 48 out of 100), it lags well behind the OECD average of 86 (World Bank, 2006).

Institutional development is strongly associated with economic growth. Patterns of colonial settlement around the world affect the quality of current institutions, which in turn affect the rate

Figure 4.1 Governance Indicators

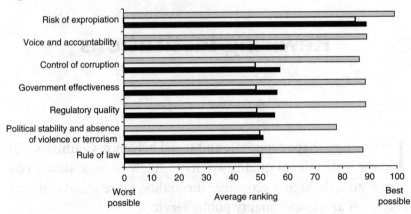

Source: For all variables calculations are based on World Bank (2009), except Risk of expropriation which is based on Acemoglu et al (2001).
Note: Variables correspond to 2009, except Risk of expropriation which is 1995.

of economic growth (Acemoglu, Johnson, and Robinson, 2001). Figure 4.2 shows that variation in income per capita is positively associated with variation in the risk of expropriation as a proxy for institutions. This relationship is particularly important in Latin America and the Caribbean. Enterprises in the region report that the most important constraints to their development are high levels of informal employment and political instability (World Bank, 2010a).

Institutional development also has an effect on economic inequality. Good institutions provide better economic opportunities to the population (Chong and Gradstein, 2007). By contrast, countries with lower institutional development tend to exclude a significant portion of the population from economic development, generating higher economic inequality. Importantly, institutional quality and income inequality not only go hand in hand;

Figure 4.2   Economic Growth and Institutions

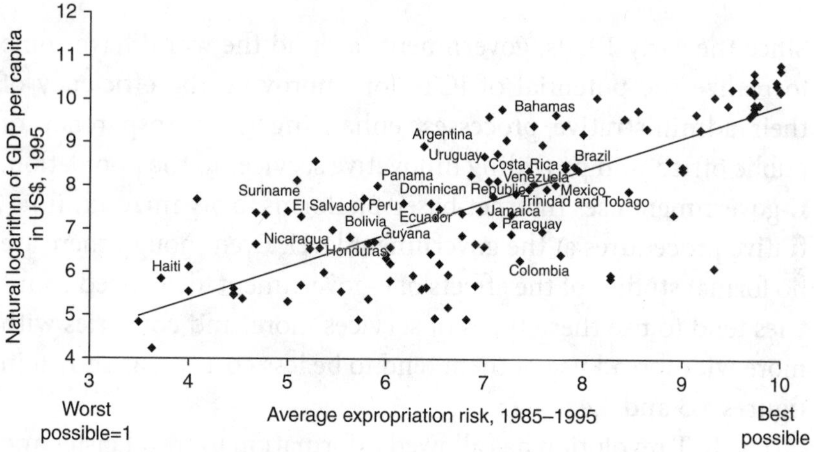

Source: Political Risk Service Group (2005) and World Bank (2010b).

they reinforce each other and the double causality holds for a wide variety of institutional indicators.

This evidence highlights the need for policies aimed at improving institutional development. However, overarching macro policies in this area are hard to formulate, demand considerable political will, require a long period of deep reforms, and yield mixed results, at best. An alternative approach is to focus on interventions that seek to change individual behavior and social norms, which are the foundation for institutional development. This chapter presents evidence pointing in this direction, focusing on recent experiences—mostly in Latin America and the Caribbean. The highlighted studies test whether information and communication technologies (ICTs) can be effective tools to improve the efficiency of government, to help the population hold the government accountable, and to change social behavior in a way that it supports better institutional development by increasing voting rates and enhancing other forms of political and social participation.

Government Goes Online

Since the early 1990s, governments around the world have come to realize the potential of ICTs for improving the efficiency of their administrative processes, enhancing the transparency of public office, and providing innovative services to the population. E-government uses Internet-based platforms to organize administrative procedures at the government level. Even though there are no formal studies of the effects of e-government, developed countries tend to use these types of services more, and countries with more widespread use of them tend to be less corrupt, as shown in figures 4.3 and 4.4.

The ICT revolution has allowed information to travel faster and in a more transparent way. The public sector has recognized these advantages and is increasingly using ICTs to improve administrative procedures and provide services more efficiently to citizens.

The region hosts several remarkable examples of online government purchasing systems. In Chile, the government is using an e-procurement system to purchase goods from the private business sector (http://www.chilecompra.cl/). Ministries, municipal governments, hospitals, and the armed forces can use ChileCompra's platform for tenders for both domestic and foreign companies. In Trinidad and Tobago, the Ministry of Finance has put in place a web-based procurement tool (http://www.Finance.gov.tt) that allows suppliers to bid online for contracts to supply goods or services.

Local governments and small communities are also exploiting the potential of ICTs to improve the efficiency of government services. In Peru, the Institute for Peruvian Studies (IEP) designed and manages the *Municipio al Día* website (http://www.municipioaldia.com), which provides management and investment support to municipalities through virtual services, with a focus on

Figure 4.3   E-government Development Index and Income

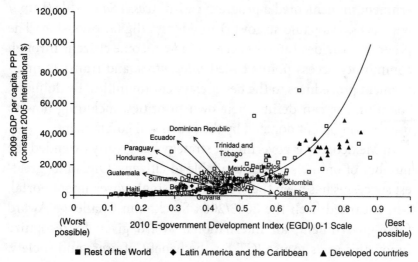

Source: United Nations (2010) and the World Bank (2010).

Figure 4.4   E-government Development Index and Corruption Perceptions Index

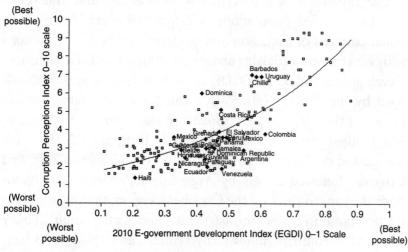

Source: United Nations (2010) and Transparency International (2009).

poor municipalities in rural areas. In Brazil, the provincial government implemented a program called *Acessa São Paulo* (http://www.acessasaopaulo.sp.gov.br) to address digital exclusion. The program provides Internet access to low-income citizens through community access points called *Infocentros*, and transfers management procedures to the beneficiary communities. By doing so, communities can define their own priorities, including how to use the equipment donated by the provincial government.

In Mexico, the e-government strategy has greatly extended the number of online services available to citizens. One of its greatest successes has been the creation of a single government portal, which earned itself the 2003/2004 Stockholm Challenge Award for e-government, an international award given to recognize innovative ways to use ICT for the benefit of users and society. Overall, however, the effectiveness of these innovations remains limited by the low level of citizen access to Internet services in Mexico (OECD, 2005). This remains a problem throughout the region.

The expansion of e-government services to rural and traditionally excluded populations is helping to break down traditional patterns of exclusion and neglect in citizens' interactions with government officials (Bhatnagar, 2002). The E-Government Development Index, or EGDI, is derived from a survey developed by the United Nations that can track the relative performance of the national governments in the region in their use of ICT (United Nations, 2010).[2] As shown in figure 4.5, the three top-ranked countries in Latin America are Colombia, Chile, and Uruguay, followed closely by Argentina and Mexico. Barbados leads the ranking among the Caribbean region, thanks to its better telecommunication infrastructure and higher adult literacy and gross enrollment, followed by Trinided and Tobago and fambica. Overall, the Caribbean region's index stands below the world average. Costa Rica and El Salvador lead the Central American nations.

Overall in the region, the use of ICTs is helping to improve many aspects of public administration. However, as yet, no formal evaluations of these types of programs yield strong conclusions about what works and what does not in the applications of these technologies to public office.

Innovation in E-government

Although the incidence of e-government in Latin America and the Caribbean is higher than in most countries around the world, the region still has a huge margin to extend the reach of public services in sectors like education, employment, and poverty relief. To cite two examples from other parts of the world, in India, an innovative e-government response to rural poverty and unemployment is an e-payment system for the National Rural Employment Guarantee Scheme, which makes use of biometric smart cards. The card uniquely identifies every citizen, with a fingerprint scanner to benefit illiterate citizens, bringing more transparency and accountability to the system. In the United States, in New York State, an e-government tool called SMART 2010 (short for Skills Matching and Referral Technology) connects unemployed New Yorkers with available jobs. A completed résumé in electronic format is fed into the New York Department of Labor's SMART 2010 system at a career center. The computer program analyzes résumés for skills and work experience and then electronically contacts unemployed New Yorkers via e-mail, recommending job openings based on their experience and skills.

Recent examples of creative uses of ICTs to improve the provision of public services have also arisen in Latin America and the Caribbean, thanks to the financial support of the Inter-American

Figure 4.5   E-government Development Index

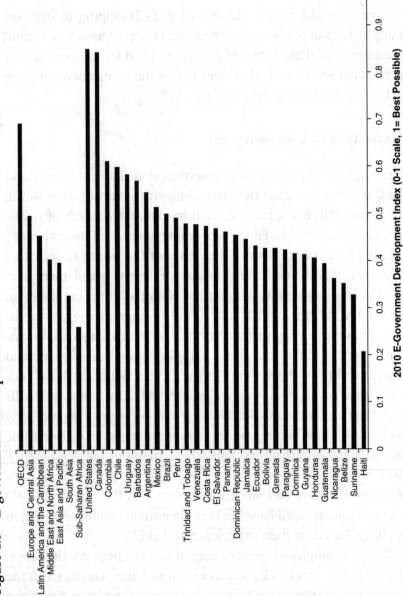

OECD
Europe and Central Asia
Latin America and the Carribbean
Middle East and North Africa
East Asia and Pacific
South Asia
Sub-Saharan Africa
United States
Canada
Colombia
Chile
Uruguay
Barbados
Argentina
Mexico
Brazil
Peru
Trinidad and Tobago
Venezuela
Costa Rica
El Salvador
Panama
Dominican Republic
Jamaica
Ecuador
Bolivia
Grenada
Paraguay
Dominica
Guyana
Honduras
Guatemala
Nicaragua
Belize
Suriname
Haiti

2010 E-Government Development Index (0-1 Scale, 1= Best Possible)

0   0.1   0.2   0.3   0.4   0.5   0.6   0.7   0.8   0.9   1

Source: United Nations (2010).

Development Bank (IDB). These cases have been rigorously evaluated, allowing conclusions to be drawn about what works and what does not in the application of ICTs to the delivery of public services.

In La Paz, Bolivia, a program was aimed at improving the renewal of the national identity card by the Identification Unit of the Bolivian Police. Chong, Machicado, and Yáñez (2010) ran a randomized control trial of the program by comparing applicants randomly assigned to a digital renewal process to those randomly assigned to a manual renewal process (see box 4.1 for another application by the police, this time in Colombia).

Adopting relatively simple information technology led to significant improvements in the quality of public service delivery. Specifically, applicants assigned a digital renewal process take 35 percent less time to complete their renewal processes and have a 12 percent higher probability of completing the renewal process, on average, as compared to those randomly assigned to a manual process. These results are encouraging, given the low-quality delivery of public service in developing countries and the challenges faced by these countries in reforming public service delivery.

In Colombia, an innovative program focuses on one of the country's most vulnerable populations, internally displaced people (IDP). Colombia has suffered from one of the longest conflicts in the world. Many IDPs have lost their assets and social networks in the conflict; 98 percent live below the poverty line, and IDPs face unemployment rates much higher than the rest of the population. Even though this group is entitled to benefit from many social programs, about 70 percent of those in the Unique Registry of Displaced People (RUPD) do not claim benefits. Blanco and Vargas (2010) carried out a randomized controlled trial in Bogotá to assess the use of short message services (SMS) to inform

Box 4.1   Going High-Tech: Improving Police Work and Saving Money in Colombia

The Colombian National Police, headquartered in Bogotá, is the national police force of the Republic of Colombia. It employs 150,000 officers, who work in 2,500 permanent sites across the country, from busy urban streets to isolated jungle villages. Until not long ago, the organization used an Internet Protocol (IP) telephony system for voice communications. Many police officers also relied on their personal mobile phones to keep in touch with one another, or used push-to-talk radios in their cars.

The audio quality of the IP telephony system was poor in spots that have lower bandwidth connectivity, such as rural offices and police cars. These technical limitations prevented the police from providing training to officers in remote areas through online audio or video presentations. Moreover, the telephony system was expensive to maintain.

The National Police needed to improve communications across all areas of the force and across a range of functions, including administration, operations, and training/education. They adopted a system that combines instant messaging, face-to-face communication, and Voice over Internet Protocol (VOIP) capabilities with integrated audio and video conferencing into one unified solution. All users of the new system can now determine the status and availability of a colleague, whether that person is in a remote jungle location or in the same office. It is now simple for police officers to place a voice call or send an e-mail message or instant message from their computers. In addition, police officers can easily schedule and conduct audio and video conferences online. "Previously, we had to send a message from headquarters to a regional capital, and then that message would be sent by boat up a river, through a forest, and finally to the officer. That process took an entire day. Now, with the new Communications Server we can communicate with remote officers instantly," says Jairo Gordillo, Colonel, Colombian National Police.

(continued on next page)

(continued)

> Lower costs are a major attraction of this innovative solution. Previously, officers in remote areas had to pay out of pocket for long-distance calls to colleagues and family. The Colombian Police also drastically cut back on travel between different regions of the country. Under the new system, "a superior officer no longer has to travel to a remote site to meet with that region's officers to give orders," Gordillo says. "That means no transportation and lodging costs. With the implementation of this new solution, we can now communicate with sites that are a 36-hour drive away—with just a click and an instant message."
>
> Police officers and other users of the new system are more efficient and productive now that they have streamlined communication tools at their fingertips. With the ability to reach people faster, police officers are able to fight crime more effectively. Some officers are equipped with smart phones that have the new communications server so they can locate criminals on the move in real time and apprehend them more effectively as well.
>
> *Source*: Microsoft (2009).

internal refugees about their eligibility to receive social benefits. SMS have proven to be a powerful tool to empower IDPs in their relation with the government. On average, households receiving SMS know their rights better than households that served as controls; however, apparently awareness varies depending on which benefits they are to receive.

Even though the findings of this study are specific to Colombia, the broader lesson from this intervention is that sending an informative SMS is an inexpensive policy intervention that can broaden the reach of social programs and greatly benefit recipients, provided that almost all of the potential beneficiaries have the means to receive it. Furthermore, this technology can complement other communication strategies quite successfully.

In Argentina, the prison system is monitoring convicts electronically. Prisoners are another vulnerable population, subject to slow judiciary procedures and even claims of human rights abuses. Society pays a high price for incarcerating a large number of people; not only is it expensive, but there is evidence that instead of rehabilitating people, prison only produces tougher criminals. These factors add up to a strong case for considering the use of electronic monitoring of some criminals. In a creative study, Di Tella and Schargrodsky (2009) provided the first causal estimates of the effects of electronic monitoring of convicts on their rates of relapsing into crime (recidivism).

Di Tella and Schargrodsky exploited the fact that the electronic bracelets used for monitoring are in short supply and that prisoners are randomly assigned to judges with different ideologies (priors) to argue that the bracelets are effectively randomly assigned. A sample of former convicts with similar characteristics were either sentenced to serve their time in prison or remained outside but were electronically monitored. Interestingly, the recidivism rate of former prisoners is considerable (22 percent), while that for those "treated" with electronic monitoring is much lower (13 percent). As promising as these low-cost technologies may seem, they are not the silver bullet of government service provision. They can and must be complemented by regular procedures and communications systems and, more importantly, they and other innovations must be continually evaluated.

Calling All Voters

People obtain much of their everyday information from the media. The amount and quality of information disseminated through the media affects the way people perceive reality and how they behave. In the literature, special attention has been paid to the effects of media exposure on public opinion, social and political participation, government behavior and accountability, and political outcomes.

The impact of the media on electoral processes is of special interest. The media provides the bulk of the information people use in elections, and the informational content of the media affects political behavior. For example, Gentzkow (2006) exploited the fact that television penetration in the United States was gradual to analyze the effects of TV exposure on voter turnout. The findings of this study are surprising: the introduction of television lowered voter turnout. Apparently, television acted as a substitute for the consumption of media with a higher content of political information, such as newspapers and radio, which inspired greater voter turnout by better-informed citizens. Both the information and turnout effects were largest in off-year congressional elections, which receive little or no coverage on television but extensive coverage in newspapers.

The concern about low turnout rates has sparked massive campaigns to encourage people to vote. Nonpartisan organizations in the United States have conducted extensive campaigns to get people to the polls on Election Day. Ha and Karlan (2009) evaluated a variety of telephone communications. They randomly assigned registered voters in North Carolina and Missouri to receive one of three types of live phone calls of varying length and content. Voters received "standard" get-out-the-vote (GOTV) calls, "interactive" calls, or "interactive calls with a request to mobilize neighbors." Which one won? People assigned to the interactive GOTV treatment were more likely to vote, while the effects of both the "get your neighbors to vote" script and the standard script were relatively weak. Along the same lines, Nickerson (2007) evaluated the effectiveness of e-mail as a voter mobilization tool. Curiously, e-mail neither increases registration rates nor boosts voter turnout; while e-mail is a low-cost form of campaign communication, it does little to boost registration and turnout. However, Dale and Strauss (2009) showed that impersonal, noticeable messages, such as text messages, can increase the likelihood that a registered voter will turn out by reminding the recipient that Election Day is approaching.

In an attempt to compare different types of GOTV interventions, Green and Gerber (2000) reported the results of a randomized field experiment in New Haven, Connecticut. Nonpartisan GOTV messages were conveyed through personal canvassing, direct mail, and telephone calls shortly before the November 1998 election. Voter turnout was increased substantially by personal canvassing, slightly by direct mail, and not at all by telephone calls.

Not only does the effectiveness of the campaigns matter, but so does their cost. Green and Gerber (2008) compared the cost-effectiveness of various GOTV techniques in the United States. They looked at some high-tech campaign tactics, such as voter mobilization through e-mail; some low-tech tactics, such as old-fashioned Election Day festivals; and some high-priced tactics, such as television, radio, and newspaper advertising. Although these strategies are quite different in terms of implementation, they all have an experimental design structure in common. The study found that although e-mail communication can reach a large number of people instantly at a low unit cost, it appears to have negligible effects on voter turnout. Personal canvassing, on the other hand, can increase voter turnout substantially. Results of the randomized field experiment involving registered voters in New Haven revealed that organizing and supervising a canvassing campaign involves significant fixed costs, but even if the effective marginal costs of canvassing were doubled, face-to-face mobilization would still be cost-effective, proving direct mail and phone calls to be less effective strategies.

In Latin America and the Caribbean, turnout is generally high compared to the United States: around 75 percent, on average. This is mainly because voting is mandatory in many countries in the region, including Argentina, Peru, and Uruguay. The fact that voting is mandatory in the region raises a whole set of new issues. In this case, the concern is not turnout, but the quality of voting and the extent to which votes represent the actual policy preferences of the population. The evidence in the United States related to GOTV campaigns indicates that information dissemination and social pressure have the potential to influence voter behavior. An interesting line of future research would be to see whether these types of campaigns are effective tools in providing voters with useful information and if more informed voters are able to elect representatives who better represent their preferences, thereby increasing the legitimacy of elected officials.

Ultimately, media content and information dissemination do affect political behavior and voting decisions. But do political biases in the news generate biases in the electoral decisions of citizens? To answer this question, DellaVigna and Kaplan (2007) exploited the natural experiment induced by the timing of the entry of a conservative television network in the United States, the Fox News Channel, in local cable markets. Cable companies in neighboring towns adopted Fox News in different years, creating idiosyncratic differences in access. The study compared the change in the Republican vote share between 1996 and 2000 for the counties that adopted Fox News by 2000 with those that did not, and found that a greater amount of news content with a conservative bias had a significant impact on the 2000 elections—an impact that was likely to have been decisive in the close presidential election.

Along the same lines, Gerber, Karlan, and Bergan (2009) focused on the written press and investigated how voter behavior and political opinion are affected by different news content. The authors randomly assigned individuals to receive a free subscription to either the *Washington Post* or the *Washington Times*, or to a control group. The *Washington Post* endorsed the Democratic candidate for governor in Maryland, while the *Washington Times* endorsed the Republican candidate. The study found that those individuals assigned to the *Washington Post* treatment group were 8 percentage points more likely to vote for the Democratic candidate for governor than those assigned to the control group.

Information influences voters; thus, it is important to be aware of how and what information is disseminated, as well as the incentives to influence information dissemination. For example, politicians can satisfy their electoral and policy objectives directly and indirectly by using public opinion to pressure other public officials. Likewise, special interest groups can finance or pressure the media to give more coverage to issues favorable to their cause (Scartascini, 2008).

For the Record

The amount of information that citizens have on hand can positively impact each of the different stages of the policymaking process by providing information to policymakers and voters alike.[3] The media can also act as a watchdog and provide additional tools for enforcing policymakers' promises. In addition, people may be able to put their own situation into perspective by comparing it to the one reported by the media.

Mass media can lead to more accountability by the government, as it helps to inform populations and better monitor the actions of incumbents (Besley, Burgess, and Prat, 2002). For example, Strömberg (2001) found that the lower the share of informed voters, the greater the share of policies associated with higher rents and corruption. Chong and Yáñez-Pagans (2010) argue that public broadcasting is associated with better institutions because it disseminates information that is not restricted by the commercial interests of advertisers.

ICTs have become powerful tools to disseminate information and knowledge to the public, transforming the way governments interact with citizens, and eventually leading to improvements in transparency and good governance. In this way, ICTs play a crucial role in the organization and coordination of political action, which enables citizens to monitor the actions of incumbents and to use this information in their voting decisions to punish or reward them.

One of the first examples of how information can provide a powerful tool to discipline the government is documented in Sen (1981, 1984). In these classic works, Sen argues that around the globe, there has never been a famine during periods of democracy. The theory is that governments respond to the needs of the citizenry when people are able to punish or reward the behavior of their elected officials with their votes. More importantly, news coverage of famines makes the government respond more quickly and efficiently.

Besley and Burgess (2002) formalize these points, arguing that citizens have imperfect information about government actions. A more informed and politically active electorate increases the incentives of the government to be responsive. Hence, democratic institutions and mass media have an important role in ensuring that voters' preferences are represented in policymaking: it is more likely that citizens will detect government inefficiencies as more and better information is available to the public. Making information transparent and accessible can therefore enhance the ability of citizens to scrutinize government actions, and lead to government that is more accountable and responsive to the needs of its citizens.

Using the New Deal expenditures of the 1940s in the United States as an example, Strömberg (2004) explored the impact of radio on public spending. The emphasis of the study was on how the introduction of new mass information technology can affect government policies by changing the number of people who are or are not informed. By comparing U.S. counties with more radio listeners to those where radio had not yet arrived or where there were very few listeners, Strömberg found that places where people are more informed received more relief funds during the New Deal.

An interesting question is whether information on a local government's performance impacts voter participation in local election processes and/or a candidate's electoral success. The identification of causal effects is generally a challenge, since information about politicians' performance is seldom provided to voters. Moreover, because information can often be politically manipulated when it is not based on independent and reliable sources, it may be potentially discounted or even ignored by citizens when casting their ballots (Ferraz and Finan, 2008).

Brazil implemented a program to audit local governments and provide voters with information about the corrupt acts of incumbents. Ferraz and Finan (2008) used this natural experiment to study the effects of disclosing information about corruption on electoral accountability and how this information shapes voters' behavior in the presence or absence of media that makes this information available to the public. The main advantage of the Brazilian program is that the federal government selected municipalities to audit at random. The fact that some municipalities were audited before or after the election allows a clear comparison between two municipalities that have similar levels of corruption—but for one, the audit reports were available before the local elections, while for the other, they were available later in the year. The release of the audit outcomes had a significant impact on the probability of an incumbent's reelection, and these effects were more pronounced in municipalities with local radio stations. Clearly, a more informed electorate makes more informed voting decisions, and the local media plays a major role in enhancing political accountability.

Sometimes, information is so scarce that even the release of information about candidates can have an effect on voters' decisions. In Brazil in 2006, three months before the election, the NGO *Transparência Brasil* released the criminal records of all incumbent federal deputies on their website. Gonçalves (2009) studied the effect of this Internet release on the reelection probabilities and overall electoral performance of incumbents. The econometric analysis suggests that Brazilian voters made use of the information compiled and published by *Transparência Brasil* to significantly punish the incumbent candidates listed with criminal charges.

Going one step further, Chong et al (2010) examined the effects of different types of negative and positive information about incumbents on voter behavior in the 2009 municipal elections in Mexico. The authors randomly assigned electoral precincts in twelve municipalities in the states of Jalisco, Morelos, and Tabasco to one of four groups: the first received information about municipalities' overall spending; the second received information about the distribution of resources to the poor; the third received information about corruption; and the fourth group served as a control group. The distributed information was taken from reports produced by the Mexican Federal Auditor's Office.

Interestingly, information about extensive corruption led to an 11 percent decrease in turnout. This drop was mainly among supporters of the incumbent's party, and their tepid participation translated into a smaller vote share. Conversely, information about overall expenditures rallied voters to the polls and boosted incumbent parties' vote share.

Most of the research relating information and participation in politics assumes that a more informed electorate is more likely to be politically active. Contrary to this assumption, the evidence from the Mexican case shows that in countries where term limits and corruption abound, information and participation do not always move in the same direction. The electoral punishment to corrupt politicians in this case was not the result of voters actively participating in the election. Rather, incumbents lost support because voters manifested their discontent by staying away from the voting booths. On the other hand, the incumbents who performed well in office were rewarded with increased voter participation. These findings suggest that information is an important aspect of good governance.

Another interesting example of how information technologies can improve the transparency of governance was the case of the electronic monitoring of the 2008 presidential elections in Paraguay. For this electoral process, the NGO Saka (which means transparency in Guaraní) trained 4,450 volunteers to report the results from about 70 percent of all the electoral booths in the country in real time. Volunteers who were present at the moment of the vote count reported the results to a central office using SMS. Overall, the system received 22,984 SMS from 9,984 electoral booths that day. These results were immediately entered into the system and published on Saka's website. As a result, the major radio and TV channels were able to report the results of the elections and irregularities as soon as they happened. SMS have also been used to report electoral irregularities to public media in other countries, such as Burkina Faso, Ghana, and Kenya (see box 4.2). Civil society's oversight of electoral processes can be fostered with these simple and cheap technologies, increasing the transparency and legitimacy of the overall process.

Enhanced civil society involvement in political processes through technologies has also occurred in extremely repressive political environments. For example, in Cuba, blogger Yoani Sanchez has demonstrated the power of the island's emerging blogging community and its use of social media applications. Sanchez's blog, *Generación Y*, has been awarded numerous international writing and journalism honors, including *TIME Magazine's* 25 Best Blogs, the Premio Ortega y Gasset, and Columbia University's Maria Moors Cabot Award. The blogger followers can bring themselves up to date on current political happenings from an independent source, thanks to the anonymity provided by the Internet. Likewise, in Iran in 2009, Twitter networks allowed people to organize to take to the streets and protest against censorship of the media.[4]

ICTs can also provide the population with tools to monitor government actions effectively. Yáñez-Pagans and Machicado Salas (2010) examined inefficiency and bureaucratic delay in the allocation of public works. A field experiment randomly equips municipal governments with a public works tracking system that provides grassroots organizations real-time information on allocations of public works. The objective of the intervention is twofold. The first goal is to involve grassroots organizations in the process of reviewing, tracking, and monitoring public works allocations. The second goal is to explicitly enhance the probability of detecting inefficiencies and bureaucratic delays within municipal governments, and therefore increase the expected cost of engaging in such practices among

Box 4.2   Technology as a Social Mobilization Tool

The rapid adoption of sophisticated communication multimedia by a significant portion of the world's population is giving rise to spontaneous social experiments of varied forms. In the political sphere, the power of persuasion, organization, and coordination have been democratized worldwide by the availability of mobile telephones and text messaging.

Critic and writer Howard Rheingold (2008) has compiled an inventory of events in which mobile communication devices led to some kind of social mobilization. Rheingold stresses that "Smart Mobs"—or groups of people equipped with high-tech communications devices that allow them to act in concert—can lead to stronger democracies, including the empowerment of citizens to demonstrate in protest of events, the capability to inexpensively and publicly monitor elections for fraud, the increased ability for volunteers to coordinate get-out-the-vote activities, and the power to disseminate information that is suppressed by authoritarian regimes and controlled mass media.

In Africa, cell phones have been used in two notable instances to combat election fraud and as political organizing tools. In Ghana, the 2004 elections went considerably more smoothly because cell phones and radio were used to report voting fraud. People at polling places used their mobiles to report fraud accusations to local radio stations, which would then air the accusation. In the 2002 elections in Kenya, mobile phones contributed not only to high voter turnout but also to the legitimacy of the results.

Mobile phones enhanced the transparency of the electoral process, improved the effectiveness of campaigns, and reduced fraud. Kenya's electoral commission and local media used SMS to distribute news about polling, and voters used mobile phones to monitor the voting in more remote areas. Local radio stations even fielded callers who alerted the listening audience to "the level of traffic at polling stations." Reports concerning Sierra Leone elections mimic reports

(continued on next page)

(continued)

from Ghana and Kenya regarding the use of phones as a powerful tool against electoral corruption. During the election that was held in 2002, a U.S.-based organization called Search for Common Ground distributed messages to journalists' cell phones. This allowed the journalists to report hourly the results of local polls. These were then announced publicly on radio stations.

Source: Rheingold (2008).

public officials. The experiment is ongoing, but the results are likely to be informative.

Change: One Person at a Time

Information technologies promote political participation and accountability. However, political involvement is not the only way in which institutions can be changed. As mentioned, social norms are a key component of any institutional system. Information technologies have shown to be an effective way to change social behavior in many aspects.

Consider TV shows, which often reinforce role models and stereotypes. Characters are usually based on urban and modern lifestyles, which TV then transmits to rural areas. Jensen and Oster (2009) documented how gender models can generate changes in gender behavior when they are diffused by the media in India. They estimated the impact of the entry of cable television on subjective measures of female autonomy, school enrollment, and fertility, and found that the entrance of cable TV generated a change in gender attitudes in the Indian population.

In Brazil, La Ferrara, Chong, and Duryea (2008) showed how the rural population mimicked the urban family models portrayed on soap operas. In the 1970s, a single television channel, *Rede Globo*, had a virtual monopoly in the country, and launched an aggressive expansion of its signal to rural areas. The most popular shows on Brazilian TV were soap operas, or *novelas*, which portrayed small, modern, urban families. The time difference in the entrance of TV signals in the country provided the opportunity to estimate the effect of *novelas* on fertility in Brazil. The finding was that the presence of the *Globo* signal led to significantly lower fertility rates. This effect was stronger for women of low socioeconomic status, and also for women who were in the middle and late phases of their child-bearing life, suggesting that television contributed more to stopping behavior than to delaying first births, consistent with demographic patterns documented for Brazil. These results may be interpreted not only in terms of exposure to television, but also of exposure to the particular reality portrayed by Brazilian *novelas*.

Exploiting this same variation in the timing of the availability of the *Rede Globo* signal, Chong and La Ferrara (2009) studied the link between television and divorce in Brazil, finding that the share of women who are separated or divorced has increased significantly since the *Globo* signal became available.

The violent content of modern TV, movies, and other media is a controversial issue. Dahl and DellaVigna (2009) analyzed the effects of violent movies on the incidence of violent crime in the United States. Surprisingly, they found that violent movies significantly decrease the incidence of violent crimes. The authors argue that crime declines because potential criminals are more attracted to these types of movies, and thus are watching them in theaters, rather than committing crimes. To support this argument, they showed that the effects are much larger for the day that movies are released, and even more so during the night hours, but crime picks up the week following the release.

Chong and Vargas (2010) built a similar argument, but put more emphasis on the content of media programs, exploring the relationship between television exposure and violent crime. The authors exploited variation in the time of entry of the three most important broadcasting networks across municipal regions over a twenty-year period in Brazil. They concluded that people living in areas covered by the television signal have significantly lower rates of homicides. The effect was strongest for lower-income men. What accounts for this benefit? One explanation is that viewers remain indoors watching TV, thus reducing the opportunity to commit violent acts. Also, considering the particular content of the commercial *novelas* in Brazil, this relationship may somehow reveal a positive connection between the progressive values and empowerment that are projected in these types of Brazilian *novelas* and the incidence of violent crimes. Finally, the paper provides evidence that the content, rather than the act of watching television in general, may be linked with the observed reduction in violent crime.

The increased information flow resulting from the widespread availability of communication technologies can also deter criminals by making it harder to commit crimes undetected (that is, by reducing the information asymmetries between criminals and potential victims), and by increasing the costs of committing a crime (that is, by increasing the likelihood of being witnessed, caught, or convicted). For example, kidnappings in Colombia were extremely common in the late 1990s. After President Uribe took power, kidnapping (along with other types of violence) began to decline significantly. Pedraza and Montenegro (2010) argued that the security policies of President Uribe were not the only reason for the significant decrease in kidnappings; the expansion of mobile phone coverage played an important role as well. The heightened level of deterrence and higher costs for perpetrating crime have resulted in a virtuous circle: improved security leads to greater investment in telecommunications around the country, which leads to faster communications between citizens and security forces, which leads to greater security. The magnitude of the effects is sizeable: mobile phones are responsible for a reduction of about 3.6 kidnappings per 100,000 people.

A related deterrent is at work in the United States. Ayres and Levitt (1998) found that the adoption of satellite detection technologies to avoid vehicle theft, known as Lojack, had a positive spillover effect on cars that were not equipped with this technology because thieves were uncertain about which cars had the device. González-Navarro (2007) ran a similar analysis in Mexico, finding that the way in which Lojack was marketed in Mexico completely eliminated the positive spillover effect on cars not equipped with the technology. For cars equipped with Lojack, theft rates fell by over 50 percent. However, the data also suggest that this deterrent effect could have been obtained by installing Lojack in 40 percent or less of the vehicles in which it was installed. Also, theft rates jumped in states where Lojack was not in use but that were close to states where Lojack was being used, at just the time when Lojack went into operation in those neighboring states.

Another way that ICTs can alter social behavior is in fund-raising. Using the Internet to raise funds has had an important impact on the way international aid is delivered. Some organizations now raise money online from private donors; the funds are generally targeted toward frontline projects and individuals in developing nations. The motivations of private donors tend to be primarily humanitarian; unlike official donors, they are less interested in foreign policy and political economy considerations (Desai and Kharas, 2009). In this sense, Internet-based private aid has come to complement, rather than substitute, official development aid.

Economic forecasting is another area in which ICTs have facilitated information sharing and altered social behavior.

Information provided by the government can be used not only to produce aggregate statistics that are helpful to businesses, but also to shape individuals' expectations about economic growth and prices, which in turn can affect their consumption patterns. Carrillo and Emram (2009) exploited a natural experiment provided by a mistake in the software that published the wrong inflation numbers for 14 months in Ecuador to show that households in developing countries rely on public signals to inform themselves about market conditions. The study showed that public signals about prices play an important role in shaping households' price expectations; the effect is stronger for older men and better educated families.

These studies have important policy implications, especially for developing countries. In societies where literacy is relatively low and newspaper circulation limited, television plays a crucial role in circulating ideas. Policymakers can use this channel to transmit important social and economic messages and thus may employ television and radio as a public policy tool.

Only the Beginning

Institutional development is an area in which significant progress is needed in Latin America and the Caribbean. Building proper democratic institutions will allow the countries of the region to grow faster, reduce poverty, and overcome social inequalities. However, traditional policies to tackle institutional failures have not delivered the expected results in the short term.

ICTs can be a useful tool to improve the efficiency of the government; e-government and digital procedures can deliver public services more successfully. These advances can help government reach the targeted population more quickly and effectively, and enhance the power of citizens to monitor government actions.

ICTs complement, rather than substitute for, macro efforts to improve institutional quality. Information diffusion has the power to influence social and political participation, fostering account-ability and allowing voters to discipline elected officials. Social preferences are also influenced by the media and the speedier, more widespread dissemination of information facilitated by the ICT revolution: effects have been observed in areas ranging from reproductive practices to violent and criminal behavior.

The experiences documented in this chapter illustrate some examples of the potential of ICTs to promote institutional develop-ment. However, the use of these technologies for development is a slow process of trial and error, which can yield lessons about what works and what does not. This learning process can be enhanced only though the rigorous testing of new and creative policies.

For all their advantages, ICTs cannot be considered the silver bullet to solve social and institutional problems in the region. They can be considered an important, sometimes cost-effective, tool to communicate and better integrate the government with their constituencies. However, these tools must be backed up by strong country-level institutional reform.

5

Tech Fever in the Health Sector

The use of information and communication technologies (ICT) in health—e-health—has been nothing short of epidemic. In developed countries, e-health has developed quickly from the provision of online medical content for health professionals and patients to the implementation of e-commerce solutions for billing, epidemiological surveillance, monitoring of health system performance, logistical support for clinical tasks, e-management of medical care processes, and support for treatment of patients with chronic conditions or disabilities. In the United States, the greatest potential for ICT may lie in systems that improve communication between health care institutions, support the ordering and management of medications, and help monitor and improve patient compliance with care regimens (Blaya, Fraser, and Holt, 2010). Mobile devices can also improve the timeliness and quality of data collection. However, before the fever becomes too contagious, there is an urgent need for more rigorous evaluations of the effectiveness and cost-effectiveness of e-health systems, especially in less developed countries (Blaya, Fraser and Holt, 2010; Kahn, Yang, and Kahn, 2010).

In developing countries, e-health could potentially help solve key health sector challenges via both public health and clinical applications. Figure 5.1 illustrates the connections between key health sector challenges, possible ICT solutions in both public health and clinical care, and potential social and economic impacts.

Figure 5.1 Applications of ICT in Health

Health Sector Challenges

1. Population aging, rise in chronic and non communicable diseases
2. New diseases due to changing lifestyles
3. Persistent inequalities in access and outcomes
4. Low quality, restricted treatment options
5. Fragmented care
6. Financing not tied to performance
7. Limited patient information, standardization and exchange
8. Knowledge management: Patient history, exams, and medication requests, research findings, etc.

Using ICT Solutions in Public Health

1. Improve awareness of risk factors, behaviors, and treatment options among the general public and high risk groups.
2. Identify disease and risk factor trends for use in decision making.
3. Model diseases in populations.
4. Collect and analyze epidemiological, demographic and social data.
5. Track and systematize patient and provider information. Enable pay for performance for public health services.
6. Access research, publications, and databases.
7. Improve epidemiological surveillance.

Using ICT Solutions in Clinical Care

1. Enable more fluid communication between patients and professionals.
2. Support diagnosis and treatment in real time.
3. Support monitoring and coordination of care for patients suffering from chronic conditions.
4. Deliver services despite distance and time barriers via telemedicine.
5. Standardize ordering, inventory management, and delivery of drugs and supplies.
6. Monitor quality and safety in patient care settings.

Potential Impact of ICT Innovations

1. Improved care; better health outcomes from more accurate, evidence-based diagnosis and treatment.
2. Faster knowledge and response to the outbreak of infectious diseases.
3. Higher cost-efficiency (faster recovery, lower hospitalization rates, fewer medical errors).
4. Economic efficiency in the management of key inputs: human resources, equipment, medicines, etc.
5. Economic benefits associated with healthier populations, requiring fewer hospitalizations and less health care.

Source: Authors' compilation based on Dzenowagis (2005) and Katz (2009).

Are ICTs likely to change health outcomes in Latin America and the Caribbean? Can ICTs improve the cost-effectiveness of health spending in the region? What are the barriers for ICT diffusion in the health sector in the region? This chapter addresses these questions and sets out a framework for thinking about the connections between common health sector challenges, ICT solutions, and potential results for the system. Building on Humpage (2010a), the chapter considers four broad categories of e-health applications: e-learning, e-health information portals and applications, telemedicine, and electronic health records.

E-learning facilitates the training of medical professionals through easier access to scholarly journals and reference materials. A successful example from Latin America is Biblioteca Regional de Medicina (BIREME), which provides access to online journals to health sciences students in Latin America for free or at a reduced cost. This e-learning facility, focusing on technical cooperation in scientific health information, is a specialized center of the Pan-American Health Organization/World Health Organization (PAHO/WHO). BIREME has had its headquarters at the Federal University of São Paulo since its creation in 1967 (http://regional.bvsalud.org/php/index.php?lang=en).

E-health information portals and applications provide basic health information online to the general public using ICT. Health prevention strategies are described, or answers to patient questions are provided, without a visit to a medical facility. Access to information via the Internet or compact discs (CDs) constitutes the core of e-health information centers. Appointment and referral systems are also common, and can support access to and continuity of care. This chapter examines the international evidence and use of such portals for public health promotion among adolescents.

Telemedicine is the exchange of medical information via any form of electronic communications to improve access to information or individual medical care in remote places. Telemedicine reduces the need to travel for medical care and includes the use of phones, mobile phones, the Internet, personal digital assistants (PDAs), radio, and television. This chapter assesses developed-country telemedicine interventions and a selection of interventions in Latin America, including some limited data on the costs and benefits of a small-scale effort in Peru.

Electronic Medical Records (eMR) or Electronic Health Records (eHR) are the core platforms for a variety of applications that offer benefits for all agents involved in health care: patients, doctors, public health officials, and researchers. An all-inclusive eHR platform ideally includes clinical and pharmaceutical administrative capabilities, such as automated information for providers and patients on prescriptions, procedure requests, and data aggregation. In systems that permit provider choice, eMR can provide greater portability, benefitting both providers and patients. Well-designed eHR improves the efficiency and accuracy of medical records, prevents duplicate procedures, and improves pharmacy inventory management. (Fraser et al, 2006a; CBO, 2008). An eMR can also be a simple electronic record (as opposed to a paper chart) of a patient's history that includes information such as test results, medication, and general history. Finally, an eMR platform that permits rapid data aggregation may be an important tool for policymakers; accurate and timely information has clear potential for improving the allocation of resources and speeding responses from governments. For these reasons, eHR and eMR are among the most promising interventions reviewed, with evidence on effectiveness coming largely from developed-country experiences.

Implementation of e-learning and e-health solutions in the region has been facilitated by the dramatic expansion in ICT infrastructure in recent years. Through the Internet and the use of computers, tablets, PDAs, and CD-ROMS, information can be updated at low cost, providing training and access to information to both patients and health care workers.

As proponents of health ICT frequently emphasize, potential gains arise from better access to information, and network effects multiply these gains as more users adopt the technologies. Better health information systems translate into better abilities to record, share, locate, and analyze information. Although ICTs are not a panacea to improving health care systems, they may be useful for monitoring patients, identifying coverage gaps, monitoring the effectiveness of different treatments, and allowing health care providers and government to respond more quickly to pandemics and infectious diseases.

Because the implementation of ICTs in the health sector is spreading feverishly across the region and the world, the appeal of taking advantage of innovative ICT applications has grown. A word of caution is needed, though, since the benefits of ICT in health remain speculative given the lack of rigorous impact evaluations or cost-benefit analyses. Only nine studies of e-health programs in developing countries include randomized controls, and only two measure effects on patient outcomes (Blaya, Holt, and Fraser, 2008). This chapter aims to assess this situation in Latin America in order to generate preliminary policy recommendations for greater adoption of ICT in the future.

Health Sector Priorities in Latin America and the Caribbean

Basic health in Latin America and the Caribbean has been improving significantly; however, equity gaps and quality remain a challenge. Access to even basic health services is not universal and quality is low. In Peru, absence rates of providers in primary health centers are about 25 percent (Chaudhury et al, 2006). In Honduras, only three-quarters of all women (only half of poor women) who received prenatal services actually received the essential content of these services, as prescribed by the Ministry of Health: blood pressure monitoring, blood and urine tests, weight and belly measurements, and advice on complications during pregnancy and what to do in case of an emergency (IDB staff estimates based on Honduras's Encuesta Nacional de Demografía y Salud, 2006). Access and quality gaps between poor and nonpoor and between indigenous and nonindigenous people are still significant in some countries. Figure 5.2 shows doctor quality in Mexico by income quintile and ethnicity; regardless of their income, indigenous people receive lower-quality care (World Bank, 2005).

Gaps in coverage of most health services with respect to developed countries have been closing, but huge quality gaps in such areas as treatments, diagnostic tools, technology, and human capital resources still persist, compared to the member-countries of the Organization for Economic Co-operation and Development (OECD) and the United States.

Latin American and Caribbean countries have undergone a swift epidemiological transition with respect to noncommunicable and chronic diseases. Chronic diseases are now the leading cause of death and illness, accounting for 68 percent of deaths and 60 percent of disability-adjusted life years (DALY). While cardiovascular disease alone is responsible for 35 percent of deaths, the combination of all other infectious diseases (malaria, tuberculosis, and others) is responsible for only 10 percent of deaths (PAHO, 2007). Meanwhile, diabetes affects up to 15 million people and causes 300,000 deaths per year. (Barcelo et. al., 2003).

Figure 5.2   Doctor Quality in Mexico by Income Quintile and Ethnicity in YEAR, Mexico, 2003 (percentile)

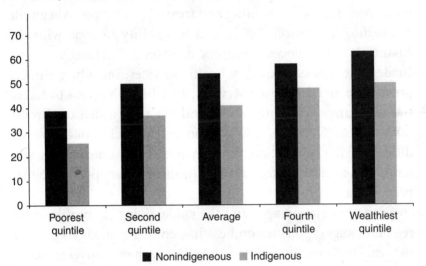

■ Nonindigeneous ■ Indigenous

Source: World Bank (2005).

Aging of the population also increases the share of disease burden attributed to chronic conditions. Predictions for the next twenty years show a near tripling of diabetic patients, ischemic heart disease, and stroke mortality in the region (Murray and López, 1996). However, to a large extent, these diseases are preventable. Up to 80 percent of heart disease, stroke, and type II diabetes could be prevented by eliminating shared risk factors, improving the dissemination of information, and increasing prevention. The region is also undergoing a "nutrition transition:" people consume too few fruits, vegetables, whole grains, cereals, and legumes, and too many foods rich in saturated fat, sugars, salt, refined cereals, and processed foods (Popkin, 1998; 2001). Furthermore, 30 to 60 percent of the region's population does not meet even the minimum recommended levels of physical activity.

Although chronic diseases affect all population groups, the poor suffer relatively more because they have higher risk factors, lower access to screening and treatment services (Abegunde et al, 2007; Anderson, 2009), and less ability to cope with the financial consequences of chronic diseases (Suhrcke et al, 2006). Inadequate access to quality health services, including clinical prevention and diagnostic services, and difficult access to essential medicine contribute significantly to the burden of chronic disease (PAHO, 2007). Information on the socioeconomic conditions of the population through integrated information systems in the health sector can help health workers practice better prevention.

As the population ages and the epidemiological profile of the region changes, pressure on health spending is likely to grow in the years to come. According to PAHO, to achieve universal access to health care services, the region must pump up public spending on health to between 5 and 6 percent of gross domestic product (GDP); however, public spending on health is significantly below that in many countries and has essentially remained flat during the past ten years.[1] Moreover, entitlements are becoming increasingly important in the access to health care and have provoked reactions from the population (such as disputes with health care providers over treatments of HIV/AIDS in Colombia). In this scenario, the efficiency of expenditure and guaranteeing evidence-based, cost-effective care is essential.

The direct economic and fiscal costs of chronic diseases are large and growing. In Mexico, it is estimated that the total health budget should increase 5 to 7 percent per year to treat the increasing number of diabetes and hypertension cases (Arredondo, Zúñiga, and Parada, 2005). Chronic disease also impacts negatively on consumption, savings, labor supply and productivity, and human capital accumulation (Suhrcke et al, 2006).

To respond to the region's health challenges and limit the pressure on health spending, policymakers agree that organizational models and provider payment mechanisms must be reformed to improve availability, quality, and continuity of health care. In the majority of countries in the region, the health sector is dominated by publicly financed and publicly provided services; the government is the main insurer and provider of services. Funding of public facilities is usually based on budgets, norms, and historical spending patterns, limiting the scope for more active management of patients and provider institutions. Chronic disease management requires a complex response over an extended period that involves coordinated inputs from a wide range of health professionals, access to essential medicines, and monitoring systems, all of which—optimally—need to be embedded within a system that promotes coordination, continuity of care, and patient participation. Yet Latin American health systems are highly fragmented. Various duplicative units or facilities are not integrated into an overall network and communicate poorly with one another and with patients. Human resources present a particular challenge in such settings; incentives to deliver quality health services to the neediest patients are scarce. Salaries bear little relationship to efficiently produced outputs such as coverage or patient outcomes.

In response to these organizational challenges, many countries are implementing new organizational models—integrated health service delivery networks based on primary care—and provider payment mechanisms. Some countries have allowed facilities managerial autonomy and improved incentives for health providers. These changes are expected to improve the performance of public health care institutions (Barnum, Kutzin, Saxenian, 1995; Jegers et al, 2002). Public-private partnerships in health care are also being explored. For instance, the public sector is pursuing various strategies—such as contracting nongovernmental organizations (NGOs) to extend health services in rural and remote areas (Guatemala and Honduras) and establishing new partnerships with private institutions that may improve access to medicines, vitamins, and micronutrients (Guatemala)—to improve access to public health services while guaranteeing efficiency, equity, and quality.

Most Latin American and Caribbean countries have developed legal frameworks and institutions to support the development of ICTs in the health sector. Information on implementation of ICTs in health is generally underreported, and many of the programs have been initiated through nongovernmental initiatives.

In 2005, the WHO passed a resolution declaring the importance of e-health and encouraging member countries to develop long-term plans to incorporate ICTs into health care.[2] In 2006, the WHO published the results of a survey on the use of ICTs in health care in their member countries. The survey shows that in 2005, three in four countries in the region had national information policies, which is slightly below the world average of about 78 percent. Latin American and Caribbean countries lag behind high-income countries in most areas, but appear to be close to world averages on many outcomes, with the exception of training health science students in ICTs.[3]

Are e-Health Innovations Treating the Region's Ills?

Prevention and e-Health Information

The Internet has significant capability to gather and deliver real-time health information. Through the Internet, patients can access wide-ranging, up-to-date information about their disease, medical treatments, costs, and preventive health practices on a 24/7 basis (twenty-four hours a day, seven days a week). Interactivity and anonymity provide patients with new communication options, the potential for accessing information tailored to their needs, and new sources of support (Anderson and Klemm, 2008; Cline and Haynes, 2001).

However, a number of pitfalls are associated with the use of the Internet as a health educational tool. The quality of the information on the Internet is uneven and at times inaccurate, which heightens the vulnerability of patients (Eysenbach et al, 2002). Patients face security and privacy issues, and access is usually inequitable, especially in developing countries (Hong, Patrick, and Gillis, 2008). These caveats notwithstanding, the literature for developed countries presents very few reported cases of harm associated with the use of poor-quality health information on the Internet (Crocco, Vallasis-Keever, and Jadad, 2002).To the contrary: a growing number of developed-country studies reveal the positive effects of Internet-based interactive and informative tools on health, health-related decision making, and well-being (see Fox, 2007).

For instance, the literature now documents that more and better health information increases the demand for preventive health care (see Lin and Hsieh, 1997). However, very little is known about the effectiveness of ITC in disseminating content-valued information regarding health prevention practices among vulnerable populations.

Some recent experiments in Latin America and the Caribbean have tried to assess the advantages of web- and mobile phone-based interventions on preventing risky behaviors among adolescents and self-monitoring of patients with chronic diseases.

Short Message Service (SMS) and the Control of Dengue in Peru

The use of cell phones and SMS suggests that SMS-delivered interventions can have positive behavioral outcomes, at least in the short term. In the United Kingdom, the use of SMS reminders for outpatient appointments has reduced the likelihood that patients will not attend their appointments (Koshy, Car, and Majeed, 2008). SMS also seems to be effective in promoting weight loss behavior among overweight people (Joo and Kim, 2007; Patrick et al, 2009).

SMS interventions are low cost, which may help less developed countries that are facing tight health budgets. To study the usefulness and efficacy of the SMS as a tool to deliver content-value information, Dammert, Galdo, and Galdo (2010) studied the effectiveness of delivering preventive information on dengue through text messaging in the district of Pariñas in Piura, Peru. The authors highlight that treatment of a single episode of dengue ranges from US$10 to US$25, reinforcing the potential of exploring low-cost innovative polices that might increase dengue preventive care. Note that households do not incur any cost when receiving a text message. The experiment focused on households in which the head of household or spouse is a cell phone user and is literate enough to read a simple message. The participant group (control) received weekly transmissions of dengue-related information—the mosquito's life cycle, the conditions in which dengue spreads, symptoms of the disease, and simple prevention strategies—through mobile phone text messages before and during the dengue season. Preliminary results suggested that households receiving any text message increased the use of mosquito nets by about 3.7 percentage points, boosted their use of screens on windows by about 7.4 percentage points, and increased the probability of covering standing supplies of water by 4.3 percentage points. However, households receiving text messages did not leave fewer tires or bottles outside their house, which could fill with water and spread the disease.

Web-based Adolescent Sexual Health Programs

Adolescents are quick to pick up new information technologies and are thus a logical target population for preventive interventions via e-health. Many countries of the region are implementing programs to provide students with computers; these, combined with the surge in mobile phone use, make the Internet and other ICT technologies such as mobile phone SMS a cost-effective vehicle to reach young people in a widespread manner.

Web-based sexual education training programs represent an important potential ICT application to prevent unwanted and risky health behaviors. Risky sexual behavior is on the rise in the region, and adolescents are becoming sexually active at increasingly younger ages. Although adolescent fertility rates have been declining, they are still higher in Latin America than in OECD countries, with the exception of the United States (Cunningham et. al. 2008).

Evidence on the effectiveness of sexual education programs is mixed. Kirby, Laris, and Rolleri (2006) reviewed eighty-three evaluations of sexual education and HIV prevention programs in developing and developed countries. In fifty-two studies tracking sexual debut, only 42 percent showed delayed debut and 55 percent showed no effect. In thirty-one studies tracking sexual frequency, only 29 percent recorded reduced frequency, 10 percent posted increased frequency, and the rest showed no effect. In fifteen studies tracking contraceptive use, 40 percent observed increased use and 53 percent observed no impact. Although the effect on risky behaviors is mixed, there is greater consensus that programs improve knowledge on safe practices. Programs also report better attitudes toward rights and safe practices, but results are smaller in magnitude and are not always long-lasting.

Kirby (2001) found that more comprehensive programs (those that incorporate information on condom and contraceptive use) seem to do better than abstinence-only programs. Comprehensive programs did not increase sexual behavior, and in the majority of cases, delayed sexual initiation, reduced the frequency of sex, decreased the number of sex partners, and increased condom and contraceptive use. Programs featuring a large menu of approaches had greater effects on behavior.

Web-based sexual education programs have delivery advantages when compared to face-to-face programs because of their higher adaptability, consistent quality, greater anonymity and confidentiality, and lower marginal costs for scaling up. According to evidence from developed countries, Internet-based programs improve the reach, engagement, and interactive involvement of sexual education programs; are more cost-effective; and are preferred by users over face-to-face interventions (Paperny, 1997; Barak and Fisher, 2003).

In developing countries, evidence of the effectiveness of web-based sexual education programs is scant. Most positive effects are concentrated on awareness and knowledge (see Chao-hua et al, 2006 for the case of China). Some sexuality information systems have also been developed based on mobile phones and SMS (see Anta, El-Wahab, and Giuffrida, 2008 for the cases of New Delhi, India and Nigeria).

A recent field experiment shed light on the potential gains of adolescent online sexual education programs in Colombia (Profamilia Educa; see Chong et al, 2010). The Internet-based sexual health education course was randomly implemented among 138 groups of ninth graders from public schools across twenty-one Colombian cities. The experimental design of this intervention allowed for a rigorous assessment of the direct impacts on the students involved in the trial, as well as the spillover effects to students not involved in the experiment. The evaluation looked at the effects of the program on improving adolescents' attitudes, knowledge, and behavior regarding sexual health, rights and sexuality, as well as positive spillover effects through social networks and within school interactions.

The results of the evaluation found that Profamilia's course caused significant and moderate improvements in sexual knowledge and attitudes in most areas (prevention of sexually transmitted diseases, STDs), condom use, pregnancy prevention, and sexual violence/abuse). The effects were relatively homogeneous across both genders, although boys improved their knowledge and attitudes regarding sexual violence more than girls. Trained students are more able to identify safe and risky sexual practices, STD symptoms, and violent/abusive sexual situations, and to understand the need to report cases in which a teenager is being sexually abused.

For sexually active girls, the course improved pregnancy prevention practices and significantly reduced pregnancies from 2.2 percent in the control group to 1.3 percent in the treatment group. There is no evidence of spillovers from students who took the course to students who did not take the course but were in the same school. This indicates that although the course was successful in improving short-term knowledge and attitudes regarding sexual health, as well as some sexual behaviors for those assigned to treatment, spillovers across classrooms do not significantly magnify the effects of the sexual education provided to the teenagers assigned to treatment.

Another important application of e-health is in the area of substance abuse, especially among adolescents, who are particularly vulnerable to substance use and abuse. Young people in Latin America are increasingly drinking alcohol simply to get drunk. Increased binge drinking and intoxication in young people—a pattern of consumption associated with countries in northern Europe, the highest in the world—is now reported in countries such as Brazil and Paraguay, and drug use among children younger than eighteen is on the rise in most of the region (Cunningham et al, 2008).

A number of preventive substance abuse programs have been introduced in developed countries through the Internet, with mixed levels of success (Bosworth, Gustafson, and Hawkins, 1994; Marsch, Bickel, and Badger, 2007; Pahwa and Schoech, 2008; Croom et al, 2009). Many interventions provide more information and awareness on the determinants, effects, and consequences of substance abuse, but have limited impact on risky behaviors and substance use and abuse, with the exception of the HeadOn: Substance Abuse Prevention for Grades 6–8 in the United States (Marsch, Bickel, and Badger, 2007). There is little evidence of success of similar programs in less developed countries (Kaplan, 2006).

A recent evaluation by Balsa, Gandelman, and Porzecanski (2010) analyzed the impact of a substance abuse Internet and SMS prevention program for adolescents in Uruguay. The three-month randomized trial found that few participants logged into the website, but most participants were reached through e-mails and SMS. The program boosted the awareness that certain substances are drugs; unfortunately, such awareness did not inspire many teens to alter their consumption habits.

Participation is a challenge in programs targeted at adolescents. The modules in HeadOn were delivered as part of the school curriculum (Marsch, Bickel, and Badger, 2007). In the Uruguayan evaluation, only a minority of those in the intervention group visited the project's website. The authors attributed this to the lack of interest in the topic, together with the unstructured and voluntary character of the intervention.

All told, web-based interventions are effective at increasing knowledge, but may be less effective at changing behaviors among youth. The limited interest in these programs suggests that they may work better as part of comprehensive preventive interventions integrated into the school curriculum or other routine programs in which adolescents participate.

e-Health Information and the Management of Chronic Disease

Treatment of chronic conditions is a growing challenge for health systems in both developed and developing countries. Successful chronic disease care involves constant patient compliance, periodic monitoring of patient progress, and, in some cases, important lifestyle changes. Evidence, mostly for developed countries, shows that most patients with cancer, chronic conditions, and disabilities using the Internet to inquire about their condition felt that they benefited from the information available. They felt they have made better treatment decisions, improved their ability to cope with their condition, undertook dieting and fitness regimes, and, in some cases, had better monitoring and outcomes (Fogel et al, 2002 and Fox, 2007 for breast cancer patients; Gustafson et al, 1999 and Benotsch and Weinhardt, 2005 for HIV/AIDS patients; Broom, 2005 for prostate cancer; Meigs et al, 2003 for diabetes patients).

Very few e-health interventions to improve access to information and treatment options for chronic disease patients exist in the developing world. In Montevideo, Uruguay, Balsa and Gandelman (2010) conducted a randomized experiment to study and evaluate the effects of an Internet-based intervention on type II diabetes patients with a personal computer (PC) and Internet access at home. Patients with type II diabetes require constant follow-up from the head physician and significant support to achieve self-control.

The intervention in Uruguay consisted of a specially designed website developed by EviMed (a private firm that develops information and educational products and services for physicians throughout Latin America; see http://www.evimed.net/) and an electronic social network where participants can navigate freely, download materials, and interact with other diabetics and specialists. The expected benefit of this intervention included better health decision making and better disease management by the patient. The evaluation found no significant impact on knowledge, behavior, or health outcome of the participants. These low effects can be partially explained because only a minority of patients logged into the website and were mostly reached by e-mail and SMS. Curiously, even among patients who initially reported having Internet access at home or using the Internet at least on a weekly basis, a majority mentioned that they did not access the Diabetes 2.0 website because they were not frequent Internet users. Participation in the website is correlated with the gender, marital status, and education level of patients. In addition, and in contrast with many of the randomized studies conducted in developed countries, recruitment to the study was not on a volunteer basis; rather, participants were selected based on their response to a baseline survey.

As opposed to mobile telephony, Web and Internet use is still not widespread in the region. To take advantage of mobile devices, some health information systems have been developed based on mobile telephone use. SMS notifications and alerts are sent to patients' cell phones, either periodically or on demand, and provide live information on waiting times, reminders for appointments, or health advice. These applications have reportedly reduced waiting times and missed appointments and hospital visits (Anta, El Wahab, and Giuffrida, 2008); however, no impact evaluations are available to assess these observations.

An on-going effort using the Internet and web-based tools is provided by Chong, Field, and Torero (2010b). Malnutrition and, in particular, anemia constitute an important concern in rural areas in the region. Low levels of iron lead to deficient performance of children in school and low productivity once they enter the work-force. However, direct distribution of iron has typically brought seemingly insurmountable sustainability challenges. Researchers conducted a randomized controlled trial with high school students in rural northern Peru to teach them the benefits of iron consumption; they were provided information via the Internet as well as other vehicles. In particular, messages were delivered via videos using (i) a popular icon (a famous soccer player) encouraging iron supplement consumption, (ii) a political figure encouraging iron supplement consumption, and (iii) a placebo message encouraging oral hygiene. To be able to clearly attribute the delivery of pills as part of the project, the local health center was equipped with iron supplements and all students requesting pills received them free of charge. They were then registered in a database controlled by a nurse, who verified their photo ID against a picture registered in a master database. The health center manned by the nurse was the only place where the pills could be obtained, and this location was specified in the messages encouraging supplemental iron consumption.

Students receiving the computer-based video encouraging iron consumption were much more willing to pick up iron pills at the health center than students who received the placebo message. Students receiving the message from the popular icon were even more willing to both pick up the iron pills and to do so consistently over time. Remarkably, grades and cognitive test scores improved significantly and anemia levels declined, in particular for students who returned to the health center consistently. In short, the intervention showed a causal relationship between information through ICTs and the way messages are provided and positive health outcomes.

Commitment Devices and ICTs

Commitment devices allow people to monitor and fulfill arrangements to which they have voluntarily entered to fulfill plans for their own future behavior. The people themselves are the source of the risk of failing to fulfill the plan (rather than changes in prices or behavior by other parties); and the arrangement affects only the person involved, not others. A "hard commitment" may involve a monetary penalty or bonus; a "soft commitment" merely entails a psychological cost.

An important area where commitment devices may be used is in managing and overcoming addiction. Bernheim and Rangel (2004) documented addicts' ability to manage the "cues" that trigger their addictive behavior. For example, recent ex-smokers avoid bars, restaurants, or other circumstances that might provide complementary cues and increase their likelihood of smoking. These are all examples of soft commitment. Some addicts also make use of hard commitments. Alcoholics are known to use certain metabolism-inhibiting drugs, such as Antabuse (also known as disulfiram), which temporarily modify the body processes that metabolize alcohol and produce a highly unpleasant physical reaction upon alcohol consumption. Field studies show that retention rates for Antabuse are poor—often less than 20 percent (Galanter and Kleber, 2008).

In a field experiment in the Philippines, Gine, Karlan, and Zinman (2008) designed and tested a voluntary commitment saving program called Committed Action to Reduce and End Smoking ("CARES"), designed specifically to help people quit smoking. In the study, a Philippine bank offered smokers an opportunity to open a savings account for the express purpose of giving them an incentive to quit. Six months after opening the account, smokers were required to take a nicotine byproduct test, putting their bank balance at risk. If the person passed the test, they got the money back; if they failed, the bank donated the money to charity. The results suggested that the intervention helped smokers quit. Intention-to-treat estimates found that access to the commitment contract increased the likelihood of passing the six-month nicotine byproduct test by 3.1 percent for the full sample and by 4.3 percent for those who reported wanting to quit at some point in their lives, respectively. The CARES treatment effects compared favorably to those found for nicotine replacement therapy in randomized controlled trials in other settings (Stead et al, 2008). The CARES take-up rate (11 percent) also compared well to nicotine replacement therapy (Bansal et al, 2004; Tipones and Fernández, 2006), suggesting that commitment contracts could help public health efforts to address the "under-use" of smoking cessation treatments (Cokkinides et al, 2005; Orleans 2007).

A recent experiment in Latin America (Karlan and Zinman, 2010) analyzed the effectiveness of the stickK.com system. Launched in January 2008, stickK.com is a web-based portal that helps users write a binding promise (a commitment contract) to achieve a goal by setting rewards, penalties, reinforcements, and accountability mechanisms to ensure success. Through stickK.com, individuals are able to create commitment contracts to encourage them to meet a wide variety of personal goals, from exercising regularly, losing weight, and quitting smoking, to going green (see chapter 7) and completing administrative or work tasks.

In 2010, the stickK program analyzed the effectiveness of stickK.com with a sample of 356 users, of whom 128 (27.5 percent) were selected from a known Latin American Internet Protocol (IP) address. Most commitments in the study included goals related to health prevention (see figure 5.3).

Figure 5.3   Types of Commitments under StickK Program, 2010 (percentage)

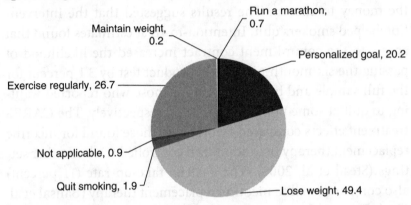

Run a marathon, 0.7

Maintain weight, 0.2

Personalized goal, 20.2

Exercise regularly, 26.7

Not applicable, 0.9

Quit smoking, 1.9

Lose weight, 49.4

Source: Karlan and Zinman (2010).

Although most contracts are ongoing, progress to date has been disappointing. Of the 304 created commitments, 65 have been completed (21.4 percent) and 239 are still in progress (78.6 percent). As demonstrated in table 5.1, most contracts failed.

A joint initiative of StickK and Compartamos Banco, a private Mexican bank specializing in microfinance, explores the role of commitment contracts in promoting beneficial behavior among employees. Compartamos employees have access to a customized web portal through the Internet and company intranet to enter into and maintain commitment contracts. The main objective is to learn if offering contracts to Compartamos employees can improve employee well-being and ultimately enhance company performance and productivity (Chong, Karlan and Zinman, 2010).

In addition to survey and contract data from StickK, there is information from Compartamos on productivity, absenteeism, and rotation. Contract activity is expected to be positively correlated with productivity indicators, since fulfilling contracts may improve

Table 5.1   Commitment Success of the StickK Program, 2010

Success Category	Number of Commitments	Percent
Total	304	100
Fail (0%)	202	66
Low (<75%)	54	18
High (>=75%)	48	16

Source: Karlan and Zinman (2010).

the mental and physical well-being of participants by helping them reach their goals; productivity may also improve. The preliminary evidence indicates that entering into a contract is negatively correlated with the percentage of employees in default (that is, employees fulfill their contracts—although the result is not statistically significant); positively correlated with productivity (that is, productivity increases—although again the result is not statistically significant); and negatively correlated with absenteeism (specifically, time at work increases by 1 percent, or four hours).

The most significant predictor of contract uptake was weekly Internet use. Each extra hour of weekly Internet use translates into a 1.5 percent higher likelihood of entering into a contract. Household income is positively correlated with contract uptake, as are physical health and energy levels. In other words, the healthier and more energetic people feel, the more likely they are to enroll in stickK.

Connecting Patients and Practitioners: Monitoring, Evaluation, and Patient Tracking Systems

Intuitively, e-health should improve short-term health outcomes and prevent long-term complications from chronic diseases. ICT enables fluid and frequent communication between patients and providers—and, in the most advanced applications, supports constant monitoring of patients' health status and timely adjustment of care. For example, the newest devices for diabetes care offer health providers real-time access to patients' blood sugar measurements, letting them adjust medications and offer advice on lifestyle changes. Computers that automatically and continuously monitor patient status, treatment protocols, and care are a realistic example of how ICT could deliver entirely new forms of care in the future.

In the case of heart disease, Bondmass et al (1999) and Jerant, Rahman, and Thomas (2001) argued that monitoring and counseling patients using ICT systems may bring significant clinical and economic benefits. In a population of U.S. patients with congestive heart failure (CHF), Roglieri et al (1997) estimated the benefits of weekly phone monitoring and mailings, finding a 63 percent reduction in readmissions for all subjects over a one-year period, as well as shorter average hospital stays and less emergency room use. Chetney (2003) evaluated a two-way interactive video technology for home care of CHF patients and found that it reduced hospital admissions by 82 percent and use of the emergency room by 77 percent.

New technologies for continuous remote clinical monitoring have produced significant benefits to patients. In the case of hypertension, home blood pressure monitoring has been effective in controlling blood pressure, diagnosing "white coat" hypertension, targeting organ damage, improving prediction of hypertension-related morbidity, improving patient compliance, and allowing faster therapy adjustment (Asmar and Zanchetti, 2000; Artinian, Washington, and Templin, 2001). In the case of diabetes, Harno, Kauppinen-Mäkelin, and Syrjäläinen (2006) conducted an evaluation of an e-health application with a diabetes management system

and a home care link. They found significantly lower levels of gly-
cated hemoglobin in blood (HbA1c, which measures blood sugar
control over several months), blood pressure, cholesterol, and fasting
plasma glucose in the study group relative to the control individuals, and fewer visits by the study patients to doctors and nurses.

**Box 5.1   Supporting Nursing Care for Cardiovascular
Disease in Chile**

In 2004, the Chilean National Ministry of Health instituted a cardiovascular disease (CVD) management program among patients
treated in the public health care system. The program aimed to identify the characteristics of patients participating in the CVD program
and the feasibility of extending the program's reach through struc-
tured nurse telephone contacts between outpatient medical visits.
Piette et al (2006) evaluated the experience of 569 low-income adults
with type II diabetes treated in public clinics in Santiago. Patients
were surveyed to assess their participation in the CVD program and
their willingness to use telephone care services. Surveys were linked
to information from medical records.

One-third of patients met the target of two visits to the CVD program in the previous six months, and another third (32 percent)
made more than three visits. Use of the CVD program was associated with greater patient satisfaction. However, contact with the
program was inadequate for 27 percent of patients—many of whom
were in poor health. Many CVD program participants reported dif-
ficulties with lifestyle changes, and greater contact with the CVD
program was not associated with healthier behaviors. Most patients
(95 percent) reported telephone access and 37 percent used the telephone to contact their clinic. The majority of patients were willing
to use telephone care for additional behavior change and emotional
support. Patients with fewer CVD program visits were particularly
likely to report willingness to use telephone care.

Source: Piette et al (2006).

In developing countries, the implementation of new tracking and monitoring devices is uncommon, mostly because such devices are not affordable or available for even the most affluent patients. But some evaluations of phone-based systems that enable providers to engage in more hands-on periodic patient checks by phone may shed light on the potential for these innovations. In Chile, a nurse-based telephone care service, linked with key clinical events and outpatient visits, resulted in improved glycemic levels, healthier eating, lower blood pressure, and better patient perceptions of their health (see box 5.1). A public health disease management program in Nicaragua based on SMS and economic incentives in the form of credit applied to prepaid phone cards improved the compliance of patients taking tuberculosis drugs (Anta, El-Wahab, and Giuffrida, 2008).

Telemedicine comprises the use of ICT to provide long-distance health care (IOM, 1996; Grigsby and Sanders, 1998). One of the most important uses of telemedicine is supporting diagnosis and treatment by physicians or nurses providing care in remote areas, or in urban areas with low population density.

In addition, long-distance clinical applications of telemedicine include remote surgery, transmission of radiological images, interactive video visits, and continuous remote analysis of self-monitored data, which has important applications for chronic diseases such as diabetes and hypertension that need constant or periodic monitoring and testing.

In Latin America, telemedicine innovations are being implemented in several countries. In Brazil, the government has sponsored a National Telemedicine Program, which currently involves about thirty universities and research institutes in nine of the twenty-seven Brazilian states. The pilot project in telemedicine for primary care involves the installation of 900 PCs, mainly support for clinical decisions. These PCs are connected to a wide area network and can also be used for videoconferencing. The system includes deployment of electronic medical records, which can be shared with other units. Priority is being given to cities where there is a family health program (*Programa Saúde da Família*), a population of less than 100,000, and geographical barriers to health care. The Ministry of Health, together with the Ministry of Education, has been investing in distance learning for training and continuing education of health professionals.

Also in Brazil, the Belo Horizonte Telemedicine Project, implemented in 2003, aims to promote the continuing education of health workers in primary care units, as well as modernize the public health system. The Belo Horizonte Telemedicine network connects primary care centers to teaching units in the fields of medicine, nursing, and dentistry at the Federal University of Minas Gerais. The network uses videoconferences for continuing education, and teleconsulting between specialists and staff at the primary care centers for second opinions and discussion of clinical cases.

The telemedicine network operates in 121 primary care centers. About 1,500 teleconsultations per year occur between specialists and staff at the primary care centers. In 2006, more than 5,000 people participated in seventy-five educational videoconferences. The results of two project evaluations showed better outcomes for health centers with telemedicine support. About 70 percent of patients stayed in basic units, with no need for referral to a specialist. The number of patients who needed to travel to the Hospital of Belo Horizonte fell by 71 percent (Tomasi et al, 2009).

In Peru, Martínez et al (2007) evaluated a telemedicine program in isolated jungle communities supported by the EHAS Foundation (Enlace Hispano Americano de Salud).[4] The EHAS program provided telemedicine systems for seven health centers and thirty-two health posts with voice communication and

Table 5.2   Cost-Benefit Analysis of a Telemedicine System in Peru

	Present Value (US$) (3% discount rate)	Present Value (US$) (5% discount rate)
Costs		
System fixed costs	196,326	196,326
System variable costs	49,946	37,303
Total costs	246,272	233,629
Health System Benefits		
Personnel trip savings	56,433	54,880
Urgent referral savings	201,209	195,672
Training costs savings	66,218	64,396
Personnel time savings	125,439	121,987
Total health system savings	449,299	436,935
Other Nonhealth Benefits	120,127	116,821
Patient productivity		
Total Benefits	569,426	553,756
Net Benefits	323,154	320,126

Source: Martínez et al (2007).

e-mail by radio in the Alto Amazonas province. Thanks to the telemedicine program, urgent patient referrals fell from a mean of 11.1 to 2.5 per year from the health posts, and from 14.0 to 8.4 per year from the health centers. Total fixed costs of the telemedicine solution were US$5,034 and average operating costs per solution were US$334.5 per year. The benefits included fewer trips by health personnel between health posts, health centers, and the provincial hospital in Yurimaguas; lower travel and accommodation expenses related to urgent patient referrals; savings in traditional training courses; and savings in the time that patients and their relatives had to spend traveling to and from the hospital for urgent referrals. Direct health care cost savings accounted for 64 percent of overall savings, and productivity gains accounted for 36 percent. The net economic effect of the telemedicine program in Peru over a four-year period (starting in 2001) was clearly positive, amounting to annual net savings of US$320,126 (using a 5 percent discount rate). Table 5.2 presents the disaggregated costs and savings from the system and its net effects (using a 3 percent and a 5 percent discount rate).

A one-way sensitivity analysis using a range of values for the discounting rate and the number of urgent referrals confirmed that the program was economically efficient (that is, it achieved net financial savings) in all cases. From the budgetary perspective of the health network, the additional operational costs (telephone and maintenance) of the telemedicine system were lower than the direct cost-savings produced for the health care network.

A more advanced application in Spain is Dermamóvil, an innovation of Spain's telecommunication giant Telefónica. Dermamóvil provides a remote diagnostic system for skin conditions. Patients can send responses to surveys and/or photos of their affected skin area to a hospital server. A doctor can download the information and send SMS medical advice through a PC. The system also provides continuous on-demand monitoring. This system has cut down the number of visits to specialists and improved the quality of health care from the patients' perspective.

ICT, by providing faster and instantaneous collection and transmission of data, is a prime innovation to enhance the efficiency of epidemiological surveillance, especially in rural areas. In Colombia, the Telematics Department of the University of Cauca has developed a computerized system for collecting, sending, processing, visualizing, and providing feedback of epidemiological information at the national level.

These epidemiological surveillance systems are developed as independent solutions. In a comprehensive e-health reform of a national health system, these surveillance systems would be designed in the context of an eMR implementation (see discussion, next section). Examples of these systems in Latin America include the *Voxiva Alerta* in Peru, which uses disease surveys on PDAs for field data collection and speeds collection time over paper collection (instantaneous collection versus up to one month). In Brazil, similar systems are being developed with the participation of Nokia (Anta, El-Wahab, and Giuffrida, 2008).

Some telemedicine solutions can also be developed based on mobile phone technologies. For example, Commcare has a program to support remote diagnostics (on Java-enabled phones or PDAs) aimed at reducing isolation and increasing professional confidence/motivation and the credibility of community health workers (Anta, El-Wahab, and Giuffrida, 2008).

Better Care, Better Monitoring, and Better Outcomes through eMR

An array of information systems is being used in the health sector. This makes the system complex and frequently prone to failure or to problems arising from compatibility and interoperability (Brender, 2006 and Heeks, 2002, cited in Blaya, Holt, and Fraser, 2008, pp. 57 and 58). eMR constitute the core platform on which other systems can be implemented and sustained, and have provided platforms for effective strategies to track patients and medications in both developed and developing countries (Fraser et al 2006; Martínez et al, 2007).

In the United States, the Veterans Health Administration (VA) has been a leader, with an advanced eMR system linking pharmacies, laboratories, and all medical providers (Perlin, Collins, and Kaplowitz, 1999). From a humanitarian point of view, the system has been invaluable for people living with diabetes and other chronic diseases (Sawin et al, 2004). Economically, it has propelled productivity by nearly 6 percent per year since it was fully implemented in 1999 (Evans, Nichol, and Perlin 2006).

In low- and middle-income countries, eMRs are increasingly being implemented as well. In several countries in South and Central America and at least nine African countries, the open-source OpenMRS platform is in use (Gerber, Brown, and Pablos-Méndez, 2010). In each case, the decision to implement an eMR system involves balancing estimated costs against expected benefits. Resistance to change by health professionals and the probability of technical problems must also be considered.

Experience with eMR in Mexico's Social Security System

One of the pioneer experiences of eMR in Latin America is that of the Mexican Social Security Institute (IMSS), which implemented eMR on a large scale in 2003. Humpage (2010b) documented this experience. The total financial cost of developing and implementing the IMSS systems between 2003 and 2008 was US$190 million, a relatively small sum when compared to other initiatives that have cost twenty to thirty times this amount (CINVESTAV, 2009). Other costs, such as lost staff productivity during training, as well as training costs, should also be considered. Table 5.3 summarizes the infrastructure, hardware, and software costs of the systems at three levels of attention: primary care, outpatient hospital care, and inpatient hospital care.

Table 5.3   Costs of the Mexican Social Security Institute's Electronic Medical Records Program

Type of Facility	Infrastructure US$	Hardware US$	Software US$	Total US$
Primary Care Centers				
Total cost	21,527,000	87,455,000	43,055,000	152,037,000
Per facility	17,939	72,879	35,879	126,698
Per user (staff)	281	1,141	562	1,984
Per computer station	552	2,242	1,104	3,898
Outpatient Hospital Care				
Total cost	3,139,000	10,118,000	6,943,000	20,200,000
Per facility	44,843	144,543	99,186	288,571
Per user (staff)	20	66	45	131
Per computer station	668	2,153	1,477	4,298
Inpatient Hospital Care				
Total cost	2,601,000	9,329,000	5,983,000	17,913,000
Per facility	44,845	160,845	103,155	308,845
Per user (staff)	55	198	127	381
Per computer station	1,351	4,846	3,108	9,305

Source: Authors' calculations based on Humpage (2010b).

Humpage (2010b) found that the IMSS eMR made great advances in data storage in the IMSS and improved delivery of medical care, especially in primary care. Patient data is more secure with automatic backups on local servers and on a central server. Real-time personnel reports for clinic directors have facilitated supervision. Both prescriptions and orders for paid medical leave days are processed much more quickly. Time savings in the production of aggregate data have been dramatic, though they have not translated into reductions in personnel.

The Mexican IMSS example suggests that implementing an eMR system in a hospital is a more complicated endeavor. Hospitals have a larger and more varied staff than clinics and attend to a wider variety of complex conditions. Humpage (2010b) argued that in the IMSS eMR, benefits to hospitals were less clear or consistent. Coverage in hospitals is much lower than in clinics, and infrastructure is insufficient to support the eMR system in some cases. Budgetary constraints have precluded installing eMR in all hospitals. Some hospitals already had their own systems in place, leaving them with little incentive to learn and use a new system, which has implications for the compatibility of data and the use of centralized information databases.

Importantly, the enormous amount of data stored in the IMSS eMR database has had a limited use for policy analysis, medical research, or patient tracking. The potential for research and policy analysis that digitally stored data offer may be one of the most important benefits of using an eMR system, especially for nationwide systems such as the one implemented by IMSS. Using these data to track patient compliance, ensure high coverage of inexpensive preventive measures, and identify individuals at risk for particular diseases is promising. However, the IMSS system has not been used for this type of analysis.

At the clinic level, the system is not used to analyze patient data beyond the moment of a patient's exam. There is potential to benefit much more from the IMSS eMR system by exploiting clinic- and systemwide data for research. During the system's first years, maximizing coverage was prioritized over exploiting the system for these uses.

Policy Prescriptions

Individuals and government alike want their health services to provide care that is patient-centered, available, accessible, safe, reliable, effective, and equitable. E-health has the potential to help improve health care provision, cost-effectiveness, and health outcomes in the region, but in most countries it is still in its infancy. Scaling up e-health will require significant investments in human resources, hardware, software, and infrastructure.

For Latin America and other developing countries to replicate the e-health solutions of developed countries is probably neither cost-effective nor feasible at this stage. The region needs to adapt the e-health solutions to each country's health priorities, existing national ICT infrastructure, and health system development.

Implementation of ICT innovations in health has demonstrated potential. However, knowledge about the effectiveness of ICT health innovations is still relatively scarce, and evaluations for a small set of applications in developing countries show mixed results. Most of the available literature, especially for Latin America, tends to be descriptive rather than evaluative, reinforcing the urgent need for projects that allow for data collection and rigorous evaluations.

Some common factors may explain the mixed results of e-health innovations. First, ICT adoption and use is heterogeneous in the region. Second, some interventions were implemented in very short time periods; in particular, in the case of prevention for adolescents, they were not included in the school curriculum. Third, interventions that aim at chronic diseases have not involved providers. By contrast, most successful interventions for chronic care in the United States have involved the use of eMR, monitoring, and tracking of patients by providers—and, in the most advanced interventions, the use of home-based testing devices.

One of the priorities for the region at this stage is piloting and implementing more comprehensive e-health interventions for chronic care. Telemedicine has been implemented with relative success, and it offers promise for reducing costs and improving patient care in isolated areas.

The next stage in ICT innovation for many of the region's health systems is the implementation of eMR in the public and social security subsectors, ideally in a coordinated manner. The implementation of eMR will allow health systems to take advantage of the full benefits of other e-health innovations, such as monitoring and tracking systems for chronic patients, telemedicine, and ICT epidemiological surveillance systems. Carefully evaluating and disseminating the results of the pioneer experiences in the region—like the IMSS eMR in Mexico—and in developed countries is key for replicating the successful experiences and learning from mistakes.

Even though e-health is generally perceived to be a key cost-effective innovation to enhance the performance of the health system, its implementation has been slow even in developed countries, especially in those with high participation by the private sector such as the United States. Only after the 2010 health reform are eMRs expected to be implemented broadly in the United States. Christensen and Remler (2007) argue that the limited adoption of ICT by health care providers, especially hospitals and insurers in the United States, can be explained by a general lack of demonstrated cost-effectiveness of ICT for them, for a variety of reasons: the fragmented nature of health provision and financing, the high financial risk of adopting new technologies, the costs and difficulty of the behavioral change needed to adopt the technology, the temporary efficiency losses and potential medical errors during the transition, and the significant legal issues concerning adoption. All of these concerns should be taken into account when considering incentives or regulation changes regarding e-health innovations. Christensen and Remler (2007) also highlight the important role of the government to pilot and be an early implementer of many of these innovations, especially eMR, using strict evidence-based criteria.

A word of caution is needed regarding the interoperability of ICT systems. The experience of the United States highlights that specific communication and technology standards in health care are needed to allow systems of ICT to "speak to each other." Such technical standards provide clear benefits and play an important role in enhancing compatibility. They reduce the technology risk faced by consumers, as they are less likely to end up stranded with an incompatible technology. Technical standards also reduce switching costs and thereby lock in users to specific technologies. These standards are regional public goods; their creation would prevent costly errors and monopolies for ICT providers.

Finally, it is important to stress that many countries in the region have not yet overcome basic problems in their health sectors. Although a serious assessment of the costs and benefits of many e-health innovations is still outstanding, the Peruvian EHAS experience suggests that many interventions may not be relatively costly when considering the current amount spent on health in the region. The risk is that these innovations—especially those that involve network effects such as eMR—may be less effective when implemented in fragmented systems that suffer from coverage, equity, provision, and financing problems. Hence, policymakers should balance the gradual implementation of e-health innovations with the urgent need to reform the health system as a whole in order to take full advantage of technology's potential benefits.

6

Computers in Schools: Why Governments Should Do Their Homework

Latin American and Caribbean countries fare poorly in terms of student learning. After significant improvements in recent decades in the enrollment of children in preschool, primary, and secondary education, the region now faces significant challenges to ensure that its students achieve adequate levels of learning. One indication of the gap is standardized test scores. Figure 6.1 presents average standardized test scores for students aged 15 and gross domestic product (GDP) per capita in 2006, by country. Countries in the region, identified in black, perform significantly worse than their counterparts with similar levels of development. For example, Argentina, Chile, and Mexico have a GDP per capita similar to Latvia, Russia, and Turkey, but these countries outperform the Latin American countries by large margins. Colombia and Brazil, with a similar GDP per capita to Azerbaijan and Thailand, fare substantially worse in international assessments.

To improve the quality of learning, countries in the region are contemplating a variety of potential interventions. In particular, many countries are vigorously pushing programs to increase students' access to computers in schools as well as at home. For example, Uruguay has recently implemented a "one computer per student" program to provide laptops to all students in public

Figure 6.1   Standardized Test Scores and Income: An International Comparison
Average Scores in Mathematics and Reading

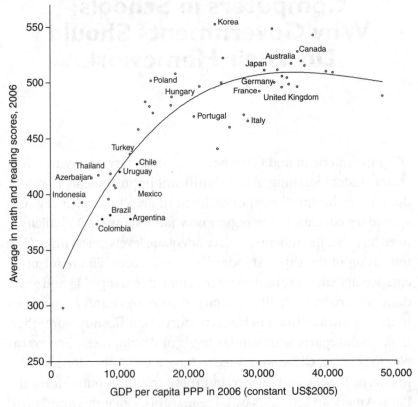

Source: OECD (2006) and World Bank (2010).

primary schools. Peru has also started distributing computers to students in rural primary schools, dramatically changing access to technology in isolated locations. A quick look at the main newspapers in the region suggests that these two countries may be soon followed by others in introducing ambitious programs that involve the use and distribution of computers in schools.

Can computers help close the learning gap in Latin American and Caribbean primary and secondary schools? This chapter seeks to provide some insight into this question and raises some important red flags for policymakers to consider. First, programs that distribute one computer per student are costly, and as such, may crowd out other interventions that may be potentially more effective. Second, the benefits of computer programs depend critically on the features of each particular project. Importantly, there are significant uncertainties surrounding their potential impact, especially for the new wave of programs that distribute laptops to students for school and home use on a large scale. The evidence so far is quite persuasive that programs that overlook teacher training and the development of software may yield low returns. Also, children may shift the time spent at home doing homework and studying to computer use that does little to boost educational achievement. Third, the use of computer-assisted instruction software in mathematics has shown promising results. Finally, using increased access to computers—not necessarily on a one-to-one basis—to teach computer skills can produce large positive effects in these competencies, virtually erasing the related "digital divide" with a limited investment.

The Next Educational Revolution?

> "I believe the motion picture is destined to revolutionize our educational system and that in a few years it will supplant largely, if not entirely, the use of textbooks."
>
> –Thomas Edison, 1922

The basic organization of the primary and secondary school system in Latin American countries—and in the rest of the world for that matter—has changed relatively little over the last 100 years. Primary schools in urban areas of Latin America are organized in grades determined by age and competence. The students follow a set national or local educational curriculum. Schools have at least one class at each grade and one teacher per class. The school is usually run by a principal, who is in charge of administrative and academic matters.

In rural areas, education is similarly organized, but when schools are located in particularly remote areas and population density is low, it is common to find multigrade schools (FAO, 2004). In these schools, one or a few teachers instruct students of different ages and competence within the same class. The school infrastructure is poor in many parts of Latin America and the Caribbean. For example, according to a study by United Nations Educational, Scientific and Cultural Organization (UNESCO) (2008), more than 10 percent of schools in Argentina, Brazil, Paraguay, and Peru lack running water.

Secondary schooling is also organized in grades related to age and competence, but the number and complexity of subjects taught increase. Thus, specialized teachers tend to be assigned to different subjects. Due to cost and feasibility considerations, secondary education organized in this fashion is mostly an urban phenomenon.

How has the advent of information and communication technologies (ICTs) changed public education? The Organisation for Economic Co-operation and Development (OECD) (2009) definition of ICT services and products includes computers and peripheral equipment, communication equipment, consumer electronic equipment, software, and telecommunications services. This definition includes anything from calculators to laptops, from radios to MP3 players, from TVs to audiovisual equipment, from landlines to cellular phones, from word processors to educational software, and from e-mail services to broadband services. Many schools have had access to some of these

ICT technologies (calculators, radios, TVs, and phones) for a long time, but—perhaps surprisingly—the basic functioning of the school system has not changed dramatically with the advent of any of these innovations.

Could the exponential decrease in the cost of communications and computers revolutionize the way schools and education function? The one laptop per child (OLPC) project has aimed to "create educational opportunities for the world's poorest children by providing each child with a rugged, low-cost, low-power, connected laptop with content and software designed for collaborative, joyful, self-empowered learning."[1] The first deployments took place in 2007, and by now close to 1 million laptops have been distributed in forty countries. What is the potential role of computers in improving educational outcomes in Latin America? A look at different modes of ICT use in schools can help answer these questions.

Computers as an Input in the Educational Process

The school system produces education by combining school infrastructure (such as school buildings, classrooms, desks, whiteboards, textbooks, and computers) and school personnel (such as administrators and teachers). School administrators hire and manage teachers and delegate to them the decision as to which combination of tools provided by the school infrastructure will allow them to achieve the learning outcomes determined by the school curriculum.

In this framework, a piece of computer equipment is just another input that teachers use at their discretion to trigger some response from their students and, ultimately, to achieve a learning outcome. Given the relative prices of the inputs and the production technology, teachers and schools choose the optimal combination of inputs to achieve their objectives. The most common uses of computers in schools can be embedded easily within this model.

Computer labs. A lab is usually installed in a specific school room, with computers shared between students. Learning is led by a specialized teacher, trained to deal with learning, software, and hardware issues.

Computer labs in schools were developed in the 1980s and 1990s with the idea of providing students with the possibility of learning computer skills, as well as introducing them to computer programming. The ultimate objective was not to produce computer programmers but to develop problem-solving skills.

Computer-assisted learning was also initially built around computer labs. In this setup, a class or a number of students in a class visit the lab with the objective of using a purpose-built software for the study of mathematics or language skills.

Computers in the classroom. With the dramatic decline in the price of audiovisual and computer equipment, many schools—particularly in urban areas—have been able to introduce a number of ICT technologies in the classroom. These technologies include computers, electronic boards, and ultimately, one computer per student.

The greater availability of computer or audiovisual equipment has let teachers introduce these pedagogical tools at their own pace and within their own day-by-day planning. For example, students can perform exercises in different areas of the school curricula and the teacher can record their progress in the computer for formative assessment. The teacher can use electronic whiteboards to present data and graphs, and manipulate information in a way that can improve visual learning.

So far, this discussion has described the use of ICT as just another input in the production of educational outcomes.

However, those that favor the idea of one computer per student view ICT as not just another input, but as a way of defining the production process. In a sense, the choice of a given ICT strategy defines the pedagogical approach and how the other inputs should be combined, given their relative prices. The one-to-one model tries to break with the traditional classroom education setting by providing a constructivist, student-centered approach to learning where students are allowed to learn and progress at their own pace.

ICT and the management of the school system. The promise of ICT in schools is not restricted to its capabilities as a pedagogical tool. Computers, cell phones, and other ICTs can be used to store, transmit, and analyze data faster than ever before.

For example, the collection, transmission, and analysis of data on enrollment, absenteeism, test scores, and infrastructure can help principals spot a problem in a given classroom, administrators spot an exemplary school, and policymakers track the performance of the educational system and the resources available. However, the gains in productivity seen in the business sector are rarely seen in the educational system, some have argued (see Carnoy, 2004), because most education managers are not knowledgeable in the use of information management tools.

The potential of ICT is not restricted to the supervision and monitoring by centralized agencies. In countries where ICT access and use by families is widespread, the possibility of using this technology to disseminate data on schools and individuals to parents is growing fast. Chile, for example, publishes the results of standardized student examinations by school on the Web. This information affects the demand for schools and is intended to improve accountability.

Computers in Schools: Placing Latin America on the Map

In the last twenty years, Latin American countries have heavily invested in ICT projects to provide students with computers and Internet connectivity. To systematically document how and when national policies on ICT in education have been implemented, Alvariño and Severín (2009) have surveyed key informants in a sample of Latin American countries. Figure 6.2 presents some general patterns regarding the timing of the introduction of national ICT policies in five areas: computer labs, connectivity, ICT training for teachers, web portals, and OLPC pilots.

A few interesting patterns emerge from the figure. First, countries have mostly followed a similar sequence of investments. Setting up computer labs has typically been the first step. Between 1996 and 2005, countries in the sample started to introduce the Internet to schools, and roughly at the same time, launched large-scale teacher training programs. Web portals have come next, as governments have tried to provide content and educational tools to schools now connected to the Internet. Finally, in the last few years, almost all the countries in the survey have implemented pilot projects to distribute a computer to each student in a school.

A similar survey to shed light on computer use in education and barriers faced by Caribbean countries was carried out in 2008 (Gaible, 2008). Availability of computers and the Internet was widespread among schools, especially for those at the secondary level. However, the investigation found that though most countries had policies regarding the introduction of ICT in education, these had limited impact in practice.

Box 6.1 describes five leading initiatives. Almost two decades ago, Costa Rica and Chile introduced computer labs

Figure 6.2   A Timeline for Adopting ICT Projects

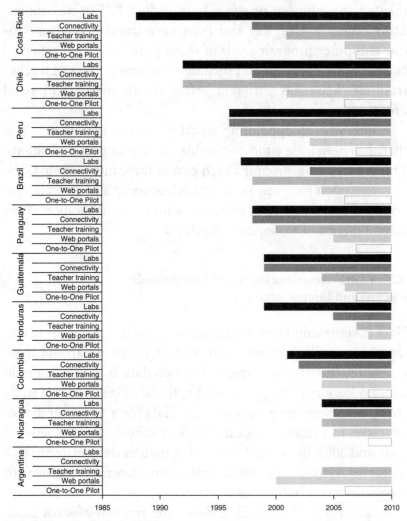

Source: Alvariño and Severín (2009).
Notes: "Labs" refers to computer laboratory. "Connectivity" refers to availability of Internet connection at the school. "Teacher Training" includes educational uses of ICT. "Web portal" refers to an educational portal at schools. "One-to-One pilot" refers to pilots that provided low-cost laptops to all students in a school. Honduras has not carried out One-to-One pilot programs. Argentina has not implemented labs and connectivity programs.

in schools on a large scale. In the late 1990s, Barbados implemented an ambitious program to introduce ICT in classrooms. More recently, Uruguay and Peru have implemented one-to-one computer programs. All of these programs have achieved countrywide coverage and include some component of teacher training. Each has different strategies in urban and rural areas.

A somewhat disappointing aspect of the five initiatives is that there has been little effort to provide credible impact evaluations. This is surprising, given the high cost of these interventions. The only exception has been Peru, which has set up a large-scale randomized evaluation of its program, with the collaboration of the Inter-American Development Bank.

ICT in Latin American and Caribbean Schools: Limited and Uneven Access

Have governments been effective at bringing ICT resources to students? How well are these resources being used? To answer these questions, this chapter exploits the rich data from the Segundo Estudio Regional Comparativo y Explicativo (SERCE). This study collected comparative representative data for a large number of countries in Latin America for primary school students between 2004 and 2007. In particular, this chapter uses data related to ICT inputs for sixth-grade students in thirteen countries, starting with computer access in the region.

Access. Figure 6.3, panel a, shows the fraction of sixth graders that have a computer at home and at school. While nearly 20 percent of students have computers at home in Paraguay and Guatemala, around 50 percent of students do in Argentina and

Box 6.1   Leading Experiences in Latin America and the Caribbean

Costa Rica. In 1988, Costa Rica introduced computers in schools as a strategy to support learning. The program relied on teaching students the programming language Logo as a way to develop skills in logic and creativity. Over the years, a number of different action lines were implemented, aimed at increasing the availability of hardware, improving teacher training, connecting schools to the Internet, and increasing digital literacy in the general population. The program presents two modalities for hardware. Computer labs are set up in urban schools. Computers are deployed directly in the classroom in rural schools—a less expensive option that responds to economies of scale. In primary urban schools, students are expected to attend two classes a week in the computer lab, one in mathematics and one in language. Classes are guided by specialized teachers, with varying participation by the regular teachers. The specialized teachers receive intense training, pedagogical support, and close supervision from technology "advisors" to ensure productive use of the computers. A special career of teachers specialized in technology has been created.

   Chile. In 1990, the Ministry of Education introduced the program Enlaces. Initially piloted in the Araucarian region, it was introduced nationwide in 1995 and today covers 98 percent of all publicly supported primary and secondary schools. Participant schools receive computers, local networks, educational and productivity software, and free or subsidized Internet access. Urban schools receive computer labs, with the number of computers installed in each school determined by the level of enrollment. In rural schools computers are installed in the classroom, with a minimum of two in each school, regardless of the level of enrollment. Unlike in Costa Rica, there are no specialized teachers. Every teacher is expected to take advantage of the computer lab to promote learning in his or her own subject, while improving students' skills in the management, presentation,

(continued on next page)

(continued)

and communication of data and ideas. For this purpose, the government created a network of universities that provide training, pedagogical support, and technical assistance.

Barbados. In 1999, the program Edutech was launched. The initiative required an investment of US$213 million, a substantial amount for a school system of only 50,000 primary and secondary school students. By 2008, students in all primary and secondary schools in the country had access to computers and the Internet. About a third of primary schools have received computers in labs and in the classrooms, whereas all secondary schools have received at least thirty computers. The program has several interrelated components. Physical infrastructure has been improved, partly to ensure that schools are ready to receive computers and network connections. The ICT component, which originally accounted for about a third of the investment, was planned to deploy about 9,000 computers in primary and secondary schools. There is also a teacher training component and initiatives geared toward improving the education curriculum.

Uruguay. The CEIBAL project (Conectividad Educativa de Informática Básica para el Aprendizaje en Línea) is a one-laptop-per-student project launched in 2007 with the goal of providing each student and his family continuous access to a computer, online resources through wireless connectivity, and free software. By the end of 2009, all students in public primary schools were covered. In 2010, the program was rolled out to secondary schools. The initial investment for CEIBAL was around US$100 million (Lasida, Peirano, and Severin, 2009) which represents 17 percent of the national budget for primary education. The laptops are designed for students. They are durable, lightweight, easy to carry, and are protected against water and dust. The battery lasts between one and two hours. They do not have a hard disk, and they store information only in flash memories. The operative system and its applications are free. Applications include a web browser, text processor, e-mail and chat service, and audio and

(continued on next page)

(continued)

video platforms. The laptops have a wireless Internet connection and can also connect to one another. A server is installed in each school (approximately 2,300 have been installed) and provides Internet connectivity. To allow teachers to become familiar with the hardware and software and develop the teaching materials, teacher training is offered two months before the laptops are officially released to the students. Approximately 56.1 percent of teachers have been trained to teach subjects using ICTs. Later, support groups visit teachers to help them integrate curricular training in specific content areas and to increase the use of technology. Forty-three percent of schools have submitted curricular innovations for the use of ICTs for educational purposes.

Peru. Peru implemented a one-laptop-per-student program with the goal of increasing the quality of public primary education, especially in rural schools in extreme poverty. Only 4 percent of beneficiary students live in urban areas, and 92 percent attend multigrade schools. Distribution of computers started in 2008. By October 2009, 170,000 computers had been distributed in 5,100 primary schools. All students and teachers received a laptop. Laptops are similar to the ones used in Uruguay. Peru selected thirty-nine different software applications, including games, measurement tools, a word processor, a calculator, chat, Wikipedia, maps, and programming software. Most are not connected to the Internet. Teacher training consists of a five-day, eight-hour-a-day course covering use of the laptops and available software. Teachers also receive ten short guides that describe how to use particular software and a manual that covers the functional use of the laptop and basic maintenance tasks.

Chile. In many countries, computer access at home is low, but this is compensated by access at school. Indeed, many believe that schools could be a powerful means of reducing inequities in access to technology (see, for example, Jara Valdivia, 2008). The

Figure 6.3   Availability of ICT at Home and at School, 2006 (percent)

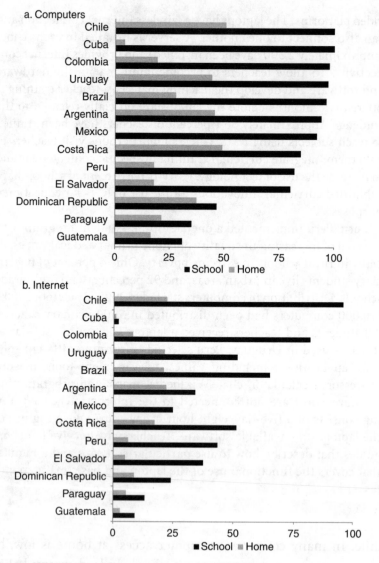

Source: Authors' calculations based on data from LLECE (2008).
Note: Data from computer and Internet access at home for Mexico is unavailable.

rationale is simple: with a limited investment—typically, a computer lab in a school—many students without outside access can use a computer regularly. Indeed, access to computers at school is practically universal in Chile, Cuba, Colombia, Uruguay, Brazil, Argentina, and Mexico.

Internet connectivity has the potential to unleash many opportunities for students in terms of accessing vast amounts of information and collaborating and communicating with peers and experts. Panel b of figure 6.3 presents data on Internet access at school and at home. Internet access at school varies widely, from 96 percent of students in Chile to only 9 percent in Guatemala: a much wider range than the measures of access to computers. Interestingly, Cuba has a 100 percent computer access at school but almost no Internet access.

Clearly, having at least one computer in a school can be interpreted as having "access" to technology, but this is not the full picture. Consider the number of minutes each student can potentially spend in front of a computer every week, which is an indicator of how many resources are available to students (figure 6.4).[2] Despite widespread access, the amount of computer time available to students is relatively low. Costa Rica, Mexico, and Chile have the highest computer time availability, with more than forty minutes of computer time per student per week. Paraguay has the lowest availability (fewer than ten minutes). It should be noted that access in public schools tends to be lower than the national average, which also includes students in private schools.

How wide is the "digital divide" when analyzed at the individual level? Figure 6.5 illustrates how much home and school "access" varies according to socioeconomic status (the education of the student's mother, classified by quartiles defined for each country). A positive link exists between access at home and socioeconomic

Figure 6.4   Potential Computer Access, 2006
Average minutes with a computer allocated to each student weekly

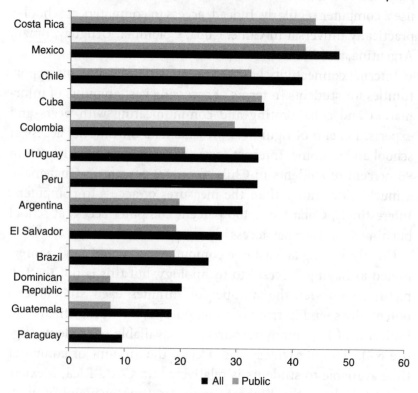

Source: Authors' calculations based on data from LLECE (2008).

status, but the relationship with school is much weaker. However, the socioeconomic gradient of access at school is more pronounced when measured in terms of intensity of access (minutes of computer time available to each student). The data suggest that the role of schools in closing differences in access is less prominent when intensity of access is taken into account.

Use. Higher access may not necessarily translate into higher utilization if schools do not make effective use of the additional resources. In economic terms, increasing access can be viewed as

Figure 6.5   Percent of Students with Access to a Computer by Mother's Education, 2006

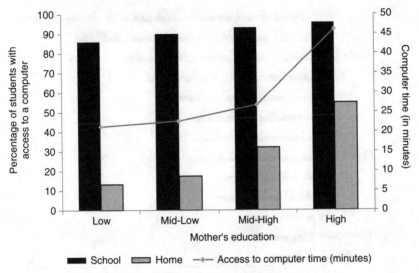

Source: Authors' calculations based on data from LLECE (2008).

an increase in the "supply" of this input at the school. However, greater use will not materialize if there is not enough demand for it. Many cases have been documented in which schools have computers available but do not use them.

To analyze this issue, students in SERCE were asked how frequently they used computers at school. Figure 6.6 shows the fraction of students by country who reported that they use computers at school at least once a week. This may be the most important indicator because it provides information regarding actual use of technology, rather than the extent or intensity of access. The figure highlights stark differences in weekly use across countries. On the high end is Cuba, where the majority of students report using a computer weekly. At the low end are Guatemala and Paraguay, where less than 20 percent of students use computers regularly.

Figure 6.6   Students Using a Computer at Least Once a Week at School, 2006 (percent)

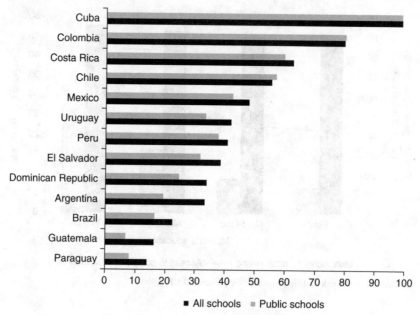

Source: Authors' calculations based on data from LLECE (2008).

Do variations in weekly use reflect disparities in access or greater efficiency in terms of technology use?[3] Apparently, computer access and school enrollment account for much of the divergence across countries in weekly computer use. Thus, the disparities can be blamed largely on the distribution of computers at school. The exceptional case is Cuba, where students enjoy much more computer time compared to other countries with similar levels of access.

Teachers' Use of ICT

Access to technology must be supported by teachers who know how to use the technology and can integrate it into their pedagogical practices so as to realize its potential benefits (see, for example,

Figure 6.7   Computer Use by Teachers, 2006

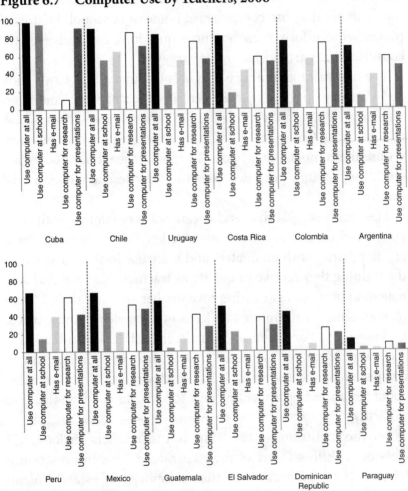

Source: Authors' calculations based on data from LLECE (2008).

Sunkel, 2006; Bruns et al., 2009). To understand the access and interaction of teachers with computers in Latin America, teacher questionnaires from the SERCE study yield summary statistics on computer access and use.

The SERCE survey provides information about whether sixth-grade public school teachers use computers regularly. For teachers who reply affirmatively to this question, the survey delves further into whether they use computers at home or at school. Figure 6.7 presents the information on these questions for twelve of the countries that participated in the survey.

The first striking finding is that only in Cuba, Chile, Costa Rica, and Uruguay do more than 80 percent of teachers use computers regularly. Although the availability of computers at school is high only in Cuba, Chile, and Mexico, more than 50 percent of teachers use the computer at school. The most frequent use of computers is for research purposes. Relatively few teachers have e-mail accounts.

The results suggest that teachers are not very familiar with computers and do not use them often. A key factor affecting teachers' familiarity with computers and their use in the classroom is the training they receive to qualify as teachers. National and subnational governments can improve teacher training in ICT since they determine minimum standards of competence and curricular knowledge. For example, countries like Chile, Colombia, Costa Rica, and Peru have mandated that teachers-in-training must be competent in the use of ICT in the classroom. However, other countries, including Argentina and Mexico, do not state that goal explicitly.

Do the institutions that train future teachers include ICT classroom skills as part of their curricula? This information is hard to come by because of the multiplicity of establishments that offer training and the option they have of either introducing ICT skills as a curricular subject or as part of the training in mainstream subjects. Countries planning to develop ICT programs should evaluate the competence of new and current teachers in the use of ICT technologies before embarking on ambitious ICT programs.

Are Latin America and the Caribbean Lagging Behind?

The Programme for International Student Assessment (PISA) periodically evaluates the performance of a nationally representative sample of fifteen-year-old students around the world. The study includes information about students and their schools, and the 2006 waves of PISA included six Latin American countries: Argentina, Brazil, Chile, Colombia, Mexico, and Uruguay. For this chapter, the computer per student ratio and the computer with Internet access per student ratio in each school were averaged for all schools in a given country. Figure 6.8 shows the relationship between these measures and GDP per capita. Each circle represents a country. The superimposed lines are fitted values from a linear model using all countries in the study, with the exception of the Latin American ones.

There is a positive relationship between computers and Internet access and GDP per capita. Although the purpose was not to assign a causal interpretation to these associations, a simple interpretation for these findings can be ventured. The demand for inputs in the educational process is a derived demand. That is, individuals do not demand computers or textbooks per se; they demand education. If education is a normal good, then as income rises, societies can be expected to demand higher levels of education and to become more educated. In turn, this will affect the demand for school infrastructure in general and ICT in particular.

Costs and Benefits of Computers for Basic Education

Although the cost of ICT products has declined significantly in recent years, providing universal access to computers is still an expensive enterprise for most Latin American and Caribbean

Figure 6.8   Computers, Internet Access, and Income

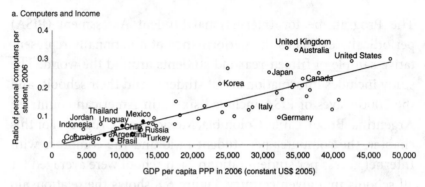

a. Computers and Income

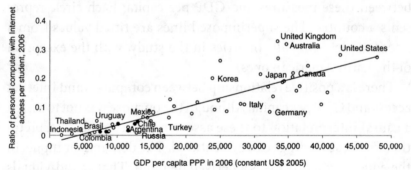

b. Computers with Internet Access and Income

Source: OECD (2006) and World Bank (2010).

countries. On one extreme of the spectrum, the most costly alternative is to provide each student with a computer to use both in class and at home (the one-to-one approach). A less expensive option is to let students share computers in school by building computer labs. This section quantifies these costs.

To compare the cost of different ICT projects in classrooms, it is useful to define the concept of "total cost of ownership" (TCO), which is typically used to capture the total cost over the life of an initial investment. It includes the original cost of the investment, which has an expected life of several years, as well as the recurrent costs required for that initial investment to work properly over its lifetime (electricity, maintenance, training, and the like).

A hypothetical analysis that reflects average parameters for the region helps explain the cost consequences of different strategies. Consider the ministry of education of a country that is evaluating whether to make the usage of computers in its schools universal. There are three alternatives. The first is a standard one-to-one program, which consists of giving one laptop to each student currently enrolled in the school system, and supporting some minimal teacher training. The second is an enhanced one-to-one program that not only provides laptops for the students, but also specially designed learning software and intensive teacher training, and allows each cohort that leaves the school system to take the computer with them (one-to-one). The third is a computer laboratory (lab) in the school that affords students two hours of access to the equipment each week.

ICT projects typically involve the purchase of large amounts of hardware and software at the onset of the program. In principle, the country can buy those resources via international competition; thus, international market prices can be used to value them. The projects usually involve teacher training. The costs will depend largely on prevailing wages and the intensity of training (hours of training and number of teachers that each instructor serves, for example). Since many costs are fixed at the country, school, or classroom level, this analysis is based on an average school in the region that has 300 students enrolled and 24 students in each class. Table 6.1 shows the resulting comparative costs for an urban school.

Assume that a relatively cheap laptop costs US$210 and has an expected life of about five years. In addition, some extra hardware is usually needed in each school to use the laptops fully (servers, disk storage, and Internet access points).[4] The annualized

Table 6.1   Annualized Total Cost of Ownership per Student (current US$)

	One-to-One	One-to-One+	Lab
Investment			
Hardware	61.9	61.9	7.1
Software	0.0	39.6	0.3
Teacher training	3.2	17.4	3.2
Internet	0.1	0.1	0.1
Other	1.7	1.7	1.6
Total	66.9	120.7	12.4
Recurrent			
Electricity	0.4	0.4	0.3
Teacher training	4.8	49.2	4.8
Internet	1.4	1.4	1.4
Maintenance	20.3	44.6	3.5
Other	0.3	0.3	0.6
Total	27.2	96.0	10.6
Total Costs	94.1	216.7	23.0

Sources: Author's calculations based on OLPC (2010) and Vital Wave Consulting (2008).
Note: All costs are calculated for a baseline school of 300 students.
One-to-One+ is similar to the One-to-One project, but it differs in the amount of training provided to teachers. It also incorporates the use of a tutorial software.

hardware cost adds up to almost US$62 per student per year.[5] The computer lab, on the other hand, is equipped with more expensive computers than the ones used in the one-to-one setting and is designed to be used by pairs of students for about two hours a week. Given that the school is open only a fixed number of hours each day, bigger schools would require several labs.[6] Despite these higher costs, the initial investment for a computer lab is much lower than in the one-to-one strategies.

All projects also require other start-up investments: software, training, and access to the Internet. Although training and software costs are relatively low in the one-to-one case, they are substantially higher for the one-to-one+ strategy. Indeed, one-to-one+ requires computer-assisted instruction software that allows children to learn according to their own capabilities. The software must be specifically designed to meet the curricular requirements of each country. Thus, it is costly.

The three strategies also create recurrent costs that are paid every year: operation costs (electricity), access to the Internet, maintenance, and teacher training. As noted, lack of teacher training is one of the main limitations of traditional one-to-one programs. This is why one-to-one+ programs place special emphasis on continuous training. Whereas one-to-one programs concentrate a high percentage of costs on deployment of hardware and peripherals, one-to-one+ programs devote a larger proportion to training and software (figure 6.9).

The cost of computers has become a paramount concern in the quest to make the one-to-one strategy feasible in developing countries. Total costs include not only the initial investment, but also sizable recurrent costs each year. Recurrent costs account for approximately 44 percent of the TCO of the one-to-one+ projects, and 29 percent of one-to-one projects. In the case of computer labs, recurrent costs are 46 percent of the total cost. High recurrent costs mean that any universal ICT project generates a permanent increase in educational spending.

Performing a hypothetical cost analysis helps reveal the relative cost of each project and the importance of each component, but it has some limitations. Indeed, if a country decides to implement one of these projects, costs would vary from those presented in table 6.1, because the specific configuration the country selects differs from the one chosen as an example, and because of the characteristics of the school system and the infrastructure available in the country. In particular, six factors can affect the cost structure

Figure 6.9   Cost Structure of Three Models of Deploying Computers, 2008 (percent)

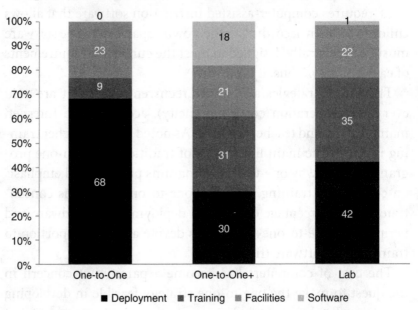

Source: Authors' calculations based on OLPC (2010) and Vital Wave Consulting (2008).
Note: Deployment refers to: Hardware, electricity, other investment, and recurrent costs. Training refers to: Training teachers costs. Facilities refers to: Internet and maintenance costs. Software refers to : Tutorial and Microsoft software costs. "One-to-One+" is similar to the "One-to-One" project, but it differs in the amount of training provided to teachers. It also incorporates the use of a tutorial software.

of any of these projects: the distribution of school size, the percentage of rural schools, the number of students per teacher, differences in teachers' wages, energy costs, and connectivity costs. Combining the hypothetical case with country-specific information on these six factors reveals how much it would cost for each country to implement the three projects from scratch.

Figure 6.10 shows the annual TCO per student of the three ICT projects as a percentage of annual current expenditure per

Figure 6.10   Cost of ICT for Primary Education in Latin America and the Caribbean, 2008

(as a percentage of current public expenditure per student in primary education)

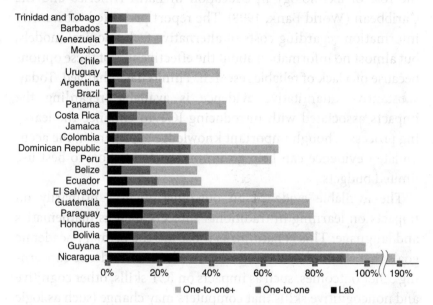

Source: Author's calculations based on CEDLAS (2010), de León (2009), LLECE (2008), UNESCO (2010), Vital Wave Consulting (2008), Viteri Díaz (2006), World Bank (2008, 2010).

Note: Calculations based on the baseline school and country information. One-to-One+ is similar to the One-to-One project, but it differs in the amount of training provided to teachers. It also incorporates the use of a tutorial software.

student in primary education. Countries are sorted from highest to lowest GDP per capita. In better-off countries, implementing even the more expensive one-to-one+ program could be affordable, in principle. In other countries, like Argentina or Costa Rica, even the less expensive option of the one-to-one strategy usually implies more than a 10 percent increase in expenditure. Because of the nature of the project, this increase would be permanent.

Benefits: Do Computers Offer Education in a Box?

In 1998, the World Bank issued its first regional report about the role of technology in education in Latin America and the Caribbean (World Bank, 1998). The report presented substantive information regarding costs of alternative technological models, but almost no information about the effectiveness of these options because of a lack of reliable research. Things have changed. Today, substantive quantitative evidence is available regarding the impacts associated with introducing ICT to enhance the learning process. Though important knowledge gaps persist, the accumulated evidence can help governments decide how to best use limited budgets.

The available evidence on outcomes focuses primarily on impacts on learning in traditional subjects such as mathematics and language. This is natural, as those are the primary academic goals that schools try to achieve. There is some evidence concerning other outcomes, such as impacts on ICT skills, other cognitive and noncognitive skills that computers may change (such as logic reasoning), and certain behavior, such as attendance and dropout rates.

Computers in schools. A vast quantitative literature attempts to estimate the impact of introducing computers to schools.[7] Typically, a treatment group of students or schools is beneficiary of some type of intervention, and a number of outcomes for the intervened "units" are compared to those from a comparison group. Among rigorous quantitative studies, two distinct groups can be identified. The first are studies that estimate the impacts associated with increasing *access* to computers, typically together with some other inputs, such as software, teacher training, and pedagogical support. The second are studies that explore the impacts associated with a particular *use* of computers in schools.

Many studies that have looked at whether increasing computer access improves educational outcomes have found either positive or negative impacts, but they cannot convincingly rule out that these interventions had no impact at all (see table 6.2, panel a). For example, Barrera-Osorio and Linden (2009) used an experimental approach to evaluate a program that deployed computers to primary and secondary schools in Colombia and found no impacts in mathematics and language. Bet, Cristia, and Ibarrarán (2010) exploited the substantial changes in ICT access from 2001 to 2006 in secondary schools in Peru to explore whether penetration of computers helped reduce the repetition rate, and also found no impacts. Under the same educational context, Cristia, Czerwonko, and Garofalo (2010) compared two sets of Peruvian public secondary schools with different levels of computer access but other similar characteristics and found no differences in math and language learning levels that could be attributed to the differential access to technology. Other studies that have focused on Israel, the Netherlands, the United Kingdom, and the United States and have analyzed programs that have increased the availability of computers or the Internet in schools have also found no statistically significant impacts (see table 6.2, panel a).

These results are rather counterintuitive; additional resources would be expected to produce better outcomes. However, the education evaluation literature has revealed many interventions that increase some inputs yet do not produce results (see, for example, Glewwe and Kremer, 2006). Still, how can these results be explained?

To have impacts, these interventions must produce a whole chain of events. If any of the links in the chain are broken, the impacts will not materialize. First, access must translate into use. Second, use must be directed to the areas measured in the exam

Table 6.2 Impacts of Access and Use on Learning

Author	Intervention Methodology	Country	Scale (Number of Schools)	Grade	Subject	Number of studies that have had a...			
						Positive Impact		Negative Impact	
						Significant	Not Significant	Significant	Not Significant
a. Impact of Increased Access to Computers or the Internet									
Angrist and Lavy (2002)	Computers, training	OLS	Israel	122	4th and 8th	Math/Language		1	1	2
Barrera-Osorio, and Linden (2009)	Computers, Training	RCT	Colombia	97	Primary	Math/Language		2		
Cristia, Czerwonko, and Garofalo (2010)	Computers, Training	Diff-in-Diff	Peru	2555	Secondary	Repetition				1
Bet, Cristia, and Ibarrarán (2010)	Computers, Training	Propensity Score Matching	Peru	202	9th	Math/Language		2		2
Leuven et al (2004)	ICT expenditure	Diff-in Diff Regression Discontinuity	Netherlands	150	8th	Math/Language				2
Goolsbee and Guryan (2006)	Internet	Diff-in-Diff	United States	~ 8,000	1st-12th	Math/Language/Science		1		
Machin, McNally, and Silvatitle (2006)	ICT expenditure	Diff-in-Diff IV	United Kingdom	591 (school districts)	Primary	Math/Language/Science	1	2		
Total							1	8	1	7

b. Impact of Computer Assisted Instruction (CAI)

Study	Type	Method	Country	Sample	Grade	Subject			
Banerjee et al (2007)	CAI	RCT	India	111	4th	Math		1	
He, Linden, and MacLeod (2008)	CAI-type	RCT	India	242	1st-3rd	English		1	
Linden (2008)	CAI	RCT	India	60	2nd-3rd	Math	1	1	
Carrillo, Onofa, and Ponce (2010)	CAI	RCT	Ecuador	16	3rd-5th	Math/Language	1		1
Rouse and Krueger (2004)	CAI	RCT	United States	4 schools, 454 students	3rd-6th	Language	1		
Dynarski et al (2007)	CAI	RCT	United States	132 schools, 439 classes	1st	Language/Math		3	
Barrow, Markman, and Rouse (2009)	CAI	RCT	United States	17 schools, 152 classes	Middle and High	Math	1		
Total							**4**	**6**	**1**

Notes: Studies were selected if they had employed a sensible identification strategy and had shown some evidence supporting the identification assumptions invoked. The last four columns show whether the results indicate positive or negative effects and also whether these were statistically significant or not. A result is statistically significant if it is unlikely that it occurred by chance. A particular study may provide a number of estimations if different grades or subjects were tested. For example, in Angrist and Lavy (2002), four estimations were reported as test scores were analyzed for math and language for students at fourth and eighth grades. In this study, one estimation showed a positive and not significant effect, two showed negative and not significant effects, and one showed negative and significant effects. RCT refers to randomized controlled trials with a reasonable number of subjects and that have not discarded randomized treatment due to noncompliance. Diff-in-Diff refers to a differences-in-differences estimator. IV refers to an Instrumental Variables estimator. OLS refers to Ordinary Least Squares. Diff-in-Diff refers to a differences-in-differences estimator. IV refers to an Instrumental Variables estimator. CAI refers to computer-assisted instruction. CAI-type corresponds to a small device (not a computer) that assists students in learning a particular subject.

(typically, mathematics and language). Third, classes in which computers are used to teach mathematics and language should have a *greater* learning effect than traditional instruction. That is, it is not enough for teaching with computers to have a positive effect on learning; it should produce *faster* learning than instruction without computers. If there is no faster learning, then "treatment" schools or students will not do better academically than their comparison counterparts. This is because the time that teachers spend in the computer lab with students cannot be used to generate learning in a traditional way. Finally, the impacts should be large enough so as to be detected in a statistical fashion. That is, studies that find evidence of "no impacts" cannot conclude that the effect is zero—only that it cannot be ruled out convincingly. Studies that find no impact with large sample sizes are far more informative than those with small sample sizes because the former are able to reject even small effects.

Which of these explanations may explain the results reviewed? In the case of Colombia, the story is quite clear. As part of the evaluation, students and teachers were surveyed regarding their use of the additional resources. The additional computer access time was used to increase the time allocated to teaching ICT skills, rather than for other subjects. Cristia, Czerwonko, and Garofalo (2010) found a similar explanation in Peru. Virtually all the increased computer access time in schools with high computer access was devoted to teaching ICT skills.

Does this mean that other programs in the region with greater computer access, such as those in Chile and Costa Rica, have also been largely ineffective in improving learning in traditional subjects? The answer to this question is highly speculative. Even though these countries were regional pioneers in the field, they did not embed their innovations in a rigorous evaluation scheme.

Hence, though these countries have played an important role in the region by generating potential models to follow, their contribution in terms of providing evidence on the actual effectiveness of these models has been much more limited.

If providing resources and letting schools choose how to use them is not an effective strategy, why not take this option away from schools and teachers and predetermine how computers should be used? A natural way to implement this strategy is by using some type of computer-assisted instruction software. These computer programs aim at producing learning in specific academic areas, such as algebra for third graders or reading skills for fifth graders. The attractiveness of the software lies in its ability to test a student's initial knowledge, tailor the content and exercises to the needs of the particular student, and provide continuous feedback to students about their progress (see Skinner, 1954). In this sense, it allows each student to have a so-called digital one-to-one tutor.

An example of this type of intervention is the "Más Tecnología" program implemented by the municipality of Guayaquil, Ecuador, in 2005. This program aims at improving the quality of education in public schools in Guayaquil. To achieve this goal, it provides computer infrastructure, Internet access, training, and computer-assisted instruction (CAI) software. The software is the critical component in the program. It was designed as a learning platform for mathematics and language, and tailors the provision of content and exercises based on an initial evaluation conducted for each student.

An experimental evaluation of this program suggests that the program was quite effective in improving test performance in mathematics, but did not attain statistically significant gains in language (Carrillo, Onofa, and Ponce, 2010). The gains in mathematics were quite large by educational evaluation standards, and are promising in terms of the potential effective use of computers in the school. Importantly, students in the program were expected to devote three hours a week to using the software. Thus, part of the gains may have been produced by the increase in the total time students spent studying math—which, in turn, may have been facilitated by the attraction the technology holds for children.

Effective impacts of interventions based on CAI software have also been documented in other developing areas (see table 6.2, panel b). Banerjee et al (2007) ran a randomized evaluation of a similar program in India in which fourth graders shared the use of software for two hours a week to improve learning in mathematics (one hour during school and one hour outside school hours). The program produced impressive results in learning, although the effect was temporary and most gains faded away a year after the program ended. Interestingly, Linden (2008) reports that a randomized evaluation in India led to *negative* impacts when the software replaced regular classes, but slightly positive impacts when computers were used outside of school. These discrepancies in results appear to relate to the quality of teaching in the school where the programs were implemented. In quality schools with effective teaching, the impacts were less; in poor schools, the potential for gains in learning was large. In the United States, where the educational system functions relatively well, these interventions have had little impact (Rouse and Krueger, 2004; Dynarski et al, 2007; Barrow, Markman, and Rouse, 2009).

How can these generally positive but not always consistent results be interpreted and compared to the null results from interventions that increased access? The first clear difference between the "use" interventions as compared to the "access" interventions is that the former, by design, alter the way that classes are conducted. While increased computer access may not change how the instructional process is executed, the "use" interventions alter it directly.

Moreover, the positive impacts usually attained by programs based on CAI software may be partly explained by the increase in total study time these interventions represent for students. Also, the fact that positive impacts are found in potentially weak educational environments but not when the use of software replaces high-quality learning time underscores the fact that the effect of introducing software on learning will be positively influenced by the quality of the software, but negatively influenced by the quality of instruction that it replaces. That is, all other things being equal, the introduction of CAI software will generate larger improvements when it replaces (or complements) low-quality learning time.

Do computers affect ICT skills? Is the effect large? In particular, is one hour of access a week enough to erase the "competencies" digital divide? The study of secondary schools in Peru by Bet, Cristia, and Ibarrarán (2010) explored these questions by exploiting a sample of two sets of schools that are similar but that have quite different computer access. The treatment schools used the additional access primarily to teach ICT skills. Hence, comparing both sets of schools can yield some evidence regarding the effects of providing one additional hour of computer access a week to learn ICT skills on these competencies. Results indicate that students in treatment schools score significantly better in a test of ICT skills. The average impact is larger than the difference in average score between children whose mothers have more than a secondary education compared to those with less. In other words, limited computer access can narrow the skills digital divide, at least in the Peruvian context studied.

Can ICT impact student behavior? In particular, could computers indirectly improve learning by making schools more attractive, and hence, increasing attendance and reducing drop-out rates? Unfortunately, computer access does not appear to reduce drop-out rates in Peru, even minimally (Cristia, Czerwonko, and

Garofalo, 2010). In India, the impact on school attendance and drop-out rates is similarly inconsequential (Banerjee et al, 2007).

Computers at home. If it is difficult to find gains from introducing computers at school, could the provision of computers at home open the path to self-learning? There are two ways of distributing computers at home. One is to give computers to selected (poor) children who probably would not otherwise have access to them. The goal is to boost access to computers at home only. An alternative policy is to give all students a laptop to use both at school and at home (the one-to-one intervention). In Chile, the *"Yo elijo mi PC"* program delivers 60,000 computers to the best students in the poorest 60 percent of the population. In Argentina, the *"Mi PC"* program aims to close the digital divide by facilitating financing and cutting the prices of computers.

Is it a good idea to provide students with computers to use at home? Proponents of this policy argue that computers may allow students to master digital skills that are in high demand in the labor market. They may also facilitate learning through the use of educational software or by providing students a plethora of content and materials via the Internet. Critics fear that children may spend too much time playing computer games instead of exercising, which could lead to weight gain. Also, children may be more exposed to violent and sexually inappropriate content and may face increased social isolation.

Clearly, these are strong cases. But what is the evidence? Establishing the causal effect of computer access on a variety of educational and social outcomes is difficult, because just comparing children who have access with those who do not may be biased, as typically students who have access come from higher-income households, attend better schools, and have better-educated parents. Two recent studies dealt with this issue using ingenious statistical tools.

A program in Romania allocated limited vouchers to buy computers to families with incomes below a certain level. Children in families with incomes just below the threshold level were compared to those with incomes just above. Before receiving the computers, these two sets of children were similar in a variety of observable dimensions (since being on one side or the other of the arbitrary cut-off was almost random); however, one group received a voucher to purchase a computer at a discounted price and the other did not. Hence, as in a randomized experiment, differences in outcomes for these children can be attributed to the effect of having a computer at home. It turns out that children in households that received the computers achieved significantly lower grades in mathematics, English, and Romanian, but demonstrated better ICT skills and performed significantly better in a test of cognitive ability (Raven's Progressive Matrices). The decline in academic achievement can be traced to a decrease in time spent doing homework and reading (Malamud and Pop-Eleches, 2010).

Children who received the computers in the previously mentioned study have had low access to the Internet, as this service was not subsidized. A question that arises is whether gaining access to the Internet may by itself produce better academic results. A second study focused on the state of North Carolina in the United States tackles this question. It exploits rich longitudinal data on test scores and local variations in when broadband Internet service was introduced. Results suggested that students who live in areas that transition from no Internet providers to several providers experience a modest but significant drop in mathematics test scores; results for reading are also negative, but not significant (Vigdor and Ladd, 2010).

Computers at school and at home. In recent years, governments around the world have shown tremendous interest in distributing laptops to students that can be used both at school and at home; interest is even greater in Latin America and the Caribbean. Unfortunately, aside from studies that use observations and reports from program participants, very little quantitative evidence exists regarding the impact of this type of program.

In 2009, a large-scale randomized evaluation was set in place by a technical team at the Inter-American Development Bank, with strong collaboration from the government of Peru. This ongoing evaluation estimates the impacts of the one-computer-per-student program implemented in Peru on learning in mathematics, Spanish, cognitive and noncognitive skills, and behavior, as well as on the mechanisms that generate these impacts. Results from this evaluation are expected to generate lessons for other countries that are contemplating implementing similar programs, as well as identifying ways to strengthen the program in Peru.

The study covered a sample of 320 schools in eight departments. About two-thirds of these schools were assigned to the treatment group, while the rest were assigned to the control group. Between April and October 2009, treatment schools received laptops for each student and teacher in the school while teachers were trained. In November 2009, data were collected to document the short-term impacts of the intervention. At that point, schools had the computers for an average of three months, but exposure time varied substantially across treatment schools.

The government did an excellent job maintaining the evaluation design, as virtually all treatment schools received computers, while fewer than 5 percent of control schools received them. Also, teacher training was completed in more than 80 percent of the schools, and typically followed the prespecified format. Lack of electricity or other logistical problems were not acute, nor were cases of theft or computer malfunction prevalent. Teachers used laptops primarily for Spanish, mathematics, art, and science. The most-used applications were word processor, sound and video recorder, calculator, paint, and Wikipedia. Some 18 percent of teachers used the computer every day for teaching purposes, 33 percent used it three to four days a week, 40 percent used it one or two days a week, and only 10 percent did not use the laptops in class. Teachers who had the laptops available longer seemed to use them less frequently in class, suggesting that some pedagogical support would be needed to ensure proper use over time.

According to surveys of parents and students, 56 percent of students took their laptop home and typically did so every day. Those who did not take it home blamed their parents' concerns that the computer could get damaged, broken, or lost. Surprisingly, the program did not affect attendance and expectations regarding the future academic achievement of students. Even more surprising, students' motivation to attend school and do their homework was significantly lower in the beneficiary schools than in the control group, though the difference was quantitatively small. On the positive side, teacher satisfaction with their relationship with peers, parents' associations, and especially with students was significantly impacted. Some 49 percent of teachers in the treatment group were very satisfied with their relationship with students, compared to 34 percent in the control group. A second follow-up is expected at the end of 2010, which may yield important evidence regarding impacts on test scores in mathematics and Spanish, as well as on measures of cognitive and noncognitive skills, behavior, and expectations.

Policy Recommendations: Strategies to Implement ICT in Schools

"Dress me slowly, for I am in a great rush."

–Napoleon Bonaparte

Experiment and evaluate. The last few years has witnessed a flurry of high-quality research on the impacts of ICT in education. However, significant uncertainty still surrounds these interventions, especially in the case of one-computer-per-student programs. Large-scale, carefully planned, and executed evaluations can generate extremely valuable information for governments in the region that want to unleash the potential of technology to improve the quality of education.

Expand interventions gradually. ICT in education programs are costly and may crowd out important alternatives with significant returns. Given their irreversible nature, the significant uncertainties regarding their impact, and the challenges for management that these complex programs pose, it is best to proceed gradually, as was done in Chile with *Enlaces,* where the roll-out took ten years. Gradual expansion allows feedback from experience and the results of pilot evaluations to improve implementation. It also allows for a better deployment of resources, as program directors can focus their attention and limited capacity on newly covered areas.

Plan (and budget) for all *necessary inputs.* The consensus among education specialists is that increasing access to computers in schools in isolation has low returns. To succeed, programs should provide six critical complementary inputs: hardware, software, electricity, teacher training, technical support, and pedagogical support. However, countries often focus too much on distributing computers and not enough on the other activities.

Focus existing computer access on uses that have proven to be effective: honing ICT skills and pursuing CAI. Certain uses of ICT can yield large positive results; hence, governments should direct limited computer access to these more promising uses. In particular, providing one or two hours of ICT training to students a week seems optimal, given the evidence regarding the large impacts of this use on ICT skills, and the expected premium that workers with these skills may attain in the labor market. CAI also has significant potential to accelerate learning in mathematics—a significant development, given the very low level of achievement in this area throughout the region. Moreover, its expected impacts will be larger in areas where the quality of teaching is lower.

Define policy goals in terms of use, not access. Policy goals are potent catalysts for prioritizing and using resources. Hence, they should be defined so as to achieve certain milestones that can generate positive impacts. Clearly, access alone does not generate impact, but certain types of use do. Therefore, countries should aim to attain goals defined in terms of achieving certain measures (and types) of use, rather than on extending access per se.

In programs that distribute laptops to students, ensure that they are used properly at home. While computer access at school has little effect on educational achievement, increased computer access at home can have *negative* consequences. These negative effects are concentrated among students with weaker adult supervision. If a program contemplates greater access at home, these considerations should be seriously taken into account and mechanisms to stimulate proper use should be implemented. In particular, computers could be loaded with interactive educational software, and competitions could be launched to stimulate use of the software. Violent and sexual content should also be blocked.

Recognize that large-scale interventions increase relative returns to investing in software. Producing CAI software requires significant fixed costs that are spread over the number of computers that will use it. In small programs, producing specialized software is economically unfeasible. As programs expand, the returns to investing in software rise dramatically. For example, for a laptop program that has distributed 1 million computers in a country, it makes perfect sense to spend US$10 per computer for software (a tiny part of the total cost of ownership). This amounts to US$10 million, clearly a budget large enough to fund the development of sophisticated software. This is not the case with other inputs, such as teacher training, whose costs are largely variable and dependent on the scale of the intervention.

Take advantage of technological capabilities to monitor program achievements. Computers have the capability to store and transmit patterns of use. If the intensity and type of use determines the potential impacts, computers can be programmed to record and transmit students' patterns of use. Privacy considerations can be safeguarded under "anonymous" reporting (reporting by individual computers without identifying the user). This type of reporting can produce free, large-scale, detailed monitoring of how the program is proceeding. Computers can also be an inexpensive way to test students to generate quick reports on trends in final academic outcomes.

Foster cooperation across countries in the development of public goods via development banks or other sources. Countries share an increasing interest in determining how to use computers effectively in education. There are important ways in which they can cooperate to increase their chances of success. They should concentrate on supporting activities that generate benefits for all (public goods): either individually, or collectively, by pooling resources. The first such activity is the implementation of large-scale rigorous evaluations. These evaluations benefit all countries in the region, as they produce evidence about what works and how to improve effectiveness. However, they are costly; they impose restrictions on governments (which cannot distribute computers to control schools); and they generate significant political risks, as some results may not be what was expected. Peru is leading the region in this area with its large-scale randomized evaluation of one laptop per child. Other countries should follow suit to generate evidence about differential impacts from different models and educational and social contexts.

A second activity is the development of CAI software. The production of this type of software resembles the development of a vaccine. Its production entails large fixed costs and the ultimate outcome is unclear. Once developed, significant testing is needed to assure its effectiveness. But once produced and tested, the marginal costs of using it an additional time are negligible. Clearly, countries could pool resources to develop (and test) a variety of software and to produce a free inventory of tested software. How can countries manage to agree to fund these activities? Development banks may be the solution. They are mandated to fund activities to foster development in the entire region. What better allocation of funds than to produce certain public goods that will benefit most of their regional members?

7

Help or Hindrance? ICT's Impact on the Environment

How do information and communication technologies (ICTs) affect the environment? To what extent do they exacerbate environmental degradation, and to what extent can they mitigate it? Technological developments have led to seemingly boundless possibilities for consumption, as new ways to communicate have brought down the barriers of geographic distance and global trade has boomed. Unfortunately, these developments have not come without environmental costs, including depleted resources and polluted commons. Interestingly, the same ICTs that have fostered these developments may also create opportunities to alleviate pressing environmental challenges and promote sustainable growth.

This chapter looks at the relationship between ICTs and the environment in Latin America. It provides an overview of ways in which ICTs might be leveraged for environmental causes in Latin America and around the globe. In line with the rest of this book, this chapter relies on robust empirical evidence and impact evaluations. To date, concrete evidence of the effects of ICTs on the environment is scarce; rigorous assessment of claims that ICTs facilitate environmental protection must be pursued in order to establish or refute the validity of such assertions. Although experimentation and evaluation are ongoing, there are substantial limits to successfully leveraging ICTs for environmental ends through information campaigns in Latin America. In terms of other ICT uses, the evidence is more encouraging, yet further and increasingly rigorous research is still needed.

Latin America's Environmental Footprint

From a global perspective, Latin American countries contribute less to environmental degradation and climate change than many other countries. However, economic development, changing population structures, increased consumption, and the rise of global trade have altered the nature and the magnitude of environmental problems in Latin America. While the regional footprint may be relatively small, Latin America's Amazonian forests and large agricultural sector make it well suited to contribute to climate change mitigation by preserving forests and improving agricultural practices (Chisari and Galiani, 2010). Moreover, Latin America is particularly vulnerable to the harmful effects of climate change, which compels the region to take an active role in environmental preservation (ITU, 2009; Chisari and Galiani, 2010; UNEP, 2010).

Figure 7.1 demonstrates the evolution of select indicators of economic development and carbon emissions in Latin America, capturing the changes described earlier.

Though low when compared to other regions, Latin America's environmental footprint can be expected to grow. For the last decade, the region has enjoyed average annual gross domestic product (GDP) growth of 3 percent, one of the highest growth rates since the 1970s. From 1970 to 2010, the overall population has increased by 51 percent (UNEP, 2010) while the urban population has grown from 61 percent to 79 percent (from 1975 to 2008), making Latin America the most urbanized region in the world (World Bank, 2010a).

Figure 7.1   Economic and Environment Indicators (Base Year 1990)

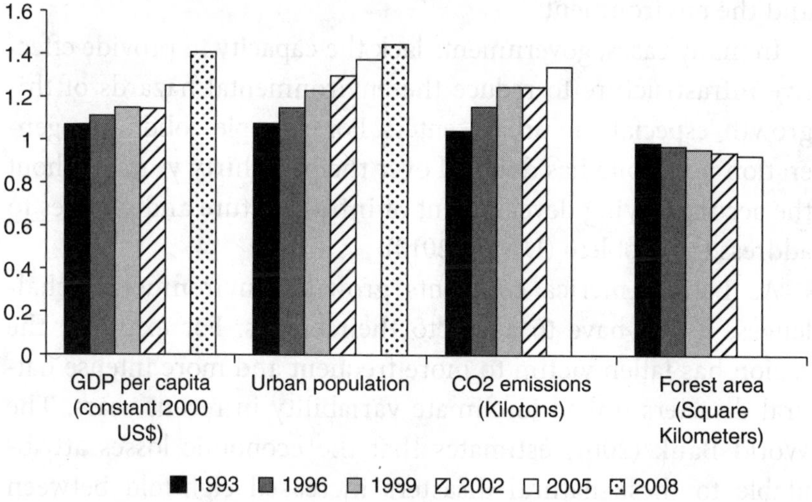

Source: World Bank (2010a).

United Nations Environment Programme's (UNEP) *Global Environmental Outlook on Latin America and the Caribbean* (2010) cites demography and shifting consumption patterns as the main drivers of environmental change in the region. Over thirty-five years, the average consumption of electricity per capita has quadrupled from 427 to 1,688 KWh. Per-capita emissions of CO_2 have also steadily increased from 1.99 metric tons in 1975 to 2.65 metric tons in 2008. Fertilizer consumption has almost doubled, from 89 kg to 146 kg per hectare of arable land in the five years between 2002 and 2007 (World Bank, 2010a). In addition to domestic consumption growth, the region still relies heavily on raw materials and natural resources exports: approximately 73 percent of exported commodities in the region are derived from natural resources, excluding Mexico[1] (UNEP, 2010). The UNEP report concludes that this model of economic growth is particularly damaging to the ecosystem and the environment.

In many cases, governments lack the capacity to provide effective infrastructure to reduce the environmental hazards of this growth, especially in urban centers. For example, solid waste generation per capita has doubled over the past thirty years, without the accompanying development of infrastructure and services to address the problem (UNEP, 2010).

As Latin America confronts growing environmental challenges, it will have to adapt to their effects. For example, the region has fallen victim to more frequent and more intense natural disasters linked to climate variability in recent years. The World Bank (2001) estimates that the economic losses attributable to these natural disasters increased eightfold between 1961–70 and 1986–95, and projects that the losses will continue to grow. In many cases, governments have been caught off guard by these natural disasters.

In the face of increased environmental pressures, environmental sustainability has slowly become a concept embedded in institutions, public policies, and business practices across the region (Ocampo and Martin, 2003). Over the past two decades, a majority of countries in Latin America have passed environmental legislation and created environmental institutions at both national and subnational levels.

Many environmental issues, however, are not being adequately addressed because of gaps in legislation, insufficient political will, and limited understanding of the issues at stake by civil society organizations and the public. Stimulating public interest and awareness is an essential starting point to addressing environmental concerns (World Bank, 2010b). The rapid expansion of ICTs may offer an effective way to spread awareness, as well as mitigate environmental pressures through other channels.

ICTs: Mitigate, Monitor, Adapt

ICTs span a wide range of technologies with exceedingly diverse uses, from e-mail to cell phones to mapping software for geographic information systems (GIS). Thus, it is not surprising that the relationship between ICTs and the environment is multidimensional. Building on prior analyses (Labelle, Rodshcat, and Vetter, 2008; Houghton, 2009; Ospina and Heeks, 2010), this chapter adopts a framework for conceptualizing the relationship between ICTs and the environment that identifies three main categories of environmental impact: mitigation, monitoring, and adaptation. *Mitigation* refers to reducing the degrading impacts on the environment. *Monitoring* refers to the potential for ICTs to collect and distribute important environmental information. *Adaptation* refers to people's ability to adapt and respond to climate change, which may include making pro-environmental behavior changes.

Mitigation: On Both Sides of the Environmental Equation

ICTs have two contrasting effects within the area of mitigation. The first is the direct (negative) effect of the ICT sector's own environmental footprint. One example is electronic waste, created by the growing quantity of discarded technological devices. The second effect is the indirect (positive) effect of ICTs, or ways in which ICTs can mitigate environmental impact in other sectors. Indirect effects include "dematerialization," such as the effect of e-mail and online media that replace physical consumption with virtual consumption. Indirect effects also include "smart" ICT devices designed to reduce energy consumption, such as lights designed to dim automatically in empty rooms.

The SMART 2020 report of the Global e-Sustainability Initiative (GeSI) estimates that in 2007, the ICT sector was responsible for 2 percent of total carbon emissions, or 830 million tons (Mt) of CO_2 (GeSI, 2008).[2] This figure is expected to grow by 6 percent each year until 2020. Three main technology sectors contribute to the ICT footprint: data centers; telecom networks and devices; and personal computers (PCs) and peripherals (GeSI, 2008). Most of the growth in emissions from the ICT sector will come from developing countries. Much of this effect is expected to be driven by the spread of mobile networks and PCs in China and India. However, Latin America's high rate of urbanization has led to rapid growth in the use of ICT equipment. The number of Internet users in Latin America, for example, grew sixfold from 2000 to 2007, and digital markets[3] grew at 14 percent, on average, annually between 2003 and 2005 (Boeni, Silva, and Ott, 2008).

There are various specific channels through which ICTs negatively impact the environment throughout the lifespan of the technology. GeSI (2008) finds that one-quarter of the emissions attributed to ICTs is generated through the equipment manufacturing and disposal processes, and the remainder is generated through the actual use of the technologies. First, producing an ICT device requires the extraction of a substantial quantity of raw materials; one United Nations University study found that approximately 1.83 tons of raw materials are needed to produce one PC desktop and monitor (Williams, 2004). Second, manufacturing ICT devices such as cell phones, computers, and monitors requires a great deal of energy. Finally, the device is inevitably disposed of. Every year, 20 to 50 million tons of e-waste—which includes hazardous substances such as lead (used in cathode ray tubes), cadmium (used in batteries), and mercury—are generated worldwide (Madden and Weissbrod, 2008). With more than 165 million Internet users in Latin America in 2008 (World Bank, 2010a), the issue of end-of-life

disposal of ICT equipment is becoming an urgent concern. A number of studies have revealed that annual e-waste has reached levels as high as 28,000 tons in Mexico; 20,000 tons in Argentina; and up to 7,000 tons in Chile, Colombia, and Peru (Boeni, Silva, and Ott, 2008). If this waste is not properly disposed of, these substances will end up polluting the atmosphere, waterways, and soil. In addition to the environmental impacts of ICT production and disposal, the use of ICT devices has even greater consequences on the environment, particularly as a result of the large quantities of electricity required to power them.

ICT companies are beginning to take steps to address their own carbon footprint. For example, Telefónica, a leading telecommunications operator with a strong presence in the Latin American market, opened a Climate Change Office in 2008 and currently has thirty projects related to climate change. It has committed to cutting its consumption of network electricity by 30 percent and its consumption of office electricity by 10 percent by 2015 (ITU, 2009). These efforts are a good start, but will need to be prioritized and expanded, since growing populations and increasing digital penetration will likely amplify the negative environmental effects of ICTs in Latin America. Understanding the direct damage that ICT devices may cause to the environment, and developing strategies for their safe disposal, will require continued research. An ongoing study conducted by Massachusetts Institute of Technology (MIT) researchers may help fill this void; the study uses small global positioning system (GPS) devices to track trash (particularly electronic waste) in order to fully understand the "removal-chain" of such waste.[4] In addition, it is important to understand the aggregate changes in technology consumption, especially as countries in Latin America attain higher levels of per capita income. Such high-level studies may also be helpful in understanding broad environmental impacts of technology.

An interesting step toward studying this aggregate relationship is a recent study entitled "Does the Expansion of ICT Carry an Environmental Cost? Evidence from Brazil" (Li, Lipscomb, and Mobarak, 2010). It looks at the connection between ICT penetration and environmental deterioration. The authors collected data on ICT penetration (specifically phone and television ownership rates) in Brazil and various measures of water quality from river monitoring stations, including dissolved oxygen (DO), turbidity, biochemical oxygen demand (BOD), chemical oxygen demand (COD), fecal coliform, total coliform, and nitrate and nitrite levels in the water. DO, turbidity, BOD, and COD are general measures of the health of a river. (Higher levels of oxygen indicate a healthier aquatic environment.) Fecal coliform and total coliform are measures of sewage levels in the water, often related to population levels, and nitrates and nitrites are measures of fertilizer runoff into rivers, which is likely the result of agricultural activities.[5]

The results suggested that there is a negative correlation between the spread of ICTs and overall water health, although this relationship is not statistically significant. Moreover, the correlation between ICT penetration and pollution does not indicate that ICTs increase pollution in a causal sense. It may simply be that the spread of ICTs is associated with other factors, such as the spread of electricity, other technologies, or industrialization itself, which are primarily responsible for changes in water quality. Indeed, the authors noted that hydroelectric dams, which generate the electricity necessary to power telephones and televisions, likely have a direct effect on water quality. It appears that ICT growth is associated with industrial development (increased population and more intense agricultural activities) and the general environmental impacts of such development.

Attempting to assess the true causal impact of increased ICT use on the environment requires examining a driver of ICT adoption that does not directly affect water quality. The authors show that electrification drives ICT adoption, but since electrification itself is likely correlated with other growth factors associated with pollution, the authors constructed a predicted measure of electrification based on geographic features that make certain areas more suitable for hydroelectric dams. As these geographic features are unlikely to directly cause changes in water quality, the authors were able to predict growth in ICT usage using predicted electrification and examine how this predicted degree of technology usage correlates with water quality.

This examination of the causal relationship between phone coverage and water quality did not reveal a statistically significant relationship between the two. However, since water quality monitoring has become widespread only recently, the analysis was conducted with a limited sample.

Although the results from this study are narrow, focusing on a limited set of ICTs and environmental outcomes, and they do not conclusively show an effect, or lack of effect, of ICT expansion on environmental health, the study represents an important step toward using robust research methodologies to better understand the causal effects of ICTs on environmental indicators.

ICTs also have positive environmental impacts that may more than offset negative impacts. Tipping the scales toward the plus side, however, will depend on government and civil society being able to take advantage of this potential and make the necessary changes in legislation and behavior. The SMART 2020 report (GeSI, 2008) argues that ICTs have the potential to reduce emissions by 7,800 Mt of CO_2 by 2020, which is five times as much as their forecasted contribution to emissions. The report outlines five key areas in which ICTs could drive increased efficiency: dematerialization, smart motor systems, smart logistics, smart buildings, and smart grids. *Dematerialization* refers to the use of online media, e-commerce, e-paper, videoconferencing, and telecommuting instead of their high-carbon alternatives. *Smart motor systems* monitor and control power use, allowing for the optimization of energy efficiency in many industrial processes. *Smart logistics* coordinate the separate processes of the global transport of goods (which comprise 14 percent of global emissions) to improve energy efficiency. *Smart buildings* are designed, constructed, and operated in ways that optimize the use of materials and energy. For example, building management systems (BMSs) moderate heat, lighting, and power so that no energy is wasted when the building is unoccupied. Finally, *smart grids* use ICTs to route power more efficiently.

While the factors discussed previously will help in global mitigation of climate change, in Latin America, the environmental promise of ICTs may actually lie outside of mitigation. The region's two critical levers for environmental change are arguably deforestation and agriculture, for which ICTs are most valuable in terms of monitoring and adaptation, discussed later in the chapter (Chisari and Galiani, 2010). Nonetheless, there are some important ICT applications for mitigation in Latin America. Telefónica offers an interesting example. The telecommunication giant is not only working to reduce its own direct impact, but has also launched *Inmotics Service,* an ICT-based system that helps companies make their buildings more energy-efficient, allowing participating companies to reduce their energy consumption by up to 27 percent (ITU, 2009).

Another particularly innovative example of how ICTs have been leveraged to mitigate climate change in Latin America is the role of information technology in the development of the natural gas vehicles market. Box 7.1 provides the example of Peru, one of the youngest and most promising markets in the region. ICTs in this context provide an interesting combination

Box 7.1   ICTs Fuel the Success of Natural Gas Vehicles

Natural gas offers numerous environmental advantages over traditional vehicular fuels, particularly with respect to air pollution. Natural gas can significantly reduce vehicle emissions, especially particulate matter, organic gases, and carbon monoxide, compared to conventional gasoline and diesel. In Latin America, abundant natural gas reserves also give natural gas an economic and strategic advantage over petrol as a vehicular fuel.

With a 35 percent share of the natural gas market, it is not surprising that the region's natural gas vehicle (NGV) market is soaring, only recently surpassed by Asia as the world's leader in the number of registered NGVs (IANGV, 2009). Argentina, Brazil, Colombia, Bolivia, and Peru, in that order, rank among the top twenty countries worldwide in terms of the number of registered NGVs.

Millions of Natural Gas Vehicles (NGV) by Region 2000–09

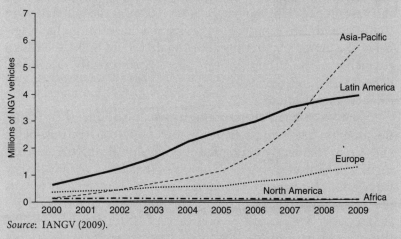

Source: IANGV (2009).

Peru's fleet of natural gas vehicles is growing geometrically thanks to a combination of forward-thinking policy and an attractive price

(continued on next page)

(continued)

differential compared to gasoline. ICTs have played a key role in this growth.

The Corporación Financiera de Desarrollo S.A. (COFIDE), a financial enterprise affiliated with the Peruvian government, has been an indispensable player in the development of this new market thanks to the establishment of a digital information management network called Sistema de Control de Carga de Gas Natural Vehicular. This system works through the mandatory installation of an intelligent chip in the gas tank of each NGV. This chip performs a necessary safety function by allowing the pump to verify in real time on a centralized database that the vehicle is certified safe to operate on natural gas and therefore is safe to refuel.

COFIDE has also established an innovative system to help drivers pay for buying or converting to NGVs. The intelligent refueling system includes an automated loan repayment mechanism. When drivers refuel, the chip installed in their gas tanks automatically applies a preprogrammed surcharge to the price of the natural gas. This surcharge is routed from the gas station to COFIDE and then remitted to the financial institution that originated the driver's loan, thus allowing drivers to make their loan payments at the filling station. This system greatly minimizes default risks and reduces transaction costs for both clients and financing institutions.

As natural gas is a cheaper alternative to gasoline, this financing program has been particularly successful in attracting people who drive frequently and stand to save significantly from converting to natural gas. A short survey of taxi drivers conducted by Innovations for Poverty Action in Lima in November 2009 reveals that less than five years after the creation of the first natural gas station, over 60 percent of taxi drivers had already converted their car to natural gas. Of these, 74 percent reported having taken a loan to finance the conversion and are taking advantage of the convenience and other benefits of this ICT-based repayment system.

of smart logistics and behavioral incentives to switch to a more efficient fuel.

Monitor and Adapt: Where Latin America Can Make a Real Difference

In Latin America and the Caribbean, ICTs can play a key role in monitoring and adapting to environmental degradation, climate change, and other environmental processes. From the creation and processing of knowledge for land use and disaster preparedness planning to disseminating information in order to inspire pro-environmental behaviors, the region can take a lead.

For Latin America, and particularly for its Amazon rainforests, a critical application of ICTs in creating information relates to preserving forests, one of Latin America's key levers for mitigating climate change. Forest coverage decreased by 782,000 square kilometers between 1990 and 2007 in Latin America, a surface larger than the country of Chile (World Bank, 2010a). Land use and tropical deforestation released 1.5 billion tons of carbon annually throughout the 1990s, amounting to almost 20 percent of global emissions. (It has been estimated that decreasing tropical deforestation by 50 percent over the next century would reduce emissions by 500 billion tons per year [Gullison et al, 2007]). ICTs such as satellites and remote sensing applications are used to monitor the condition of Amazonian rainforests and, if successful, could inform and facilitate conservation endeavors. (Chisari and Galiani, 2010).

Two additional areas where ICTs can make a strong contribution to monitoring and adaptation are biodiversity and agriculture. Latin America includes five of the world's ten most biodiverse countries (Brazil, Colombia, Ecuador, Mexico, and Peru), and climate change and economic growth put much of this natural wealth at risk (ITU, 2009). ICTs can play an important role in monitoring biodiversity through "geomapping," where data is collected using remote sensing, analyzed using GISs, and mapped using freely accessible tools like Google Earth (Labelle, Rodschat, and Vetter, 2008). Aggregating and processing this information efficiently allows for more timely and effective actions aimed at preserving biodiversity.

ICTs can also deliver important information related to agriculture, allowing farmers to adapt to and mitigate the effects of climate change. Mungai (2005) highlights the "M-vironment Framework" in Kenya, a mobile telephone platform facilitating a wide variety of environmental initiatives in agriculture. For example, a cell phone text messaging (or short message service, SMS) reduces the need for transportation by providing farmers with information on market prices without having to travel to market, and GISs can enable better resource management. In Latin America, a study by Centro Peruano de Estudios Sociales (CEPES) found that in the Huaral Valley in Peru, telecenters and information kiosks improved the distribution of irrigation water, helping communities adapt to water shortages (Bossio, 2007).

Finally, ICTs can help countries respond better to natural disasters, including hurricanes, earthquakes, and even volcano eruptions. Telecommunications, for example, are critical for education, early warning, and relief operations in the case of natural disasters (Wattegama, 2007).

In the aftermath of the March 2010 earthquake in Chile, the Chilean government launched several efforts to leverage ICTs for early warning efforts in case of future disasters. In May 2010, the Ministry of Transport and Telecommunications announced a new SMS alert system. The system uses a technology called Cell Broadcast Service (CBS), which sends automatic text messages to specified geographic regions, ensuring that the messages arrive even when cellular networks are overwhelmed by traffic. Starting in 2012, all cellular phones in Chile will be required to include this technology (and 70 percent already do). The Chilean government has adopted several related measures, including a national education effort to promote communication via SMS text messages in cases of emergency, new energy requirements for antennas so that they are not dependent on the electric grid, higher standards for cell phone service quality, and a new online information system for emergencies (Morandé, 2010).

In addition to early warning efforts, ICTs have been shown to be vital in the aftermath of natural disasters. In August 2007, ICTs were employed directly after the earthquake in Peru: satellites were used to reestablish communication in remote areas, providing critical information to rescue and relief operations (ITU, 2009). After the earthquake in Haiti in January 2010, a group of researchers from the Karolinska Institute and Columbia University, in collaboration with Digicel Haiti, used cell phones to track population movements, providing a useful description of people's movements and internal displacement (Bengtsson et al, 2010).[6]

In addition to assisting with government response, ICTs can help individuals communicate with and support one another financially in the event of a natural disaster. This was the case in Rwanda, (Blumenstock, Gillick, and Eagle, 2010); Rwandans used airtime transfers to provide financial support to friends and families in areas affected by an earthquake. Crowdsourcing—the use of the general public to accomplish tasks—further demonstrates the capacity of ICTs to independently create and organize knowledge in the event of natural disasters. One of the most remarkable crowdsourcing tools is the Ushahidi platform, which collects information from citizens, nongovernmental organizations (NGOs), and media to create an early warning system for violence and unrest, as well as natural disasters (such as forest fire prevention in Italy), and to facilitate data visualization during response and recovery (such as tracking responses to earthquakes in Chile and Haiti).

In addition to generating information, ICTs have been used to distribute information, with the goal of encouraging pro-environmental behavior. Economic theory predicts that people will not naturally exhibit pro-environmental behavior, since both individuals and firms ignore externalities, such as environmental degradation, as long as costs are borne by others. People's reticence to take responsibility for environmental consequences is even greater because environmental effects are often highly uncertain, delayed, and geographically distant (Gattig and Hendrickx, 2007). In addition, the world often lacks markets for environmental goods, which makes it difficult to accurately value and efficiently allocate these goods (Shogren and Taylor, 2008).

Standard economic solutions in the face of such externalities and market failures aim to change incentives to better align private and social benefits, often by applying taxes and subsidies. Recent advances in behavioral economics, however, suggest that individuals do care about factors other than their material self-interest. This would imply that merely spreading effective messages about environmental issues could change behavior. In Latin America, ICTs such as cell phones, SMS, and e-mails are uniquely suited for such information dissemination because of their increased prevalence and the cost effectiveness with which information can be transmitted.

Across the globe, there is evidence of ICTs being used to promote environmentally friendly behavior by disseminating information. In Indonesia, officials set up a public information database rating the degree of firm compliance with pollution discharge limits. A rough analysis found that within the first fifteen months of the program, about one-third of the low-rated firms came into compliance (Afsah, Blackman, and Ratunanda, 2000). A similar intervention occurred in the Philippines, where drivers were encouraged to report smoke-emitting vehicles to authorities via Internet, fax, phone, or SMS (Dongtotsang and Sagun, 2006). In the United States, a campaign involving electronic highway signs was used to encourage drivers to adopt behaviors to improve air quality (Henry and Gordon, 2003).

These interventions represent innovative uses of ICTs as information dissemination devices to promote environmental aims, and evaluation studies generally suggest that they are successful. The number of studies using experimental research methodology, however, is limited. Many studies approach the problem qualitatively or use quasi-experimental research designs and are, therefore, unable to incontrovertibly establish the effectiveness of the campaigns.[7] While there exists a body of experimental evidence on environmental information campaigns, it generally does not deal with ICT technology and focuses on developed countries.

Several recent studies begin to address the lack of rigorous assessments of this type in Latin America. The studies, in Peru and Mexico, have adopted randomized control trial (RCT) methodology to evaluate the effect of information campaigns, delivered through ICTs, on pro-environmental behaviors.

ICTs and Recycling in Peru

In Peru, solid waste management has become an area of increasing concern. Nearly 20,000 tons of solid waste are produced in the country every day, most of which is still being dumped in rivers and in the ocean, or left in informal dumps (Chauvin, 2009). In the face of this challenge, a number of programs to reduce the environmental impact of solid waste have sprung up across the country. One such program, administered in Piura (northern Peru) by the national NGO Prisma, provides technical assistance and training to help informal recyclers develop and launch small formal recycling associations. The aim is to expand incomes and improve working conditions for informal recyclers, as well as boost the level of recycling in Peru. The program, started in 2002, has facilitated the creation of several recycling cooperatives.

Despite an intensive canvassing process that lasts four weeks, participation in the program is far from universal; the take-up rate is only about 34 percent of households residing in areas served by the program. Moreover, dropouts are high, as registered families' participation declines and households stop contributing their recyclables to the cooperatives.

Several information campaigns were designed to address these compliance issues, with the objective of both increasing the percentage of families in new areas joining the program and the level of participation among existing participants. The campaigns utilized text messages, as they have proved effective in other contexts (Karlan, McConnell, Mullainathan, and Zinman 2010) and represent a cost-effective tool to maximize reach. Each household received six text reminders over five weeks, in addition to the normal canvassing conducted by Prisma. To include households that did not have cell phones, flyers that encouraged participation were delivered before the traditional canvassing process started. Since prior research has suggested that interventions that directly reduce the cost of recycling are more effective, this study included a subgroup that received bins to store recyclables, facilitating a comparison between the effectiveness of these bins and text reminders to recycle. The goal of the study was not only to evaluate the impact of the information campaign, but also to understand the limitations of ICT-based campaigns in a context where not all households have cell phones or are willing to share their numbers.

The study was broken into two parts, one designed to assess the issue of take-up, while the other focused on increasing participation levels among existing participants. A total of 6,721 families were included in the take-up study, while 1,802 households were included in the participation study. All households were administered a brief survey collecting basic demographic information. Approximately 10 percent of the households answered a longer survey that included more detailed questions on attitudes toward the community, recycling, and the environment.

Drawing on lessons from economics and social psychology, a number of messages encouraging households to participate in the recycling program were tested (such as messages emphasizing the environmental benefits of recycling versus the economic benefits to collectors, or mentioning that many of the household's peers participate in the program). Households in the take-up study were randomly assigned to receive one of the messages (through flyers and text messages if they provided a phone number), or to be in a control group that did not receive a message. Households in the participation study received text messages reminding them that the collector was coming for their recyclables the following day, a bin in which to store recyclables, neither, or both.

The data obtained from the demographic surveys reveal some important limitations in using ICTs to facilitate environmental information campaigns, which must be balanced against the advantage of cost effectiveness. Primarily, the data make clear that the spread of technology is not universal, particularly in developing countries, which may limit the potential of ICTs as a medium for information campaigns. This was the case in the particular context of northern Peru, where more than half the respondents either did not have a cell phone (44 percent) or did not want to share their number (12 percent).

These findings raise important questions about the ability of information campaigns delivered via cell phones to attain sufficient reach in developing countries. The most advanced technology may not always be the most desirable; other ICTs (such as radio, for example) or communication channels might be preferable. In addition, delivering messages through ICTs such as cell phones inadvertently selects a particular sample of individuals to receive the messages, which may have implications for the effectiveness of the campaign. For example, if wealthy households predominantly own cell phones, it may be that they are already predisposed to recycling (perhaps because of higher average education levels) or, conversely, that their opportunity cost of recycling is much higher, both of which could affect these households' receptiveness to messages encouraging them to recycle. In the study sample, there was a significant difference in terms of socioeconomic indicators and interest in local affairs between those providing a cell phone number and those who did not own cell phones or were unwilling to share their contact information. On average, the first group earned about 10 percent more per day than the second group, and also tended to have an overall higher level of education.

The groups also differed in terms of their interest in receiving information about recycling; cell phone owners were more interested than nonowners. This may indicate that cell phone owners are predisposed toward recycling and already do so, or that they would be especially receptive to messages about recycling. Data obtained from the control group in the take-up study allow comparisons in recycling behavior among households that gave their phone numbers and others, independent of any encouragement to recycle. Figure 7.2 shows that households in the control group that

Figure 7.2   Interest in Recycling as Indicated by Cell Phone Ownership and/or Willingness to Reveal Cell Phone Number, 2010 (Percent)

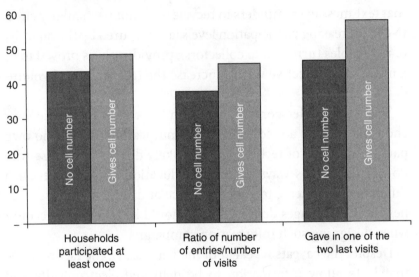

Source: Chong et al (2010a).
Note: "Visits" refers to the number of times the collector came to the household. "Entries" refers to the number of times the household gave recyclables.

shared their contact information were more likely to recycle and participate than others in the control group.

In light of these differences, comparing the end result of using text messages with people who provided their cell phone number with those who refused or do not have a cell phone would yield erroneous conclusions. Differences would be incorrectly attributed to the messages rather than some other factor correlated with cell phone ownership and willingness to receive text messages. As the various messages encouraging participation in the recycling program were randomized within both the group that provided phone numbers and the group that did not, the study avoids this pitfall. The study, however, found that neither the text messages nor the flyers affected households' likelihood of enrolling in the program. Turning to the study designed to increase participation among those already enrolled in the program, figure 7.3 reveals that text message reminders to recycle were not particularly effective in increasing participation levels (as measured by the quantity of recyclables turned in to collectors); providing bins proved to be a much more effective way to increase the frequency and volume of recyclables.

The study underscores an important practical issue whenever choosing ICTs as a medium for communication: those who own particular forms of technology will likely differ from those who do not in various ways, including education and income. Such differences may serve to either enhance or diminish the effectiveness of the messages delivered, and should be taken into account when designing such information campaigns.

Despite the caveats revealed in the Peru study, the fact remains that ICTs allow information to be delivered electronically and may thus represent a cost-effective substitute for traditional information campaigns. Over time, ICTs may actually be a more effective means by which to promote pro-environmental behavior and other social messages. As individuals become increasingly familiar with and dependent on electronic devices and media, they may become more receptive to messages delivered through these channels than in other ways.

Reusable Shopping Bags in Mexico

While the Peru study did not distinguish between the effects of an SMS and a paper flyer, a recent study in Mexico offers one test of the relative effectiveness of electronic versus physical messages. The study evaluated the effectiveness of an information campaign designed to induce shoppers to reduce their consumption

Figure 7.3   Average Kilograms of Recyclables per Household per Week across Treatments, 2010

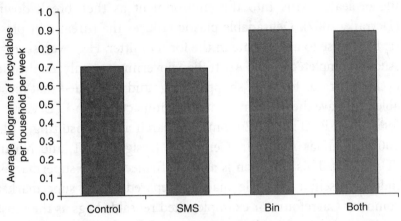

Source: Chong et al (2010a).

of disposable plastic bags, largely through the use of reusable shopping bags. In addition to varying the specific content of the appeal to consumers to bring their own reusable bags to stores, the study also randomized the delivery mechanism used to convey that message; one group of supermarkets used a visual campaign relying on banners at store entrances, while another group of stores conducted the campaign using digital audio messages on the supermarket's overhead public announcement system. This design allows a direct test of the relative effectiveness of each medium.

The environmental rationale for this study is the well-documented environmental consequences of disposable plastic bags. Between 500 billion and 1 trillion plastic bags are consumed worldwide each year, with Mexico City using an estimated 20 million bags per day (Inma, 2010). Although precise estimates on the percentage of plastic bags that enter the recycling stream is unavailable, the vast majority are not used again and end up as waste, landfill, or litter. Discarded plastic bags pose a threat to ecosystems because they are often ingested by wild and marine life or leak toxins into the environment as they break down (Derraik, 2002). Degradable plastic reduces the threat that plastic bags pose to animal life in the form of litter. However, several studies completed by the Australian government analyzed the life cycle of various forms of shopping bags and concluded that reusable bags have the least environmental impact (Nolan-ITU, Centre for Design RMIT, and Eunomia Research and Consulting, Ltd., 2002; ExcelPlas Australia, Centre for Design RMIT, and Nolan ITU, 2004). This assertion is also confirmed by the supermarket industry itself; a life-cycle analysis prepared for the supermarket company Carrefour, for example, cited reusable bags as the most environmentally friendly option, provided they are used at least four times (Ecobilan, 2004).

In June 2009 the UNEP called for a worldwide ban on thin-film plastic bags (UNEP, 2009). Since then, there has been a growing movement in cities of both the developed and developing world to reduce the consumption of single-use plastic bags.

Policymakers' attempts to curb the harmful effects of disposable plastic bags are generally focused on two distinct methods. One approach focuses on the post-consumption stage, using initiatives to improve plastic bag collection and recycling facilities. Another approach aims to reduce the amount of plastic bags used in the first place, with initiatives aimed at consumers. Policies can attempt to modify consumer behavior by offering new and beneficial technology, providing incentives, appealing to basic values, modifying institutional structures, changing attitudes and beliefs with education and information, or enacting regulations designed to directly impact the extent to which plastic bags are used (Stern, 1999).

In 2009, the Legislative Assembly of the Federal District of Mexico City chose to adopt the latter technique, banning the

use of nondegradable plastic bags within Mexico City and fin-
ing shops that dispense free plastic bags. In an effort to encourage the purchase and regular use of reusable bags, Innovations for
Poverty Action partnered with Comercial Mexicana, a Mexican
hypermarket group, to launch and evaluate an information campaign to increase the use of reusable bags. A variety of messages
were constructed, informing shoppers about the sheer number of
bags used in Mexico and the environmental impact these bags
have, and encouraging them to use reusable bags to improve the
environment and make the world a cleaner place for future generations. A total of 199 supermarkets participated in the study;
69 received no information (the control group); 66 stores put up
banners at store entrances with a written message encouraging
reusable bag use; and 64 stores played the same message over the
in-store digital audio system.

Although the study is ongoing, preliminary results are available. First, the authors consider the impact of the information
campaign on the number of plastic bags used per day by stores.
Results, shown in figure 7.4, indicate that shoppers exposed to
the information campaign appear to consume fewer bags. This
preliminary analysis, however, was conducted with only partial
data and the differences are not statistically different from one
another (in other words, they might be due to random chance);
additional data collection is under way. Moreover, no clear differences emerge between those exposed to the visual campaign and
those who heard the audio messages.

Turning to the purchase of reusable bags from Comercial
Mexicana, which offers a variety of reusable bags (including jute,
cotton, and thermal bags, as well as reusable boxes) for sale, the
initial results suggest that those customers exposed to the information campaign actually purchased fewer reusable bags in the
study period, as displayed in figure 7.5. Again, these results are

Figure 7.4   Number of Standard Shopping Bags (Type 40) Used per Store per Day

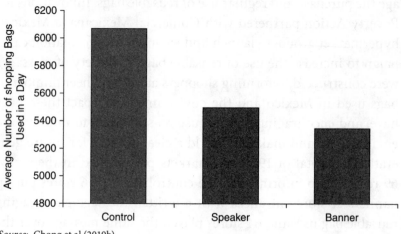

Source: Chong et al (2010b).

preliminary and the differences are not statistically different from one another. Thus, these initial results may be a statistical artifact, or perhaps consumers exposed to the campaign have begun to more consistently bring their own receptacles to carry their groceries and are purchasing fewer reusable bags. As additional data become available, the robustness of these observations will be established and an assessment of the relative effectiveness of visual banners or recorded digital announcements played over the grocery store's public address system will be completed.

Environmental Commitments

In addition to providing information, as was done in Mexico and Peru, ICTs can help people adopt pro-environmental behaviors in other ways. One promising area is the design of appropriate commitment mechanisms (Hepburn, Duncan, and Papachristodoulou,

Figure 7.5   Number of Reusable Bags and Boxes Sold per Month

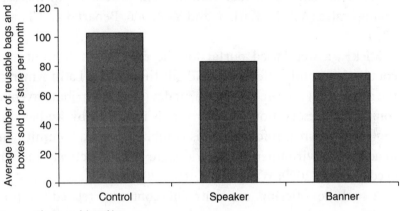

Source: Chong et al (2010b).

2010), and ICTs can play an important role in the development of commitment contracts and platforms. A *commitment device* can be defined as an arrangement that commits an individual to a future choice or action and specifies penalties if the action is not taken. Crucially, a commitment contract is primarily aimed at helping a person keep a promise regarding his or her own future behavior when that person represents the greatest source of risk of failure (for example, planning to diet but never starting the diet).

Recent studies have proven the effectiveness in both developed and developing countries of using commitment devices and incentives to achieve goals. A field experiment in the Philippines (Gine, Karlan, and Zinman, 2010), for example, randomly offered smokers a commitment contract to stop smoking. Smokers pledged their own money and signed contracts to commit themselves to passing a nicotine-byproduct test six months later. If they passed the test, they received their money back; if they failed, the money was donated to charity. This increased smoking cessation rates by 30 percentage points, making it far more effective than other interventions aimed at reducing smoking. Similarly, other studies have demonstrated that commitment products can increase savings rates (Ashraf, Karlan, and Yin 2006; Benartzi and Thaler 2004).

StickK, a web-based portal for the creation of commitment contracts, recently offered individuals throughout Latin America the opportunity to use commitment devices to contribute to environmental preservation.[8] The project is informed by studies that suggest that when information is combined with a commitment to act, pro-environmental behaviors are more effectively encouraged (Kazdin 2009; Wang and Katzev, 2006).

A website offering commitment contracts related to pro-environmental behaviors was launched across twelve Latin American countries starting in May 2010.[9] Individuals had the opportunity to create their own custom-made contract related to common environmental issues, such as saving energy and recycling. The website also included a series of default offerings, such as commitments to turn off lights when exiting rooms, unplug appliances, and recycle.[10] Initial findings on the number of clicks on ads for the stickK website and contracts created through the website provide insights into the interest in web-based commitments to undertake pro-environmental behavior.[11]

Figure 7.6 shows the total number of clicks compared to the number of Internet users by country. Clearly, interest in web-based environment commitments is highly correlated with general Internet penetration. Similarly, the number of commitment contracts that were attempted or completed is also strongly correlated with Internet penetration. However, the number of contracts created to date was small compared to the number of visits: 132 contracts were attempted, and only 52 were created. These results are consistent with the notion that interest in web-based environmental commitments in Latin America is low.

Figure 7.6   Number of Internet Users and Clicks by Country, 2010

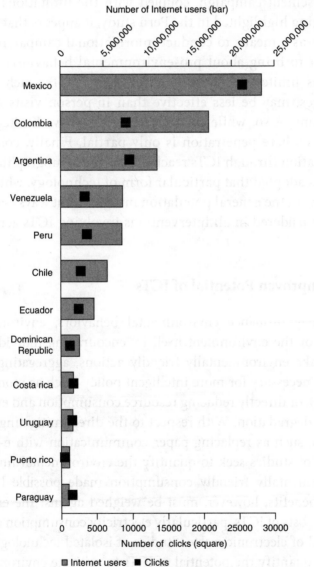

Source: Karlan and Zinman (2010), and World Bank (2010a).

In light of the limited success of the StickK Internet-based advertisement campaign, coupled with the limitations of text messaging highlighted in the Peru study, it appears that the use of ICTs as a means to conduct informational campaigns in an attempt to bring about pro-environmental behavioral change remains limited in Latin America. Some ICTs, such as text messages, may be less effective than in-person visits or conversations. Also, while cost effective, ICTs have limited reach in areas where penetration is only partial. Finally, conveying information through ICTs reaches only the demographic group that has adopted that particular form of technology, which may differ from the general population in significant ways—a caveat to be considered in all interventions involving ICTs across the region.

The Unproven Potential of ICTs

ICTs may influence environmental behaviors, environmental policy, or the environment itself by encouraging individuals to undertake environmentally friendly actions, aggregating information necessary for more intelligent policy (such as monitoring climate), or directly reducing resource consumption and environmental degradation. With respect to the direct mitigating effects of ICTs, such as replacing paper communication with e-mail, a variety of studies seek to quantify the environmental impact of environmentally friendly consumption made possible by ICT. These benefits, however, must be weighed against the environmental costs of ICTs, particularly electricity consumption and the disposal of electronic waste. Studies of isolated technologies will help to quantify the potential of ICTs to mitigate environmental concerns directly. More research is needed to understand these tradeoffs, particularly at an aggregate level.

Similarly, clear evidence is scarce concerning the impact of ICT-enabled information creation and aggregation on environmental policy, the actions of firms or other agents, or environmental outcomes. At a national and regional level, considerable resources have been invested in developing ICT monitoring systems, primarily to track climate change, deforestation, and wildlife, as well as to improve responses to natural disasters and humanitarian crises. The task of rigorously evaluating the environmental consequences of such investments using statistical approaches is formidable; thus, qualitative study of the spread and uses of the information generated by these systems may be optimal. At a micro scale, however, ICT-generated information may be useful in solving localized environmental challenges. Understanding whether these efforts result in a solution to or mitigation of localized issues will be important to policymakers concerned with environmental issues and to officials tasked with the aggregation of local environmental information. Rigorous statistical research is suited to evaluate the effectiveness of information creation in localized situations.

The results from several recent RCTs designed to test the effectiveness of ICT information campaigns in inspiring pro-environmental behaviors offer little evidence that this strategy is effective. Moreover, though the number of users is rapidly increasing in the region, employing the Internet or cell phones to engage individuals in actions to reduce their environmental footprint is not an effective way to reach the entire population. Thus, leveraging ICTs to change the costs and benefits of pro-environmental choices directly, instead of merely providing information, will be more effective in generating behavioral change. Innovative uses of ICTs to do so are emerging and represent a promising development, such as the use of smart chip technology to make the financing of natural gas vehicles more efficient.

From a policy perspective, national actors may be able to boost the environmental impact of ICTs by enacting policies that encourage individuals and firms to adopt technologies with a proven net-positive environmental impact. In addition, governments should consider leveraging ICTs to create more efficient information aggregation and communication systems, which can facilitate more rapid and efficient responses to natural disasters and other environmental developments. Multilateral agencies can contribute to this process by encouraging experimentation and innovative uses and applications of ICTs for environmental preservation, as well as supporting rigorous evaluation of new ideas to reduce environmental impact.

8

Development.com: Using ICTs to Escape Poverty

A potato grower in Honduras turns on his mobile phone and sees a text message saying that the price of potatoes has gone up in the Tegucigalpa market. He has been receiving price information twice a week for the last two months, and now sees that the prices he has negotiated with the wholesaler have slowly been improving. As a small producer, he used to sell his products directly from his farm using the prices in his local area as his only benchmark. Many times, these prices were lower than actual market prices.

In a small town in Colombia, a young woman lands a job at the local community center thanks to the knowledge of spreadsheets and word processing that she acquired during her daily visits to the local telecenter near her home. In Peru, another young woman, unemployed for several months, also gets a job after receiving text messages on her mobile phone listing job opportunities that match her labor profile.

Examples like these illustrate the earning opportunities that can be achieved thanks to the diffusion of information and communication technologies (ICTs) among various sectors of the population in Latin America and the Caribbean. This chapter focuses on the poor. In 2005, 17 percent of Latin Americans were living on less than US$2.00 a day, and 8 percent were living on less than US$1.25 a day (World Bank, 2010). What does being poor mean?

Living in poverty is not only about not having enough money to purchase valuable goods and services; it is also about lacking access to the resources to break out of poverty and guarantee well-being. Access to information can enable the poor to use their own knowledge and strengths to escape poverty traps.

There are compelling reasons to expect significant economic development from the adoption of ICTs. One way in which these technologies can help bring about economic improvement is by reducing disparities and gaps in information (asymmetric and imperfect information) in markets. For example, individuals and firms can use ICTs to research prices of products, look for jobs, or locate potential buyers of their products. This may be especially relevant for certain groups that are at a disadvantage with respect to others, either because they lack information or because their access to it is delayed or in a lower quality form. Low-cost access to useful information can help low-income families find economic and social opportunities that could benefit them. ICTs can become a powerful tool to alleviate poverty, reducing uncertainty, promoting inclusion, and increasing income.

Another channel through which ICTs can help reduce poverty is the production of ICT goods and services. The development of the ICT sector can offer jobs and income-generating opportunities and, in some cases, create entirely new livelihoods. Moreover, a vibrant ICT sector can facilitate and sustain more widespread use of these technologies throughout the rest of an economy.

A number of conceptual and empirical studies have been conducted to trace the direct and indirect economic linkages between ICTs and poverty reduction. The variety of views about ICTs indicate that its role in development is unclear, especially without convincing evidence of its impact (Torero and von Braun, 2006; Harris, 2004). An emerging body of research focuses on the reduction in communication costs associated with the greater use of ICTs—particularly mobile phones—and their effects on development.

Information is a key component in enabling economic agents to make optimal decisions, which may help decrease income inequality and in turn alleviate poverty. This chapter explores different channels through which ICTs can help people boost their incomes through more, better, and faster information. Closing information gaps reduces the ability of the better informed to extract unfair profits (rents) from the less informed, and thus helps enhance resource allocation, increase income, and improve welfare among those living in more disadvantaged areas, or those who, because of their socioeconomic status, lack access to information (Chong, Galdo, and Torero, 2009). With this in mind, this chapter emphasizes certain mechanisms that help lessen uncertainty and improve the availability of information, thereby creating conditions propitious for higher levels of employment, more human capital formation, and better-performing markets and small producers.

Asymmetric information and search costs are particularly detrimental in two specific markets: agriculture and labor. In the agricultural sector, small producers usually sell their products knowing only prices in their local area. Cell phones give producers access to prices in other markets and open their eyes to the relative worth of their produce. Expanded mobile phone service, together with needed complementary public services (gathering, processing, and disseminating information in real time by agriculture and production ministries), give poor farmers the fodder they need to negotiate higher prices with intermediaries and wholesalers.

ICTs have also proven their worth in the performance of labor markets. Job search activities require time and resources, and may lead workers to many dead ends (Mortensen, 1986). ICTs can help reduce job search time and costs, and therefore impact positively on unemployment rates. ICTs also influence labor markets by improving applicant's skill levels, and thus their employment prospects.

When it comes to the poor, telephony is the ICT that will have the greatest penetration and impact. Telephony is important not only as a channel to improve access to information and communications, but also as a prerequisite for the widespread use of more advanced technologies such as the Internet. However, Internet service penetration is still low; the majority of Internet users are in developed countries and the more affluent segments of developing country populations. Mobile telephony, on the other hand, has emerged as the most important ICT for low-income countries, and as the principal gateway to increased ICT access and use. Among its numerous advantages, mobile telephone infrastructure can be installed without ever deploying the expensive network of wires necessary for land-based phones.

The use of mobile phones has tangible economic benefits, improving agricultural and labor market efficiency, as well as producer and consumer welfare, in specific circumstances and countries (Jensen, 2007; Aker, 2008, 2010; Aker and Mitbi, 2010; Klonner and Nolen, 2010). These effects can be particularly dramatic in places where mobile phones represent the first modern telecommunications infrastructure of any kind. Rural areas of developing countries had the least access to telecommunications technology before the introduction of mobile phones, which are now being adopted at break-neck rates.

The explosion in mobile phone penetration rates in developing countries points to the role of mobile telephony as a "digital bridge" that will help many developing countries reduce the connectivity divide that separates them from others with a more developed fixed-line infrastructure. Figure 8.1 shows the

Figure 8.1   Mobile Telephone Subscribers per 100 Inhabitants

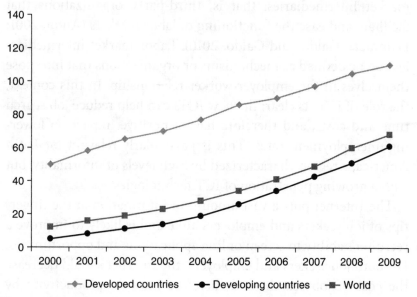

Source: ITU (2010).

evolution of mobile phone subscribers per 100 inhabitants in the developed and developing world. Although in 2009 mobile phone penetration was almost twice as high in developed economies as in developing ones, the divide is expected to narrow in the next few years, as mobile markets reach the saturation point in developed economies and continue their spectacular growth in developing countries.

Do ICTs Work in Labor Markets?

The labor market is replete with imperfect and asymmetric information. Search activities require time and resources. The costly nature of exchange when labor information is incomplete and asymmetric would suggest that there may be room for labor market intermediaries: that is, third-party organizations that facilitate and ease the functioning of labor markets (Autor, 2001; Dammert, Galdo, and Galdo, 2010). Labor market intermediaries can be defined as mechanisms or organizations that interpose themselves in the employer-worker relationship. In this context, the role of ICTs is clear: the new ICTs can help reduce job search time and costs, and therefore have a positive impact on lowering unemployment rates. This is particularly relevant for Latin America, a region characterized by high levels of informality, but with a growing penetration of ICT technologies.

The Internet puts a vast amount of information at the fingertips of job seekers and employers alike and is likely to improve a recruiter's ability to screen online applications and opportunities. For both job seekers and employers, the Internet should decrease the cost of job search, and therefore improve productivity by matching skills to jobs (Pissarides, 2000).

Although Internet access has gained ground in several developing countries, the percentage of households with a connection to the Internet is still low. Access to mobile phones, on the other hand, has been the most rapid technology ever adopted in developing countries (ITU, 2010). In particular in Latin American countries, in only five years, the percentage of households with access to mobile phones soared from 28 percent in 2003 to 74 percent in 2008 (ECLAC, 2009). The possibility that a third party (labor market intermediary) can disseminate customized information about job openings to unemployed individuals via short message service (SMS) may lower search costs for the unemployed, particularly when access to such information otherwise would have required access to the Internet. Texting in labor markets may constitute a relatively inexpensive policy option with potentially desirable effects on labor outcomes.

Job seekers are using this kind of service around the world, with countries in Asia taking the lead. Babajob, in Bangalore, India, is a matching resource for blue-collar workers looking for jobs, and offers services via text message. Souktel, in the Palestinian territories, offers job-hunting services via text message. It allows users without Internet service or fancy phones to register by texting information about themselves. Users who then text "match me" will receive a listing of suitable jobs, complete with phone numbers to dial for applying (Giridharadas, 2010).

To test the effectiveness of this type of search mechanism, Dammert, Galdo, and Galdo (2010) performed a randomized experiment in Peru to analyze how information technologies—particularly the use of text messaging to provide vacancy referrals—may reduce job search frictions and increase employability. Their empirical analysis was based on an experimental design built on a state-run social program, the PROEMPLEO program. PROEMEPLEO provides nondigital labor mediation to job seekers who voluntarily show up at any labor mediation office, complete an application, and answer a detailed labor survey. On average, 180 individuals apply daily for the program. Each day, thirty randomly selected individuals who applied to the program are assigned to one of three groups: control, nondigital treatment, and digital treatment. The treatment consists of three months of transmission of cellular phone text messages to each individual in the digital treatment group informing them of job opportunities that match their labor profile. Information based on a baseline survey reveals that the groups are fully comparable in terms of their observable characteristics, including their current labor status and previous employment history.

Given the three-month treatment scheme, the follow-up survey asked individuals to report on their employment status each month after initiating the program. The results suggested that the labor intermediation program had a positive short-term effect on employability. The results also suggested short-term gains of using digital technology in the labor intermediation process. One month after initiating the program, individuals who received SMS messages were 7 percent more likely to be employed, compared to those who were in the control group. After two months, this number fell to 6 percent and was barely significant statistically. After three months, this number fell to 3.9 percent, and the difference between the two groups was not statistically different. The employment rates of the three groups in the first, second, and third months after treatment are illustrated in figure 8.2.

ICTs have also proven to be important in the performance of labor markets through the influence that ICT skills have on the possibility of employment. Acquisition of ICT skills, at both a

Figure 8.2   Employment Rate of Participants in the Labor Intermediation Program

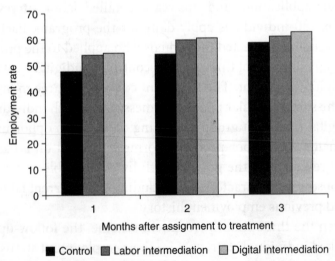

Source: Dammert, Galdo, and Galdo (2010).

country and individual level, can be extremely powerful for the inclusion of marginalized groups in the labor market.

People can be excluded from consideration for employment simply because they cannot demonstrate basic ICT knowledge. In this case, no amount of effort to conduct an online job search, write a résumé, or receive assistance in other areas will make a noticeable difference. A study conducted by Lopez-Boo and Blanco (2010) evaluated the impact that the acquisition of ICT skills had in the labor markets of two Latin American cities: Buenos Aires and Bogotá. Fictitious curricula vitae (CVs) were sent to real job vacancies. Every variable included in these CVs was controlled for similarity, except the gender and ICT skills level of each applicant. After sending the CVs, the study measured whether applicants with ICT skills received significantly more or less callbacks or e-mails for future interviews than applicants who lacked ICT skills. The study found that having ICT skills on the resume boosted the probability of receiving a callback by around 1 percent. This advantage is much greater in Bogota than in Buenos Aires. The conclusion is that having basic knowledge of informatics tools could generate higher employment opportunities.

The Fruits of Technology in Agricultural Markets

Access to information in rural areas is limited and costly. Small producers, especially those who live in poor rural areas, tend to be at a disadvantage because they usually sell their products on their farms knowing only prices in the immediate area where they live. When dealing with intermediaries, these small producers lack timely information about other market prices. In rural areas, increased access to mobile phones and associated applications and services may have a particularly important impact on poverty. In many developing countries, markets are dispersed and communications infrastructure is poor, so the potential for inefficiency in the allocation of goods across markets is great. By improving access to information, ICTs may help poorly functioning markets work better and thereby increase incomes, lower consumer prices, or both.

A growing literature provides micro-level evidence in this field. Jensen (2007) used survey data to show that the adoption of mobile phones by fishermen and wholesalers in Kerala, a state in India with a large fishing industry, was associated with a dramatic reduction in price dispersion, the complete elimination of waste, and near-perfect adherence to the Law of One Price. Aker (2008) exploited the quasi-experimental nature of cell phone coverage in Niger between 2001 and 2006 to estimate the impact of the staggered introduction of information technology on market performance. In Niger, the population is made up largely of rural subsistence farmers, who depend upon rain-fed agriculture as their main source of income. Aker found that cell phones reduced grain price dispersion across markets by at least 6.4 percent and price variation by 10 percent. Cell phones have a greater impact on price dispersion for markets that are located far away from each other and separated by poor-quality roads. This effect becomes magnified as more and more markets enjoy cell phone coverage.

Camacho and Conover (2010) and Pineda Burgos, Agüero Rodríguez, and Espinoza (2010) evaluated ICT information systems for agricultural producers for Colombia and Honduras, respectively. These programs are innovative interventions to increase profitability among agricultural producers in the region. For years, support programs for farmers and small producers in the region have focused on providing technical assistance, credit, and infrastructure investment. In very few cases have interventions focused on reducing information gaps between farmers and markets that allow intermediaries and wholesalers to take advantage of the asymmetries.

Pineda Burgos, Agüero Rodríguez, and Espinoza (2010) evaluated whether ICTs could help Honduran vegetable growers better negotiate prices for their produce and obtain higher returns. Vegetable growers assisted by the Entrenamiento y Desarrollo de Agricultores (EDA) served as a representative sample of Honduran vegetable producers. Farmers in the treated group were sent SMS text messages containing market prices for high-value vegetables in the markets of Tegucigalpa and San Pedro Sula. Then these farmers were asked about the benefits of having price information (see figure 8.3). More than 90 percent of the farmers surveyed answered "Yes" to the question of whether they obtained some benefit from receiving the information.

For six of nine crops, the farmers who received market price information via SMS lowered price differentials against average market prices, compared to farmers who did not receive the SMS messages. Farmers with access to SMS reported landing prices

Figure 8.3   Reasons Why Honduran Farmers Feel that Price Information Was or Was Not Beneficial

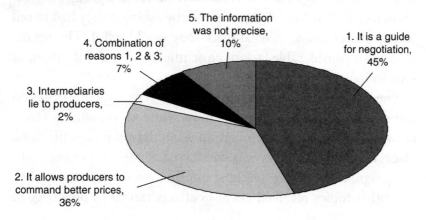

5. The information was not precise, 10%

4. Combination of reasons 1, 2 & 3; 7%

1. It is a guide for negotiation, 45%

3. Intermediaries lie to producers, 2%

2. It allows producers to command better prices, 36%

that were 12.5 percent higher, on average, thanks to better market information. Interestingly, the effect of the intervention was lower among farmers who received technical assistance or farmers with larger plots of cultivated land. This suggests that more underprivileged farmers reaped greater benefits from the SMS messages. This may be because farmers who received technical assistance may have developed stronger relationships with their buyers; thus, the prices they receive when they have price information do not change significantly (some producers said they had pre-negotiated the price of their production before the harvest). Moreover, the producers who have less power to negotiate (in this case, because they have planted less land) were empowered and benefited more from the intervention.

Many agricultural products in Colombia today are commercialized inefficiently because farmers lack information, particularly on prices. Colombian farmers make production decisions based on informal sources of information, such as family members, neighbors, or tradition. In a randomized study of the agricultural sector, Camacho and Conover (2010) explored how providing information to farmers via SMS text messages can improve welfare. Knowledge of price is the simplest possible outcome that can be tested in the experiment. A baseline survey of a group of farmers assessed their knowledge of prices by asking if they had to sell their product today, at what price they would sell it. The results revealed a considerable lack of basic information about prices, as seen in figure 8.4.

The randomly selected farmers who received the information were assigned to the treatment group, while the remaining farmers were placed in the control group. After the randomization took place, a follow-up survey was conducted. Under this experimental design, the study tested how information on prices, weather, and other topics received via SMS affects farmers' knowledge of

Figure 8.4   Farmers' Knowledge of Prices in Colombia

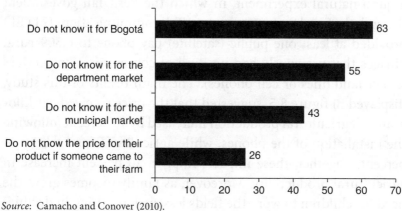

Source: Camacho and Conover (2010).

prices, sales prices, decisions to change and store crops or delay harvest, substitute sources of information, share information, or combine produce with other farmers. Relative to the farmers who did not receive SMS information, the farmers who did receive information obviously had better knowledge of prices, giving them an advantage when negotiating with middlemen; consequently, the dispersion in the expected price of their crops was narrower—although there was little difference in the actual sales price. The farmers considered the text messages useful and an important source of information for sales. Even though crop losses declined, farmers' revenues or household expenditures did not change significantly. All told, the study indicated that inexpensive technological interventions quickly become useful sources of price information and reduce the probability of weather-related crop loss.

For the case of Peru, Beuermann (2010) examined the impact of installing public pay phones in isolated villages in rural areas to identify the effects of telecommunication technologies on agricultural productivity and child labor. The author exploited a quasi-natural experiment, in which the Peruvian government through the Fund for Investments in Telecommunications (FITEL) provided at least one public (satellite) pay phone to 6,509 rural villages that previously had no kind of communication services (either land lines or cell phones). The main results of this study, displayed in figure 8.5, suggested that the price received per kilogram of agricultural production increased by 16 percent following the installation of the phones, while agricultural costs fell by 24 percent. Together, these impacts imply a 20 percent increase in agricultural productivity. Moreover, as family incomes grew, the need for children to work the fields lessened, resulting in declines in child labor and child agricultural labor of 32 percent and 26.3 percent, respectively. Importantly, this intervention differs from the previous studies in that it involves public (satellite) pay phones rather than cell phones or Internet kiosks. This study was carried out in areas in Peru where neither cell phones nor fixed-line phones were available.

Figure 8.5   Effect of Provision of Public Pay Phones on Agricultural Productivity and Child Labor in Rural Peru

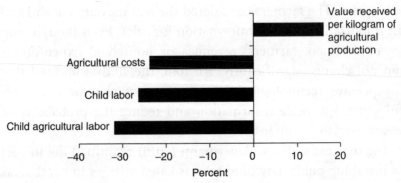

Source: Beuermann (2010).

Beefing Up Quality for the International Market

To improve market access, food products must meet escalating safety and quality requirements around the world. To help Argentine cattle ranchers meet these market demands and improve their competitiveness in the international meat market, a project backed by the Inter-American Development Bank (IDB) and the Multilateral Investment Fund (MIF) turned to technology, developing a new system for tracing Argentine beef.

The system, called TRAZAR (from the English word, "traceability"), is a successful example of the application of ICT methods in rural areas to increase the efficiency and potential of small- and medium-scale farmers. This program used ICT to track the production cycle of cow herds in Santa Fe province, Argentina, between 2004 and 2006. TRAZAR is a software program that stores all the information related to the identified animals, and can be accessed and managed through the Internet. Traceability involves tracing each animal from the time it joins the herd until the meat is distributed, and is a requirement to export meat to high-value markets, such as the European Union (EU).

Originally, the main objective of the program was to equip small- and medium-scale cattle farmers with this tool so that they could export the best-quality Argentine beef. The field work started with workshops in Santa Fe to make cattle farmers aware of the advantages of the system. More than 100 cattle farmers attended, but only 40 enrolled. These forty initial beneficiaries created a cooperative called Progan to commercialize their products. The farmers as a group had more market power, better possibilities of reaching high-value markets, greater social capital, and better knowledge of the business. Before the program was launched, many of these same farmers sold their cows and calves to the nearest meat processing company for cold storage. Once they started using the TRAZAR software and participating in Progan, they became involved in all the links of the beef production chain: primary production of animals, commercialization, industrialization, and distribution. TRAZAR can be regarded as another case of applying ICT methods to help solve market failures due to problems of coordination and asymmetric information.

To evaluate the impact of TRAZAR on the income and welfare of the small-scale farmers, Galiani and Jaitman (2010) created a control group consisting of forty farmers from Santa Fe who shared similar pre-program characteristics in terms of scale, region, income, and problems as those who enrolled in TRAZAR. The treatment group consisted of the forty initial beneficiaries; of these, only twenty-four (60 percent) decided to continue using TRAZAR software once the financial support dried up, and the remaining sixteen (40 percent) left the program.[1]

According to the evaluation, TRAZAR fulfilled its overall objective of strengthening the competitiveness of cattle farmers in the international meat market by complying with traceability requirements for the herd. Since 2005, Progan has been assigned a portion of the Hilton quota (the highest-value exports to the EU). The farmers' improved competitiveness has boosted the profitability of the small- and medium-scale enterprises involved. Figure 8.6 shows that by selling to Progan, farmers received a higher price than if they sold their production to the nearest meat processing firm. (This differential would represent their opportunity cost.) Furthermore, Progan members also participated in the profits of the cooperative. Therefore, when Progan pays out dividends, the income of its members increases even more. In recent years, the income of the beneficiaries that sold to Progan was between 8 percent and 20 percent more per kilogram of high-quality export beef sold, considering the higher baseline

Figure 8.6   Income of Progan Farmers

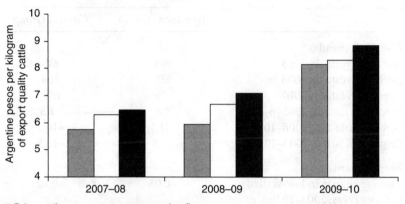

■ Price at the nearest meat processing firm
□ Farmers' profit per kilogram before distributing Progan's dividends
■ Farmers' profit per kilogram after distributing Progan's dividends
Source: Galiani and Jaitman (2010).

price paid by Progan and their share in the paid-out dividends of the cooperative.

Recent years have brought hard times to the beef industry, in spite of high international prices for meat, in part because government rules have changed constantly. In response to losses, approximately 60,000 producers left the business and many others have liquidated part of their cattle herd. Table 8.1 shows that during the years of the program (2004–6), the TRAZAR members increased their cattle herd by 8.8 percent, while the control group started a liquidation phase. After the program ended, the initial beneficiaries also began decreasing the number of heads on average, but to a lesser extent than the control group. The combination of discouraging policies in the sector and the worst drought ever forced the smallest and most-liquidity constrained producers to leave the program. Overall, between 2003 and 2010, heads of livestock contracted 15.5 percent in the control group, but only by 3.3 percent among the initial beneficiaries.

Table 8.1   Main Results of TRAZAR Evaluation

	Treatment Group	Control Group
Livestock (heads)		
Average livestock, 2003	908	816
Average livestock, 2006	988	804
Average livestock, 2010	879	690
Percent variation, 2003–6	8.8	–1.5
Percent variation, 2006–10	–11.1	–14.2
Percent variation, 2003–10	–3.3	–15.5
Employment		
Average change in low-skilled rural workers, 2003–10 (no. of workers)	–0.08	–0.02
Average change in high-skilled rural workers, 2003–10 (no. of workers)	1.20	0.00
Animal Welfare		
Change, 2004–10 (percentage of farmers who implemented improvements)	70	30
Quality of Animals		
Change, 2004–10 (percentage of farmers who implemented improvements)	80	0

Source: Galiani and Jaitman (2010).

Farmers had to alter their production methods to comply with the high standards of sanitation, quality, and animal welfare requested by high-value markets. Therefore, most of the producers introduced improvements that in turn increased the efficiency of their production and their income. For example, they began using flags to manage the herd (instead of more aggressive and invasive methods), improved reproduction selection, reduced animal stress to obtain better meat, and registered their activities in TRAZAR software. This required an investment in training workers and an increase in the number of highly skilled rural employees. In the TRAZAR group, there was a shift from low-skilled to higher-skilled employment that did not occur in the control group.

Narrowing the Digital Divide

Telephony is the primary infrastructure that facilitates access to ICTs. When it comes to a direct link to poor communities and poor people, the telephone plays a key role (Torero and von Braun, 2006). Telephony is important not only as a channel for improved access to information and communications, but also as a prerequisite for the widespread use of more advanced technologies such as the Internet. In most countries, especially developing countries, there is a large gap in the availability of ICTs between urban and rural locations. Rural populations in low-income economies often lack access to fixed telephony, and while mobile penetration in rural areas is rising, it is still low in some least developed countries. At the end of 2008, almost half the rural population in the least developed countries was still not covered by a mobile signal (United Nations, 2010).

Rural telecommunications services constitute a crucial rural infrastructure since they provide the means for transferring information in a context where alternatives are less accessible. Investing in this kind of infrastructure can narrow information gaps and shorten the distance between economic agents, thus reducing transaction costs—and enhancing the efficiency of resource allocation (Leff, 1984; Tschang, Chuladul, and Thu Le, 2002; Andrew and Petkov, 2003). However, even though telecommunications infrastructure has long been recognized as a key ingredient for promoting economic growth, it has not been a central investment issue in many developing countries.[2]

In an attempt to establish a link between access to telephone services and household income, Chong, Galdo, and Torero (2009) took advantage of a quasi-natural experiment in Peru in which the privatized telecommunications company, Telefónica del Peru, was required by the government to randomly install and operate public pay phones in small and isolated rural towns following privatization in 1994. Public telephones were distributed across the country, although somewhat more heavily in the Andean region, where poverty is more acute than in the rather unpopulated Amazon region in the west, or the relatively richer coastal region. The authors designed and administered a household survey to a representative sample of towns in rural areas of the country. At the time of the survey, half the towns had at least a public telephone installed by the privatized company in the most accessible part of the town, such as the municipal authority building or the town's main shop. The control group consisted of the remaining towns, where the lack of public telephone service reflected a supply constraint more than lack of demand.

To better understand the channels by which access to public telephones may impact households, the study used three measures of per capita income: total annual household per capita income, regardless of source; non-farm per capita income; and farm per capita income only. Analyzing farm and non-farm income separately takes into consideration the economics of rural households. Non-farm income helps families make ends meet when farm income goes through its typical cyclical declines. As shown in figure 8.7, the availability of a rural public telephone installed by the privatized firm in the town or village is associated with approximately 20 percent higher per capita income, 16 percent higher per capita non-farm income, and 18 percent higher per capita farm income.

Figure 8.7   Effect of Access to Public Telephones in Rural Areas on Household Income in Peru

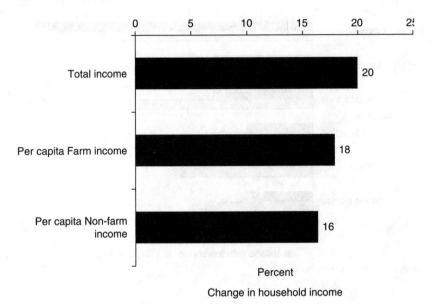

Percent

Change in household income

Source: Chong, Galdo, and Torero (2009).

Also in Peru, a survey was conducted in four rural departments in the southern part of the country in 2000 to report the perceived benefits of public phones by rural users (Torero and von Braun, 2006). Sample households attributed significant benefits to public telephone access, including the ability to communicate faster, avoid travel, and save money and time (see figure 8.8).

Beuermann, McKelvey, and Sotelo-Lopez (2010) evaluated the impact of cellular coverage on household well-being in rural Peru by exploiting the roll-out of mobile phone infrastructure between 2001 and 2007. Mobile phone coverage raised the income and expenditures of rural consumers; however, there was no significant impact on the profits of home businesses. These results are important for understanding the overall impact on well-being

Figure 8.8 Perceived Benefits of Public Phones by Rural Users in Peru, 2000

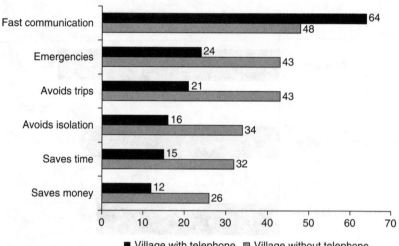

Source: Torero and von Braun (2006).

in an environment such as Peru, where 85 percent of households operate a home farm.

Another widespread strategy for extending benefits of ICTs to poorer communities is to encourage telecenters: that is, public facilities where people can access ICTs. How can telecenters support the livelihood of people living in poverty? Telecenters can foster the development of technical and business skills, provide access to key information, facilitate access to government services and financial resources, and offer support to budding microentrepreneurs (UNCTAD, 2007).

A number of governments of developing countries, including Colombia, have launched programs aimed at providing ICT access through community centers in rural areas. In the late 1990s, the telecommunications infrastructure in Colombia was concentrated in the major urban centers and along main roads.

Small localities and rural areas were bypassed by the established and traditional telecommunications providers. According to the Telecommunications Regulation Commission of Colombia, average teledensity was 17 percent and differences among the regions of the country were great.[3] As a response to this critical situation, in 1999, the Ministry of Information Technology and Communications in Colombia launched Compartel, a social tele-communication program whose main goal is to allow distant areas, or those with lower socioeconomic development, to benefit from telecommunications technologies like rural telephony and Internet service.

The program is based on a competitive bidding scheme for the deployment of telecenters by private companies. Bidders can benefit from economies of scale by bundling together hundreds of telecenters. Thus, operators can establish telecenters run by local entrepreneurs, but backed by the support and resources of a larger regional network and a professional management organiza-tion. In Colombia, in partnership with global network provides BT (British Telecom), Compartel sites have been located in small population areas, police stations, and villages with more than 100 inhabitants that did not have any type of communication. Access to telephony has been provided to around 5 million Colombians, with 1,393 telecenters operating throughout the country in 2009. According to a survey of 922 telecenters conducted in 2006 by Universidad de los Andes,[4] students and teachers are the main users of telecenters, along with vulnerable sectors like unemployed workers or handicapped people. Figure 8.9 shows the distribution of Compartel telecenter users by monthly income, in Colombian pesos. In general, telecenters target low-income populations.

Individuals who have used the telecenters for a longer period tend to have a higher level of income, after controlling for intrin-sic characteristics of the individuals, like education, employment,

Box 8.1   A Conditional Cash Transfer Program in the Dominican Republic

The Solidaridad program, launched in 2005 by the government of the Dominican Republic, provides conditional cash transfers to poor households, provided that they invest more in education, health, and nutrition. Eligible families receive between US$20 and US$40 per month if they attend nutrition training courses, immunize their children, and ensure that the children go to school. Some 460,000 families are covered by Solidaridad, approximately 74 percent of the population living in poverty in the Dominican Republic.

From the onset, the payment system has operated through a debit card to enhance transparency, reduce transaction costs—such as time spent waiting in line for payment or the time spent converting payments to cash—and lower the risk of having cash on hand that can be stolen or spent on day-to-day activities. The debit card can be used in the Red de Abasto Social, which basically consists of local grocery stores, known as colmados. To encourage the stores to participate in the program and set up the necessary technology, a minimum number of beneficiaries per neighborhood was guaranteed, giving the colmados a certain degree of local market power.

The colmados vary in terms of the numbers of competitors they face, the products they sell, and the levels of quality in their establishments. Thus, consumers encounter different prices for the same products, even when these consumers live in similar areas. The program is going through an expansion phase, and the number of colmados will be increasing.

Currently, researchers are conducting an experimental evaluation to analyze the impact of this expansion on the level of market competition (Busso, Chong, and Galiani, 2010). Two groups of variables will be considered. The first takes into account characteristics of the colmados (price and quality of products, investment in capital goods, quality of service, sales). The second group looks at characteristics of the beneficiaries (price paid, consumption of the basic food basket, distance to the closest shop, changes in points of sale).

(continued on next page)

(continued)

The experiment will increase market competition for products that are part of the program, while the market for products that are not permitted should not vary significantly. After the expansion in store locations, prices are expected to fall, along with the time families spend going to the stores, while the quality of the service is expected to increase.

Figure 8.9 Distribution of Compartel Telecenter Users by Monthly Income, 2006 (percent)

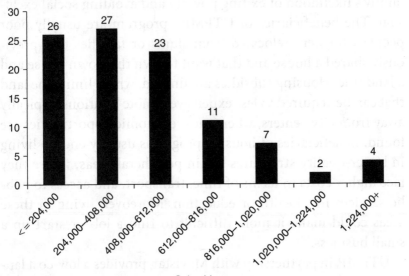

Colombian pesos

Source: Ministry of Communications, Republic of Colombia (2007).

and knowledge of ICTs. The program has evolved so that it now includes rural broadband strategies for public institutions, like basic and secondary schools in underprivileged municipalities that lack technical infrastructure and have a high percentage of registered students. The program also aims to improve the administrative processes of the mayor's offices, health institutions, military outposts, and other local institutions.

Another initiative to narrow the digital divide is being pursued in Chile by *Un techo para mi País* (UTPMP), a nongovernmental organization (NGO) that partnered with Movistar, a large multinational company that specializes in offering communication services such as phone lines and Internet connection, to provide housing to people who live in slums (Multilateral Investment Fund, 2010). The main objective of UTPMP's housing program is to improve household welfare and increase the family's likelihood of exiting poverty and avoiding social exclusion. The beneficiaries of UTPMP's program are usually poor people who were relocated from slums or families that previously shared a house and that want to own their own house and a land title. Housing subsidies are limited, which limits the land that can be acquired to less expensive remote locations, typically away from city centers, where most economic opportunities are found. Beneficiaries of housing programs usually end up living in better-quality structures but in peripheral areas, where they face higher costs in terms of time, transport, and access to public services like health or education. Moreover, living in these areas could make it more difficult to find a job or start up a small business.

UTPMP, in partnership with Movistar, provides a low-cost laptop to households that have upgraded their home from a slum dwelling to permanent construction or have upgraded their home but still live in a poor sector and have limited access to opportunities. The *Conectando a mi País* program targets households that reside in permanent structures in poor and marginalized neighborhoods and do not have access to a computer at home. The *Conectando a mi País* low-cost laptop includes Internet connection through a Universal Serial Bus (USB) modem and a set of social and technological tools (the "Tech-O" software) specially designed for this still on-going program.

Dreaming of the Future

ICTs are a potentially effective weapon for fighting poverty. They can help close information gaps, spread the knowledge available to a broader sector of the population, and expand the opportunity frontier of the most vulnerable sectors. Armed with more and better information, the poor can be better equipped to act on their own behalf, boost their earning potential, and use their own knowledge and abilities to lift themselves out of poverty.

The role of ICTs in improving social and economic conditions in the world's poorest countries has been strongly advanced by the international community. The Millennium Development Goals (MDGs) envision a global partnership for development that includes as one of its objectives making the benefits of ICTs available to all the world's inhabitants. ICTs can also play a major part in achieving other goals, such as eradicating extreme poverty and hunger. The MDGs assign three main roles to ICTs: increasing access to market information and lowering transaction costs for poor farmers and traders; increasing the efficiency, competitiveness, and market access of firms in developing countries; and enhancing the ability of developing countries to participate in the global economy and to exploit their comparative advantage in factor costs, particularly skilled labor.

This chapter described several ICT strategies that can help people improve their incomes. One example is the strong potential of ICT services to reduce asymmetries in the price information that small farmers and producers face in rural areas. ICTs can also influence labor markets, reducing job search time and costs, and enhancing the skill level of job seekers, making them more employable. In Latin America, with its high levels of informality, the galloping penetration of ICT technologies holds particular promise. Initiatives to narrow the digital divide, like providing rural telephony and Internet service, are also extremely relevant.

However, people with low levels of education are still at a disadvantage and unlikely to reap the full benefits of new technologies, including broader access to knowledge and information. The poor may face special constraints in accessing ICTs and using them for their specific needs. ICTs are not a magic wand that put dreams of wealth and progress in everyone's hands. Improving the skills of the population and the quality and level of physical infrastructure are crucial to make these dreams come true.

Notes

1 A Field of Dreams or a Dream Come True?

1. This book considers ICT to be the application of both traditional and modern communications and computing technologies to the creation, management, and use of information. This definition encompasses both equipment and services that facilitate the electronic capture, processing, display, and transmission of information, and includes the computing industry, the Internet, electronic and display telecommunications and related services, and related audiovisual equipment.
2. Roller and Waverman (2001) and Waverman, Meschi, and Fuss (2005), among others, have studied the macroeconomic link between ICTs and economic growth. Although they find a positive association between both, the results have remained open to question, as it is unclear whether ICT is the driving force of economic growth or economic growth is driving the use of ICTs. Furthermore, it is not clear whether there is an additional variable, not included in their empirical work, that may be responsible for their findings. These two issues deem these and other related findings as promising— but perhaps not credible enough.
3. About 80 percent of the world's websites are in English (Kenny, 2006).
4. In a natural experiment, the assignment of treatment has been made "by nature" and was not "designed" by experimenters.

2 The Region's Place in the Digital World: A Tale of Three Divides

1. For example, more than 330,000 customers started to use mobile broadband in Chile in 2008–09 (Anta and Albi, 2010).

2. As mobile phone technology is evolving quickly (for example, with the arrival of smart-phone technology), the concept of a mobile phone itself is changing from a simple instrument of communication to a far more sophisticated digital tool with multiple applications. Although the overall access gap between countries of Latin America and the Caribbean and OECD countries might be narrowing, a burgeoning mobile phone "quality" gap cannot be disregarded, if, as expected, new mobile phone technologies are spreading faster in the OECD countries than in Latin America and the Caribbean.

3. The available international indicators for access to computer hardware do not control for differences in the "quality" of the equipment, so the difference between Latin America and the Caribbean and OECD regarding information storage, processing capacities, and applications may not be fully reflected in the raw numbers. A recent study shows that the differences in hard disk storage capacity per capita between OECD and Latin American and Caribbean countries dramatically increased, rising from 3,780 megabits in 1996 to 750,000 megabits in 2006 (Peres and Hilbert, 2009)

4. Beyond penetration rates, consider Latin America's considerable delay in terms of connection quality. Vicente and Gil-de-Bernabé (2010) computed a "Broadband Quality Score," an index that combines three key performance parameters for the quality of a connection (upload and download speeds and latency). Brazil and Mexico, the only two Latin American countries included in the index, performed poorly, ranking thirtieth-eighth and fortieth out of forty-two countries, respectively.

5. A national innovation system is the "network of institutions in the public and private sectors whose activities and interactions initiate, import, modify and diffuse new technologies" (Freeman, 1987, p. 1).

6. For example, Stoneman, Battisti, and Girma (2010) report that India did not match the level of phones per capita in the United States as of 1910 until 90 years later.

7. Following Pritchett, Woolcock, and Andrews (2010), this study first determined the annual rate of progress in diffusion for each country in the region, computing the difference between the current and initial rates of penetration and then dividing it by the number of years since the moment when the technology was made available: 1975 for PCs, 1980 for mobile phones, 1988 for the Internet, and 1998 for broadband. For fixed telephony,

the initial values reported by ITU in 1960 or the earliest year were used. Second, the digital gap in 2008 between the OECD average and each country of Latin America and the Caribbean was computed, and this gap was divided by the diffusion annual rate of progress (obtained from the previous step). This methodology renders information about the number of years it would take for each country in the region to reach current OECD average levels under a business-as-usual scenario.

8. The ICT production function suffers from economies of scale and scope in the different services, generating a type of natural monopoly barrier to entry. Efficient provision of ICT services requires adequate regulation in order to keep prices close to the average production costs.

9. Trade openness is included under the assumption that in countries with more open economies, inhabitants will value connectivity more for business purposes.

10. This result is in line with the literature on the determinants of ICT adoption using microdata, which highlight the strong role played by income and education (see, for example, Vicente and Lopez, 2006; Grazzi and Vergara, forthcoming).

11. Data on broadband are not included, as household surveys do not report data on the access of this technology yet.

12. Households in the highest quartile in the OECD have 2.25 times more access to the Internet than households in the lowest quartile; inequality is about ten times lower than the averages of Latin America and the Caribbean (EUROSTAT, 2009; ECLAC and ICA, 2010).

13. The use of the number of subscriptions as an indicator of the diffusion of a technology in a country is open to criticism. These supply-side data collected by Internet operators have many limitations, mainly due to possible double counting of individuals with more than one subscription, the lack of distinction between commercial and private subscriptions, the presence of inactive accounts, and the sharing of a subscription among multiple users (see ITU, 2010).

14. The EU15 comprised the following fifteen countries: Austria, Belgium, Denmark, Finland, France, Germany, Greece, Ireland, Italy, Luxembourg, Netherlands, Portugal, Spain, Sweden, United Kingdom (OECD, 2007).

15. When comparing Internet use between Latin America and the Caribbean and Europe, the data do not control for the duration of use, as such

information is not available. Thus, the gaps discussed in this section are likely to be severely underestimated.

16. Robert Solow, "We'd Better Watch Out," *New York Times Book Review*, July 12, 1987, p. 36.

17. There are a few exceptions. See, for example, the work of Gordon (2000, 2003).

18. Providers of ICTs services tend to focus on the development of solutions for large firms and traditional sectors, such as finance, insurance, logistics, agro-industry, and wholesale trade, but the supply of solutions is limited for SME needs. Working with this group of firms is normally complex because the group is heterogeneous and transaction costs are high.

19. Data are from the World Economic Forum's Executive Opinion Survey. Survey questions ask for response on a scale from a low of 1 to a high of 7. For each survey question, individual responses from the 2008 and 2009 editions of the survey are combined and aggregated in order to produce country scores. For more information on the Executive Opinion Survey, see chapter 1 (WEF, 2010).

20. Productivity is measured by income per capita. Human capital is proxied by years of schooling. Regulatory quality and infrastructure are measured by Internet subscriptions per 100 inhabitants.

3   Banking on Technology for Financial Inclusion

1. These figures come from a recent study by Demirgüç-Kunt, Beck, and Hohohan (2008).

2. For a summary of the evidence on the importance of finance for economic well-being, see Claessens (2006).

3. A POS device is the machine used in many commercial establishments around the world to make electronic payments for purchases. It looks like a small box with a screen and a keypad, and has a slot through which a debit or credit card can be slid.

4. Three-quarters of the world's 4 billion cell phones are used in developing countries, according to *The Economist* ("The Power of Mobile Money," September 24, 2009). (Accessed May 2010).

5. Unfortunately, there is no proper evaluation of this arrangement. In the near future, research is likely that could suggest improvements for the initiative.

6. Ivatury and Pickens (2006) note that although the users of WIZZIT are low-income people, they are not the poorest people in South Africa. The early users of WIZZIT were wealthier and more technologically and financially sophisticated than the average low-income person in the country.

7. See Wishart (2006) for a discussion.

8. A detailed discussion on the determinants of productivity is found in Pagés (2010).

9. The figures report the estimated impact from a regression in which the dependent variable is sales growth in the past three years and the independent variables are a dummy indicating if the firm has a bank account; and interaction between that dummy and a country variable indicating Internet penetration (the logarithm of the share of population with Internet usage or the logarithm of the cost of accessing the Internet); size dummies indicating if a firm is small (fewer than 20 workers), medium (21–99 workers), or large (100 or more workers); and a country-sector-year fixed effect. The standard errors of the regression estimated with the Ordinary Least Squares (OLS) econometric technique are clustered at the country level.

4   Rewiring Institutions

1. The index uses protection against risk of expropriation as a proxy for institutions and includes constraints on government expropriation, independent judiciary, property rights enforcement, and institutions providing equal access to education and ensuring civil liberties.

2. The EDGI is a weighted average of three normalized scores on the most important dimensions of e-government: scope and quality of online services, telecommunication connectivity, and human capacity.

3. Hughes (2010) provides a detailed analysis of the role of the media in policymaking in Latin America.

4. Information for political purposes can be used by citizens and governments alike. Hsieh et al (2010) analyzed how the Venezuelan government made use of voters' names and ID numbers posted on the website of a progovernment legislator.

5   Tech Fever in the Health Sector

1. Spending around 3.6 percent of GDP for 2004–05.
2. Resolution WHA58.28, May 2005.
3. The WHO uses the World Bank definition of high-income countries; additional information is available at WHO (2006).
4. EHAS also supports projects in Colombia, Cuba, and Ecuador, and is starting activities in Bolivia. Other groups have applied its methodologies and technology solutions for telemedicine in rural areas in Mexico and Nicaragua.

6   Computers in Schools: Why Governments Should Do Their Homework

1. www.laptop.org/en. Last accessed April 2010.
2. This is computed by considering a typical twenty-five-hour school week and assuming that allocation of computer time to students in each school is efficient so that each computer is used all the time.
3. Alternatively, they may reflect the fact that in some countries, such as Cuba, all students are assured weekly access, while in other countries, differences in frequency across different groups of students may explain these results.
4. A more complete budget table that explicitly details all the assumptions used is available from the authors upon request.
5. As it is standard in the literature, annual costs were computed according to the formula: $c \dfrac{[r(1+r)^n]}{[(1+r)^n - 1]}$, where c is the cost of the asset, r is the social discount rate assumed to be 10 percent, and n is the expected life of the asset (five years).
6. Unlike one-to-one programs, the computer lab requires other expenditures in addition to computers, such as renovations for a computer room and the deployment of a network. The following assumptions are made: Each class has a maximum of twenty-four students and each class uses the lab two hours each week either to learn basic computing skills or to support math and reading learning. Classes use the lab jointly. Each computer

is used by two students at a time. The lab is open while students are in school (approximately thirty hours a week). Given these assumptions, the number of computers in each lab and the number of labs required in each school can be calculated. For instance, if the school has 40 students, one lab with ten computers would suffice; if the school has 250 students, it would require one lab with twelve computers; if it has 500 students, it would require two labs with twelve computers.

7. A large qualitative literature has also documented interesting experiences, such as the "hole in the wall" pilots. These experiences were dubbed as "the hole in the wall" because a computer with Internet access was embedded in a brick wall in a slum to explore the hypothesis that even disadvantaged children can acquire computer skills on their own (Mitra, 2003).

7   Help or Hindrance? ICT's Impact on the Environment

1. Mexico's export pattern is mainly linked (74 percent) to the manufacturing sector.
2. $MtCO_2e$ stands for Metric Ton Carbon Dioxide Equivalent. This is the standard measurement for CO_2 emissions. $GtCO_2e$ stands for Gigaton Carbon Dioxide Equivalent.
3. Digital markets include ICTs as well as consumer electronics.
4. TrashTrack Program of the SENSEable City Laboratory, MIT.
5. Turbidity measures suspended matter in the water, and is measured by the translucence of the water. Turbidity levels are increased by the presence of organic pollution in the water, but can also be increased by other pollutants with high levels of suspended content. BOD and COD are measures of the organic matter in the water. They measure how much organic matter can oxidize either through interaction with a chemical agent (COD) or through microbes (BOD). High levels of either COD or BOD suggest high levels of organic matter. High levels of organic matter are suggestive of fertilizer runoff, sewage, or organic industrial waste. Coliform bacteria are bacteria associated with raw sewage. Fecal coliform is the most dangerous of the coliform bacteria, as water with high fecal coliform levels is likely to contain other pathogens as well. Raw sewage often contains more than 10 million raw coliform

bacteria per 100 mL. Nitrates and nitrites are nutrients, typically originating from fertilizer runoff, but they can also come from landfills and sewage.

6. Internal Population Displacement in Haiti. Preliminary analyses of movement patterns of Digicel mobile phones: 1 December 2009 to 18 June 2010. Report update: 31 August 2010. Authors note that the analyses in the report are being complemented by more in-depth studies for forthcoming scientific, peer-reviewed publishing.

7. Geller (1981) assesses the effectiveness of energy conservation workshops by administering questionnaires and visiting households. Henry and Gordon (2003) used pre- and post-survey data to evaluate campaigns to raise awareness of threats to air quality and change behavior related to air pollution. Syme, Nancarrow, and Seligman (2000) reviewed the evidence regarding save-water campaigns to promote household water conservation and concluded that more experimental research is needed.

8. StickK.com was launched in January 2008. Individuals can choose to meet a wide variety of goals, from personal (exercising regularly, losing weight, quitting smoking) to environmental (conserving energy in the office), to work-based (completing reports). StickK requires users to track and report their progress each week.

9. Argentina, Chile, Colombia, Costa Rica, Dominican Republic, Ecuador. Mexico, Panama, Peru, Puerto Rico, Uruguay, and Venezuela.

10. In addition to investigating the general use of the website as a means to encourage pro-environmental behavior, this study looked at how ICTs might be used to encourage enrollment in contracts. StickK conducted a Google Ad Words advertisement campaign testing twenty-two different types of ads with a maximum length of ninety-five characters. A randomized trial was set up in order to test various theories about which messages effectively encourage people to create environmental commitments.

11. Clicks are defined as the number of times users clicked an ad for the website over the designated period (May and June 2010).

8   Development.com: Using ICTs to Escape Poverty

1. The treatment group investigated the forty beneficiaries of the program, irrespective of their status after 2006 when the funding ended. Including

only those twenty-four farmers who kept on using the system after 2006 would overestimate the effect of the program.

2. Low-income countries account for only 9 percent of the world's telephone mainlines, which equals approximately twenty-eight lines per 1,000 inhabitants. In contrast, high-income countries account for 52 percent of the world's telephone mainlines, or 585 lines per 1,000 inhabitants. In rural areas in developing countries, the contrast is even more dramatic: fewer than one line per 1,000 inhabitants (International Telecommunications Union, 1998).

3. Ministry of Communications, International Communication Unit, Republic of Colombia (2004).

4. Ministry of Communications, International Communication Unit, Republic of Colombia (2007).

References

Abegunde D, C. D. Mathers, T. Adam, M. Ortegon, and K. Strong. 2007. The Burden and Costs of Chronic Diseases in Low-income and Middle-income Countries. *Lancet* 370:1929–38.

Abraham, R. 2007. Mobile Phones and Economic Development: Evidence from the Fishing Industry in India. *Information Technologies and International Development* 4(1): 5–17.

Acemoglu, D., S. Johnson, and J. A. Robinson. 2001. The Colonial Origins of Comparative Development: An Empirical Investigation. *The American Economic Review* 91(5): 1369–1401.

Afsah, S., A. Blackman, and D. Ratunanda. 2000. "How Do Public Disclosure Pollution Control Programs Work? Evidence from Indonesia." Resources for the Future Discussion Paper 00–44. Resources for the Future, Washington, DC.

Aker, J. 2008. Does Digital Divide or Provide? The Impact of Mobile Phones on Grain Markets in Niger. BREAD Working Paper 177.

———. 2010. Information Markets Near and Far: Mobile Phones and Agricultural Markets in Niger. *American Economic Journal: Applied Economics* 2(3): 46–59.

Aker, J, and I. Mbiti. 2010. Mobile Phones and Economic Development in Africa. *Journal of Economic Perspectives* 24(3): 207–32.

Alvariño, C. and E. Severín. 2009. Aprendizajes en la Sociedad del Conocimiento: Punto de Quiebre para la Introducción de las TICs en la Educación de América Latina. Unpublished document. Santiago, Chile: ECLAC (Economic Commission for Latin America and the Caribbean).

Anderson, G. F. 2009. Missing in Action: International Aid Agencies in Poor Countries to Fight Chronic Disease. *Health Affairs* 28(1): 202–05.

Anderson, A. S., and P. Klemm. 2008. The Internet: Friend or Foe when Providing Patient Education? *Clinical Journal of Oncology Nursing* 12(1): 55–63.

Andrew, T. N., and D. Petkov. 2003. The Need for a Systems Thinking Approach to the Planning of Rural Telecommunications Infrastructure. *Telecommunications Policy* 27: 75–93.

Angrist, J. and V. Lavy. 2002. New Evidence on Classroom Computers and Pupil Learning. *The Economic Journal* 112(482): 735–65.

Anta, R., S. El-Wahab, and A. Giuffrida. 2008. Mobile Health: The Potential of Mobile Telephony to Bring Health Care to the Majority. Innovation Note, Inter-American Development Bank, November 2008. Washington, DC.

Anta, R., and N. Albi. 2010. Analisis del Sector de Telecomunicaciones en Chile. Recomendaciones para acelerar el desarrollo de la Banda Ancha. Technical Note, Science and Technology Division, Washington, DC: Inter-American Development Bank.

Arredondo, A. A., A. Zúñiga, and I. Parada. 2005. Health Care Costs and Financial Costs of Epidemiological Changes in Latin America: Evidence from Mexico. *Public Health* 119(8): 711–20.

Artinian, N. T., O. G. Washington, and T. N. Templin. 2001. Effects of Home Telemonitoring and Community based Monitoring on Blood Pressure Control in Urban African Americans: A Pilot Study. *Heart and Lung* 30(3):191–99.

Ashraf, N., D. Karlan, and W. Yin. 2006. "Tying Odysseus to the Mast: Evidence from a Commitment Savings Product in the Philippines." *Quarterly Journal of Economics* 121(2): 635–72.

Asmar, R., and A. Zanchetti. 2000. Guidelines for the Use of Self-Blood Pressure Monitoring: A Summary Report of the First International Consensus Conference. *Journal of Hypertension* 18(5): 493–508.

Autor, D. Wiring the Labor Market. *Journal of Economic Perspectives* 15(1): 25–40.

Ayres, I. and S. Levitt. 1998. "Measuring Positive Externalities from Unobservable Victim Precaution: An Empirical Analysis of Lojack." *Quarterly Journal of Economics* 113(1): 43–77.

Balsa, A. and N. Gandelman. 2010. The Impact of ICT in Health Promotion: A Randomized Experiment with Diabetic Patients. Unpublished document. Inter-America Development Bank, Washington, DC.

Balsa, A., N. Gandelman, and R. Porzecanski. 2010. The Impact of ICT on Adolescents' Perceptions and Consumption of Substances. Unpublished document. Washington, DC: Inter-American Development Bank.

Banerjee, A., S. Cole, E. Duflo, and L. Linden. 2007. Remedying Education: Evidence from Two Randomized Experiments in India. *The Quarterly Journal of Economics* 122(3): 1235–64.

Bansal, M., M. Cummings, A. Hyland and G. Giovino. 2004. Stop-Smoking Medications: Who Uses Them, Who Misuses Them, and Who Is Misinformed about Them? *Nicotine & Tobacco Research* 6(Supplement 3, December 2004): S303–10.

Barak A., and W. A. Fisher. 2003. Experience with an Internet-based, Theoretically Grounded Educational Resource for the Promotion of Sexual and Reproductive Health. *Sexual and Relationship Therapy* 18(3): 293–308.

Barcelo, A., C. Aedo, S. Rajpathak, and S. Robles. 2003. The Cost of Diabetes in Latin America and the Caribbean. *Bulletin of the World Health Organization* [online] 81(1): 19–27.

Barnum H., J. Kutzin, and H. Saxenian. 1995. Incentives and Provider Payment Methods. *International Journal of Health Planning and Management* 10(1): 10–45.

Barrera-Osorio, F. and L. Linden. 2009. The Use and Misuse of Computers in Education. Evidence from a Randomized Experiment in Colombia. Policy Research Working Paper 4836. Washington, DC: World Bank.

Barro, R., and J. Lee. 2000. International Data on Educational Attainment: Updates and Implications. CID Working Paper No. 42. Center for International Development, Harvard University, Cambridge.

Barrow, L., L. Markman, and C. Rouse. 2009. Technology's Edge: The Educational Benefits of Computer-Aided Instruction. *American Economic Journal* 1(1): 52–74.

Basant, R., S. J. Commander, R. Harrison, and N. Menezes-Filho. 2006. ICT Adoption and Productivity in Developing Countries: New Firm Level Evidence from Brazil and India. IZA Discussion Paper No. 2294. Institute for the Study of Labor, Bonn.

Beck, T., A. Demirgüç-Kun, and R. Levine. 2007. "Finance, Inequality and the Poor." *Journal of Financial Economics* 12(1): 27–49.

Beck, T., A. Demirgüç -Kunt, and M. Martínez Peria. 2006. "Banking Services for Everyone? Barriers to Bank Access and Use around the World." World Bank Policy Research Working Paper 4079. World Bank, Washington, DC.

Beck, T., R. Levine, and N. Loayza. 2000. "Finance and the Sources of Growth." *Journal of Financial Economics* 58(1–2): 261–300.

Benartzi, S. and R. Thaler. 2004. "Save More Tomorrow: Using Behavioral Economics to Increase Employee Saving." *Journal of Political Economy* 112(1): 164–87.

Bengtsson, L., X. Lu, R. Garfield, A. Thorson, and J. von Schreeb. 2010. "Internal Population Displacement in Haiti: Preliminary Analyses of Movement Patterns of Digicel Mobile Phones: 1 December 2009 to 18 June 2010." Columbia University and Karolinksa Institutet. Available at: www. reliefweb.int/rw/RWFiles2010.nsf/FilesByRWDocUnidFilename/MMAO-88UCCQ-full_report.pdf/$File/full_report.pdf. Last accessed October 14, 2010.

Benotsch, E. G., and L. Weinhardt. 2005. Health-Related Internet Use, Coping, Social Support, and Health Indicators in People Living with HIV/AIDS: Preliminary Results from a Community Survey. *Qualitative Health Research* 15(3): 325–45.

Bernheim, B. D., and A. Rangel. 2004. Addiction and Cue-Triggered Decision Processes. *American Economic Review* 94(5): 1558–90.

Besley, T., Burgess, R. and A. Prat.2002. "Mass Media and Political Accountability." In: R. Islam ed. *The Right to Tell: The Role of Mass Media in Economic Development.* WBI Development Studies, World Bank, Washington, DC.

Besley, T., and R. Burgess. 2002. The Political Economy of Government Responsiveness: Theory and Evidence from India. *The Quarterly Journal of Economics* 117(4): 1415–51.

Bet, G., J. Cristia, and P. Ibarrarán. 2010. ICT Access, Use and Outcomes in Secondary Schools in Peru. Unpublished document. Washington, DC: Inter-American Development Bank.

Beuermann, D. 2010 Telecommunications Technologies, Agricultural Productivity, and Child Labor in Rural Peru. Unpublished document. College Park: University of Maryland.

Beuermann, D., C. McKelvey, and C. Sotelo-Lopez. 2010. The Effects of Mobile Phone Infrastructure: Evidence from Rural Peru. Unpublished document. College Park: University of Maryland.

Bhatnagar, S. 2002. E-government: Lessons from Implementation in Developing Countries. Regional Development Dialogue 24. United Nations Centre for Regional Development (UNCRD). Nagoya, Japan: UNCRD.

Blanco, M., and J. F. Vargas. 2010. Empowering IDP with SMS: A Randomized Controlled Trial in Bogotá. Unpublished document. Washington, DC.: Inter-American Development Bank.

Blaya, J., B. Holt, and H. Fraser. 2008. Evaluations of the Impact of E-Health Technologies in Developing Countries: A Systematic Review. Prepared for the Making the E-Health Connection conference, Bellagio, Italy, July 13–August 8.

Blaya, J., H. Fraser, and B. Holt. 2010. E-Health Technologies Show Promise in Developing Countries. *Health Affairs* 29(2): 244–51. Available at http://ejournals.ebsco.com/direct.asp?ArticleID=42FF8EF7D8E43664EE14. July, 2010.

Blinder, A. S. 1973. Wage Discrimination: Reduced Form and Structural Estimates. *The Journal of Human Resources* 8: 436–55.

Blumenstock, J., D. Gillick, and N. Eagle. 2010. "Who's Calling? Demographics of Mobile Phone Use in Rwanda." *AAAI Symposium on Artificial Intelligence and Development,* Forthcoming.

Blumenstock, J. E., N. Eagle, and M. Fafchamps. 2010. "Calling for Help: Risk Sharing over the Rwandan Mobile Phone Network." Unpublished document. University of California, Berkeley.

Boeni, H., U. Silva, and D. Ott. 2008. "E-Waste Recycling in Latin America: Overview, Challenges, and Potential." In: B. Mishra, C. Ludwig, and S. Das eds. *REWAS 2008: Global Symposium on Recycling, Waste Treatment, and Clean Technology.* John Wiley & Sons.

Bondmass, M., N. Bolger, G. Castro, and B. Avitall. 1999. The Effect of Physiologic Home Monitoring and Telemanagement on Chronic Heart Failure Outcomes. *The Internet Journal of Asthma, Allergy and Immunology* 3(2). Available at: www.ispub.com/ostia/index.php?xmlFilePath=journals/ijanp/vol3n2/chf.xml. Last accessed April 2010.

Bossio, J. 2007. "Sostenibilidad de proyectos de desarrollo con nuevas tecnologías: el caso de la organización de regantes y su sistema de información en Huaral." *The Journal of Community Informatics* 3(3). Special Issue: Community Informatics in Latin America and the Caribbean. Available at: www.ci-journal.net/index.php/ciej/article/view/394/375. Last accessed May, 2010.

Bosworth, K., D. H. Gustafson, and R. P. Hawkins. 1994. The BARN System: Use and Impact of Adolescent Health Promotion via Computer. *Computers in Human Behavior* 10(4): 467–82.

Brender J., Ammenwerth E, Nykanen P, Talmon J. 2006. Factors Influencing Success and Failure of Health Informatics Systems—a Pilot Delphi Study. *Methods Inf Med* 45(1):125–36.

Bresnahan, T., E. Brynjolfsson, and L.M. Hitt. 2002. Information Technology, Workplace Organization and the Demand for Skilled Labour: Firm-level Evidence. *Quarterly Journal of Economics* 117(1): 339–76.

Broom, A. 2005. Virtually Healthy: The Impact of Internet Use on Disease Experience and the Doctor-Patient Relationship. *Qualitative Health Research* 15(3): 325–45.

Bruhn, M., and D. McKenzie. 2009. In Pursuit of Balance: Randomization in Practice in Development Field Experiments. *American Economic Journal: Applied Economics* 1(4): 200–32.

Bruns, B., M. Trucano, R. Hawkins, J. Hinostroza, and C. Cutolo. 2009. ICT Policy in Chilean Primary and Secondary Education: 2010 and Beyond. Policy Note. Santiago, Chile: Chilean Ministry of Finance.

Bryan, G., D. Karlan, and S. Nelson. 2010. "Commitment Devices." Yale University, New Haven, CT. Available at: http://karlan.yale.edu/p/AnnualReviewEdits4.pdf. Last accessed August 2010.

Busso, M., A. Chong, and S. Galiani. 2010. Evaluación de la Expansión de la Red de Abasto Social del Programa Solidaridad. Unpublished document. Inter-American Development Bank, Washington, DC.

Camacho, A. and E. Conover. 2010. The Impact of Price and Climate information in Colombia's Agricultural Sector. Unpublished document. Inter-American Development Bank, Washington, DC.

Carnoy, M. 2004. ICT in Education: Possibilities and Challenges. Inaugural lecture of the 2004–2005 Academic Year. Universitat Oberta de Catalunya, Spain. Available at: www.uoc.edu/inaugural04/eng/carnoy1004.pdf. Last accessed July 2010

Carrillo, P., and M. Emram. 2009. Public Information and Household Expectations in Developing Countries: Evidence from a Natural Experiment. Working paper IIEP-WP-2009-8. Institute for International Economic Policy, George Washington University. Washington, DC.

Carrillo, P., M. Onofa, and J. Ponce. 2010. Information Technology and Student's Achievement: Evidence from a Randomized Experiment in Ecuador. Unpublished document. Washington, DC: Inter-American Development Bank.

Carvajal, A., H. Monroe, C. Pattillo, and B. Wynter. 2009. "Ponzi Schemes in the Caribbean." IMF Working Paper Series WP/09/95. International Monetary Fund, Washington, DC.

CBO (U.S. Congressional Budget Office). 2008. Evidence on the Costs and Benefits of Health Information Technology. Testimony of Peter R. Orszag before the Subcommittee on Health, Committee on Ways and Means of the U.S. House of Representatives, May 2008.

CEDLAS (Centro de Estudios Distributivos Laborales y Sociales) and The World Bank. 2010. Socio-Economic Database for Latin America and the Caribbean (SEDLAC). Available at: http://sedlac.econo.unlp.edu.ar/eng/. Last accessed September 2010.

Chauvin, L. 2009. "Peru's Scavengers Turn Professional." *Time Magazine* February 10, 2009.

Chisari, O. and S. Galiani. 2010. "Climate Change: A Research Agenda for Latin America and the Caribbean." Technical Note IDB-TN-164, Inter-American Development Bank, Washington, DC.

Chong, A., and A. Micco. 2003. "The Internet and the Ability to Innovate in Latin America. *Emerging Markets Review* 4: 53–72.

Chong, A., and M. Gradstein. 2007. Inequality and Institutions. *The Review of Economics and Statistics* 89(3): 454–65.

Chong, A., V. Galdo, and M. Torero. 2009. Access to Telephone Services and Household Income in Poor Rural Areas Using a Quasi-natural Experiment for Peru. *Economica* 76(304): 623–48.

Chong, A., and E. La Ferrara. 2009. Television and Divorce: Evidence from Brazilian Novelas. *Journal of the European Economic Association* 7(2–3): 458–68.

Chong, A., de la O, A., Karlan, D. and L. Wantchekron. 2010. Information Dissemination and Local Governments' Electoral Returns: Evidence from a Field Experiment in Mexico. Forthcoming working paper, Yale University. New Haven, CT.

Chong, A., E. Field, M. Torero. 2010. Measuring the Power of Information. Unpublished document. Inter-American Development Bank, Washington, DC.

Chong, A., M. Gonzalez-Navarro, D. Karlan, and M. Valdivia. 2010. Effectiveness of Online Sexual Health Education: A Randomized Controlled Trial among Urban Public Schools in Colombia. Unpublished document. Inter-American Development Bank, Washington, DC.

Chong A., D. Karlan, J. Shapiro, and J. Zinman. 2010a. "Experiments to Improve Participation in a Recycling Program in Northern Peru," Forthcoming working paper, Yale University.

Chong A., D. Karlan, J. Shapiro, and J. Zinman. 2010b. "Information Campaign to Reduce Plastic Bags Consumption in Mexico," Forthcoming working paper, Yale University.

Chong, A., D. Karlan, and J. Zinman. 2010c. "Promoting Beneficial Consumer Behavior in Latin America." Unpublished paper. Yale University. New Haven, CN.

Chong, A., R. La Porta, F. Lopez-de-Silanes, and A. Shleifer. 2010. Government Efficiency in Its Simplest Case. Unpublished document. École des Haute Etudes Commericales du Nord (EDHEC).

Chong, A., G. Machicado, and M. Yáñez. 2010. Public Service Delivery and Information Technologies in Bolivia: Evidence from a Randomized Natural Experiment. Unpublished document. Washington, DC: Inter-American Development Bank.

Chong, A., and P. Vargas. 2010. Long-Run Exposure to Television and Homicides: Some Evidence for Brazil. Unpublished document. Washington, DC: Inter-American Development Bank.

Chong, A., and P. Yáñez-Pagans. 2010. Does Public Television Promote Better Institutions? Unpublished document. Washington, DC: Inter-American Development Bank.

Chao-hua Lou, Q. Zhao, E. Gao, and I. Shah. 2006. Can the Internet Be an Effective Way to Conduct Sex Education for Young People in China? *Journal of Adolescent Health* 39(5): 720–8.

Chaudhury, N., J. Hammer, M. Kremer, K. Muralidharan, and F. Halsey Rogers. 2006. Missing in Action: Teacher and Health Worker Absence in Developing Countries. *Journal of Economic Perspectives* 20(1): 91–116.

Chetney, R. 2003. Home Care that Doesn't Miss a Beat. *Home Healthcare Nurse* 21(10): 681–6.

Chinn, M., and R. Fairlie. 2006. The Determinants of the Global Digital Divide: A Cross-country Analysis of Computer and Internet Penetration." *Oxford Economic Papers* 59(1) 16–44.

———. 2010. ICT Use in the Developing World: An Analysis of Differences in Computer and Internet Penetration. *Review of International Economics* 18(1): 153–67.

Christensen, M., and D. Remler. 2007. Information and Communications Technology in Chronic Disease Care: Why Is Adoption So Slow and Is Slower Better? NBER Working Paper No. 13078. National Bureau of Economic Research, Cambridge, MA.

CIDE (Centro de Investigación y Desarrollo de la Educación), Invertec IGT, and Universidad Alberto Hurtado. 2004. Informe Final Evaluación en profundidad del programa Red Tecnológica Educacional – Enlaces. Santiago, Chile: Ministry of Education.

CINVESTAV (Centro de Investigación y de Estudios Avanzados del Instituto Politécnico Nacional). 2009. Evaluación Integral del Expediente Clínico Electrónico en el IMSS. Mexico City: Secretaría de Salud de México.

Claessens, S. 2006. "Access to Financial Services: A Review of the Issues and Public Policy Objectives." *World Bank Research Observer* 21(2): 207–40.

Cline R. J. W., and K. M. Haynes. 2001. Consumer Health Information Seeking on the Internet: the State of the Art. *Health Education Research*, 16(6): 671–92.

Cokkinides, V., E. Ward, A. Jemal, and M. Thun. 2005. Under-Use of Smoking Cessation Treatments: Results from the National Health Interview Survey, 2000. *American Journal of Preventive Medicine* 28(1): 119–22.

Crespi, G., C. Criscuolo, and J. Haskel. 2007. Information Technology, Organisational Change and Productivity. CEPR Discussion Paper 6105. Center for Economic Policy Research, London.

Crocco, A. G., M. Vallasis-Keever, and A. R. Jadad. 2002. Analysis of Cases of Harm Associated with Use of Health Information on the Internet. Journal of the American Medical Association 287 (21): 2869–71.

Croom K, D. Lewis, T. Marchell, M. L. Lesser, V. F. Reyna, L. Kubicki-Bedford , M. Feffer, and L. Staiano-Coico. 2009. Impact of an Online Alcohol Education Course on Behavior and Harm for Incoming First-Year College Students: Short-term Evaluation of a Randomized Trial. *Journal of American College Health* 57(4): 445–54.

Cristia, J., A. Czerwonko, and P. Garofalo. 2010. Does ICT Increase Years of Education: Evidence from Peru. OVE Working Paper 0110. Washington, DC: Office of Evaluation and Oversight (OVE), Inter-American Development Bank.

Cunningham, W., L. McGinnis, R. Verdú, C. Tesliuc, and D. Verner. 2008. *Youth at Risk in Latin America and the Caribbean: Understanding the Causes, Realizing the Potential.* The World Bank: Washington, DC.

Dahl, G., and S. Della Vigna. 2009. Does Movie Violence Increase Violent Crime? *The Quarterly Journal of Economics* 124(2): 677–734.

Dale, A., and A. Strauss. 2009. Don't Forget to Vote: Text Messages Reminders as a Mobilization Tool. *American Journal of Political Science* 53(4): 787–804.

Dammert, A., J. Galdo, and V. Galdo. 2010(a). Wiring Labor-Market Intermediation: Evidence from a Randomized Social Experiment in Peru. Unpublished document. Inter-American Development Bank, Washington, DC.

Dammert, A., J. Galdo, and V. Galdo. 2010(b). Dengue and ICT: Evidence from a Field Experiment in Peru. Unpublished document. Inter-American Development Bank, Washington, DC.

Daude, C. 2010. Innovation, Productivity and Economic Development in Latin America and the Caribbean. Working Paper 288, OECD Development Centre, Paris.

Dellavigna, S., and E. Kaplan. 2007. The Fox News Effect: Media Bias and Voting. *The Quarterly Journal of Economics* 122(3): 1187–234.

Demirgüç-Kunt, A., T. Beck, and P. Honohan. 2008. *Finance for All: Policies and Pitfalls in Expanding Access.* Washington, DC: The World Bank.

de León, O. 2009. Perspectivas de las Tecnologías de Telecomunicaciones y sus Implicancias en los Mercados y Marcos Regulatorios en los Países de América Latina y el Caribe. Santiago, Chile: ECLAC (Economic Commission for Latin America and the Caribbean). Available at: www.eclac.org/ddpe/publicaciones/xml/2/37322/W271.pdf. Last accessed August 2010.

Derraik, Jose G. B. 2002. "The Pollution of the Marine Environment by Plastic Debris: A Review." *Marine Pollution Bulletin* 44(9): 842–52.

Desai, R., and H. Kharas. 2009. "Do Philanthropic Citizens Behave Like Governments? Internet-based Platforms and the Diffusion of International Private Aid." Working Paper 12. The Brookings Institution, Washington, DC.

DiMaggio, P., and E. Hargittai. 2001. From Digital Divide to Digital Inequality: Studying Internet Usage as Penetration Increases. Working Paper 15, Center for Arts and Cultural Policy Studies, Princeton University (Summer).

DiMaggio, P., E. Hargittai, C. Celeste, and S. Shafer. 2004. Digital Inequality: From Unequal Access to Differentiated Use. In K. M. Neckerman, ed., *Social Inequality.* New York: Russell Sage Foundation, 355–400.

Di Tella, R., and E. Schargrodsky. 2009. Criminal Recidivism after Prison and Electronic Monitoring. National Bureau of Economic Research. Working Paper No. 15602.

Dongtotsang, D. T. and R. A. Sagun. 2006. *Mobile Telephony as an Enabler of Environmental Action in the Philippines.* Winnipeg, Manitoba, Canada: International Institute for Sustainable Development (IISD).

Duryea, S., and E. Schargrodsky. 2008 "Financial Services for the Poor: Welfare, Savings and Consumption." Inter-American Development Bank, Washington, DC. Available at: www.google.com/url?sa=t&source=web&cd=1&ved=0CBMQFjAA&url=http%3A%2F%2Fsiteresources.worldbank.org%2FINTFR%2FResources%2FDuryeaSchargrodsky150208.pdf&ei=4APYTPr8I4Wclgfdv-n8CA&usg=AFQjCNFrVEfd7uljg7AZ6rL-0Zj91SLsng. Last accessed May 2010.

Dynarski, M., R. et al. 2007. Effectiveness of Reading and Mathematics Software Products: Findings from the First Student Cohort. Report to Congress. Publication NCEE 2007–4005. Washington, DC: U.S. Department of Education.

Dzenowagis, J. 2005. Connecting for Health: Global Vision, Local Insight. Geneva: World Health Organization. Available at www.who.int/kms/resources/wsis_report/en/index.html. Last accessed July 26, 2010.

ECLAC (Economic Commission for Latin America and the Caribbean). 2009. Observatory for the Information Society in Latin America and the Caribbean (OSILAC) Statistics. United Nations, Santiago de Chile, Chile.

ECLAC (Economic Commission for Latin America and the Caribbean) and ICA (Instituto para la Conectividad en las Américas (ICA). 2010. OSILAC (Observatory for the Information Society in Latin America and the Caribbean). 2010. Available at: www.eclac.org/cgi-bin/getprod.asp?xml=/socinfo/noticias/paginas/6/34206/P34206.xml&xsl=/socinfo/tpl/p18f-st.xsl&base=/socinfo/tpl/top-bottom.xsl. Last accessed March and June 2010.

Ecobilan, 2004. *Évaluation des impacts environnementaux des sacs de caisse Carrefour.* (Evaluation of the Environmental Impact of Carrefour Merchandise Bags). Price-Waterhouse-Coopers/Ecobilan (EcoBalance). Available at: www.ademe.fr/ htdocs/actualite/rapport_carrefour_post revue_critique_v4.pdf. Last accessed February 2010.

Estache, A., M. Manacorda, and T. Valletti. 2002. Telecommunications Reform, Access Regulation, and Internet Adoption in Latin America. *Economia* 2(2): 204–17.

EUROSTAT (European Commission Eurostat database). 2006. Eurostat databases. Available at : http://epp.eurostat.ec.europa.eu/portal/page/portal/information_society/data/comprehensive_databases. Last accessed February 2010.

———. 2009. Available at: http://epp.eurostat.ec.europa.eu/portal/page/portal/statistics/search_database. Last accessed February 2010.

Evans, P., and T. Wurster. 1997. Strategy and the New Economics of Information. *Harvard Business Review* September–October: 71–82.

Evans, D. C., P. W. Nichol, and J. B. Perlin. 2006. Effect of the Implementation of an Enterprise-wide Electronic Health Record on Productivity in the Veterans Health Administration. *Health Economics, Policy and Law (2006)* 1(2): 163–69.

ExcelPlas Australia, Centre for Design RMIT, and Nolan ITU. 2004. "The Impacts of Degradable Plastic Bags in Australia." Final Report to the Department of the Environment and Heritage, Commonwealth Government of Australia, Canberra.

Eysenbah G., J. Powell, O. Kuss, and E. Sa. 2002. Empirical Studies Assessing the Quality of Health Information for Consumers on the World Wide Web: A Systematic Review. *Journal of the American Medical Association* 287 (20): 2691–700.

FAO (Food and Agriculture Organization). 2004. Educación para la población rural en Brasil, Chile, Colombia, Honduras, México, Paraguay y Perú. Rome: Food and Agriculture Organization.

Ferraz, C., and F. Finan. 2008. Exposing Corrupt Politicians: The Effects of Brazil's Publicly Released Audits on Electoral Outcomes. *The Quarterly Journal of Economics* 123(2): 703–45.

Fogel, J., S. M. Albert, F. Schnabel, B. A. Ditkoff, and A. I. Neugut. 2002. Internet Use and Social Support in Women with Breast Cancer. *Health Psychology* 21(4): 398–404.

Forman, C., A. Goldfarb, and S. Greenstein. 2003. How Did Location Affect Adoption of the Commercial Internet? Global Village, Urban Density, and Industry Composition. NBER Working Paper No. 9979. National Bureau of Economic Research. Cambridge, MA.

Foray, D. 2007. Enriching the Indicator Base for the Economics of Knowledge. In *Science, Technology and Innovation Indicators in a Changing World, Responding to Policy Needs*. Paris: Organization for Economic Co-operation and Development.

Fox, Susannah. 2007. E-patients with a Disability or Chronic Disease. Washington, DC: Pew Internet and American Life Project. October 8, 2007. Available at: www.pewinternet.org/~/media//Files/Reports/2007/ EPatients_Chronic_Conditions_2007.pdf. Last accessed March 2010.

Fraser, H., J. Blaya, S. Choi, C. Bonilla, and D. Jazayeri. 2006. Evaluating the Impact and Costs of Deploying an Electronic Medical Record System to Support TB Treatment in Peru. AMIA Annual Symposium Proceedings 2006: 264–8 [PubMed: 17238344].

Freeman, C. 1987. *Technology Policy and Economic Performance: Lessons from Japan*. London: Pinter.

Gaible, E. 2008. Survey of ICT and Education in the Caribbean: A Summary Report, Based on 16 Country Surveys. Washington, DC: infoDev/World Bank. Available at: www.infodev.org/en/Publication.441.html. Last accessed March 2010.

Galanter, M., and H. D. Kleber. 2008. *The American Psychiatric Publishing Textbook of Substance Abuse Treatment 4th Edition*. American Psychiatric Publishing.

Galiani, S., and L. Jaitman. 2010. Traceability Applied to SMEs in Argentina. A Case Study. Unpublished document. Inter-American Development Bank, Washington, DC.

Gattig, A., and L. Hendrickx. 2007. "Judgmental Discounting and Environmental Risk Perception: Dimensional Similarities, Domain Differences, and Implications of Sustainability." *Journal of Social Issues* 63(1): 21–39.

Geller, E. S. 1981. "Evaluating Energy Conservation Programs: Is Verbal Report Enough?" *The Journal of Consumer Research* 8(3): 331–5.

Gentzkow, M. 2006. Televisionand Voter Turnout. *The Quarterly Journal of Economics* 121(3): 931–72.

Gerber, A., D. Karlan, and D. Bergan. 2009. Does The Media Matter? A Field Experiment Measuring the Effect of Newspapers on Voting Behavior and Political Opinions. *American Economic Journal: Applied Economics* 1(2): 35–52.

Gerber, T., K. Brown, and A. Pablos-Méndez. 2010. An Agenda for Action on Global e-Health. *Health Affairs* 29(2): 235–38.

GeSI (Global e-Sustainability Initiative, Climate Group). 2008. *SMART 2020: Enabling the Low-carbon Economy in the Information Age*. London: Creative Commons.

Gine, X., D. Karlan and J. Zinman. 2008. "Put Your Money Where Your Butt Is: A Commitment Savings Account for Smoking Cessation" (December). Available at http://karlan.yale.edu/p/CARES_dec08.pdf. February 2010.

Giné, X., D. Karlan, and J. Zinman. 2010. "Put Your Money Where Your Butt Is: A Commitment Contract for Smoking Cessation." World Bank Policy Research Working Paper No. 4985. The World Bank, Washington, DC

Giridharadas, A. 2010. Where a Cellphone Is Still Cutting Edge. *The New York Times*, April 11, page *WK4*.

Glewwe, M. and M. Kremer. 2006. Schools, Teachers, and Education Outcomes in Developing Countries. In: Handbook of the Economics of Education, Vol. 2, E. Hanushek and F. Welch, eds, chap. 16, 945–1017. Amsterdam: Elsevier.

Gonçalves, S. 2009. Does Exposing Corruption on the Internet Affect Electoral Performance? Chapter 3, Ph. D. Thesis, London School of Economics and Political Science, Department of Economics. London.

González-Navarro, M. 2008. "Deterrence and Displacement in Auto Theft." Working Papers No.1098, Princeton University, Department of Economics, Center for Economic Policy Studies. Princeton, NJ.

Goolsbee, A., and P. Klenow. 1999. Evidence on Networkand Learning Externalities in the Diffusion of Home Computers. NBER Working Paper 4148, National Bureau for Economic Research, Cambridge, MA.

Goolsbee, A. and J. Guryan. 2006. The Impact of Internet Subsidies in Public Schools. *The Review of Economics and Statistics* 88(2): 336–47.

Gordon, R. 2000. Does the New Economy Measure up to the Great Inventions of the Past? *The Journal of Economic Perspectives* 14(4): 49–74.

———. 2003. High-Tech Innovation and Productivity Growth: Does Supply Create Its Own Demand? NBER Working Paper No 9437. National Bureau for Economic Research, Cambridge, MA.

Goyal, A. 2010. Information, Direct Access to Farmers, and Rural Market Performance in Central India. *American Economic Journal: Applied Economics* 2(3): 25–45.

Grazzi M. and Vergara S. (forthcoming) "Determinants of ICT Access" in Balboni, M., Rovira S. and Vergara S. eds. "On the Different Dimensions of ICT in Latin America. Exploring the Benefits and Constraints of Microdata Analysis," ECLAC-IDRC, Santiago de Chile.

Green, A., and D. Gerber. 2000. The Effects of Canvassing, Telephone Calls, and Direct Mail on Voter Turnout: A Field Experiment. *The American Political Science Review* 94(3): 653–63.

———. 2008. *Get Out the Vote: How to Increase Voter Turnout*. Washington, DC: Brookings Institution Press (second edition).

Grigsby, J., and J. Sanders. 1998. Telemedicine: Where It Is and Where It Is Going. *Annals of Internal Medicine* 129(2): 123–7.

Gullison, R., et al. 2007. "Tropical Forests and Climate Policy." *Science* 316(5827): 985–6.

Gustafson, D., et al. 1999. Impact of a Patient-centered, Computer-based Health Information/Support System. *American Journal of Preventive Medicine* 16(1): 1–9.

Ha, S., and D. Karlan. 2009. Get-Out-the-Vote Phone Calls: Does Quality Matter? *American Politics Research* 37(2): 353–69.

Hall, B. 2006. Innovation and Diffusion. In: J. Fagerberg, D. Mowery, and R. Nelson, eds., *The Oxford Handbook of Innovation*. Oxford, England: Oxford University Press.

Harno, K., R. Kauppinen-Mäkelin, and J. Syrjäläinen. 2006. Managing Diabetes Care Using an Integrated Regional e-health Approach. *Journal of Telemedicine and Telecare* 2006 12 (Suppl 1): 13–15.

Harris, R. 2004. *Information and Communication Technologies for Poverty Alleviation*. One of the e-premier series published by the United Nations Development Programme/APDIP. Available at www.apdip.net/publications/iespprimers/eprimer-pov.pdf. Last accessed August 2010.

Hastings, J., O. Mitchell, and E. Chyn. 2010. "Fees, Framing, and Financial Literacy in the Choice of Pension Manager," Pension Research Council Working Paper WP2010–09. The Wharton School, University of Pennsylvania, Philadelphia, PA.

He, F., L. Linden, and M. MacLeod. 2008. How to Teach English in India: Testing the Relative Productivity of Instruction Methods within the Pratham English Language Education Program. Unpublished document. Boston, MA: The Abdul Latif Jameel Poverty Action Lab, MIT.

Heeks, R. 2002. Information Systems and Developing Countries: Failure, Success, and Local Improvisations. *The Information Society* 18:101–12.

Henry, G. T., and C. S. Gordon. 2003. "Driving Less for Better Air: Impacts of a Public Information Campaign." *Journal of Policy Analysis and Management* 22(1): 45–63.

Hepburn, C., S. Duncan, and A. Papachristodoulou. 2010. "Behavioral Economics, Hyperbolic Discounting, and Environmental Policy." *Environmental Resource Economics* 46(2): 189–206.

Hong, Y., T. B. Patrick, and R. Gillis. 2008. *Protection of Patient's Privacy and Data Security in E-Health Services.* International Conference on BioMedical Engineering and Informatics, 2008. bmei, vol. 1, 643–47, 2008.

Houghton, J. 2009. "ICT and the Environment in Developing Countries: Opportunities and Developments." In: *ICTs for Development. Improving Policy Coherence*, OECD and InfoDEV/World Bank, Washington, DC.

Hsieh, C., D. Ortega, E. Miguel, and F. Rodríguez. 2010. The Price of Political Opposition: Evidence from Venezuela's Maisanta. Working Paper No. 14923. National Bureau of Economic Research

Hughes, S. 2010. "The Latin American News Media and the Policymaking Process." In: Scartascini, C., Stein, E. and M. Tommasi, eds. *How Democracy Works: Political Institutions, Actors, and Arenas in Latin American Policymaking.* Inter-American Development Bank, Washington, DC. and David Rockefeller Center for Latin American Studies, Harvard University, Cambridge, MA.

Humpage, S. 2010a. Information and Communications Technology in Health: Focus on Latin America and the Caribbean. Unpublished document. Inter-American Development Bank.

Humpage, S. 2010b. Benefits and Costs of Electronic Medical Records: The Experience of Mexico's Social Security Institute. Technical Note No. IDB-TN-122. Inter-American Development Bank, Washington, DC.

ICT in Latin America. "Exploring the Benefits and Constraints of Microdata Analysis," ECLAC-IDRC, Santiago de Chile.

IANGV (International Association for Natural Gas Vehicles). 2009. *Natural Gas Vehicle Statistics.* International Association for Natural Gas Vehicles, Dataset available at: www.iangv.org. Last accessed July 2010.

INE (Instituto Nacional de Estadística). 2006. Encuesta Nacional de Demografía y Salud (ENDESA) 2005–2006. Available at http://www.measuredhs.com/pubs/pdf/FR189/FR189.pdf. Last accessed July 2010.

Inma, G. 2010. "Ciudad de México y la Cruzada contra las bolsas de plástico." BBC Mundo. México, August 18, 2010.

INDEC (Instituto Nacional de Estadistica y Censos) and SECYT (Secretaria de Ciencia y Técnica) 2006. Argentina. Encuesta Nacional a Empresas sobre Innovacion, I+D y TICs [2002–2004]: Analisis de sus Resultados. Buenos Aires, Argentina.

IOM (Institute of Medicine). 1996. *The Nation's Physician Workforce: Options for Balancing Supply and Requirements.* Washington, DC: National Academy Press.

ITU (International Telecommunication Union. 2010). *ICT Indicators Database*. Available at: www.itu.int/ITUD/ict/publications/world/world.html. Last accessed August 2010. Geneva: International Telecommunications Union.

———. 1998. World Telecommunication Development Report: Universal Access. Geneva: International Telecommunications Union.

ITU (International Telecommunications Union). 2006. *World Telecommunication/ ICT Development Report 2006. Measuring ICT for Social and Economic Development*. Geneva: International Telecommunications Union.

———. 2009. "ITU Background Report: Symposium on ICTs and Climate Change." Report prepared for Symposium on ICTs and Climate Change, Quito, Ecuador, July 8–10, International Telecommunication Union.

———. 2009a. *Measuring the Information Society, The ICT Development Index*. Geneva: International Telecommunications Union.

———. 2009b. World Telecommunication/ICT Indicators Database. Geneva: International Telecommunication Union.

———. 2009c. Information and Communication Technology Statistics Online. Available at: www.itu.int/ITU-D/ICTEYE/Indicators/Indicators.aspx#. Last accessed May 2010.

———. 2010a. *Measuring the Information Society*. Geneva: International Telecommunications Union.

Ivatury, G., and I. Mas. 2008. "The Early Experience with Branchless Banking." Focus Note No. 46. Consultative Group to Assist the Poor (CGAP), Washington, DC.

Ivatury, G. and M. Pickens. 2006. *Mobile Phone Banking and Low-income Customers. Evidence from South Africa*. Consultative Group to Assist the Poor (CGAP)/The World Bank and United Nations, Washington, DC.

Jack, W., and T. Suri. 2010. "Mobile Money: The Economics of M-PESA." Available at: www.google.com/url?sa=t&source=web&cd=1&ved=0CBc QFjAA&url=http%3A%2F%2Fwww.mit.edu%2F~tavneet%2FM-PESA. pdf&ei=ig3YTPrhOYSdlgeA_uj8CA&usg=AFQjCNEY6QL9pm4UijtCf5R I6BhgEgPxEw. Last accessed August 2010.

Jann, B. 2008. "A Stata Implementation of the Blinder-Oaxaca Decomposition. ETH Zurich Sociology Working Paper 5. Swiss Federal Institute of Technology, Zurich.

Jara Valdivia, I. 2008. Las Políticas de Tecnología para Escuelas en América Latina y el Mundo: Visiones y Lecciones. Santiago, Chile: ECLAC

(Economic Commission for Latin America and the Caribbean). Available at: www.eclac.org/ddpe/publicaciones/xml/8/34938/W214.pdf. Last accessed August 2010.

Jegers, M., K. Kesteloot, D. De Graeve, and W. Gilles. 2002. A Typology for Provider Payment Systems in Health Care. *Health Policy* 60(3): 255–73.

Jensen, R. 2007. The Digital Provide: Information (Technology), Market Performance, and Welfare in the South Indian Fisheries Sector. *The Quarterly Journal of Economics* 112(3): 879–924.

Jensen, R., and E. Oster. 2009. The Power of TV: Cable Television and Women's Status in India. *The Quarterly Journal of Economics* 124(3): 1057–94.

Jerant, A., A. Rahman, and N. S. Thomas. 2001. Reducing the Cost of Frequent Hospital Admissions for Congestive Heart Failure: A Randomized Trial of a Home Telecare Intervention. *Medical Care* 39(11): 1234–45.

Joo, N., and B. Kim. 2007. Mobile Phone Short Message Service for Behavior Modification in a Community-based Weight Control Program in Korea. *Journal of Telemedicine and Telecare* 13(8): 416–20.

Jorgenson, D. W., 2001. Information Technology and the U.S. Economy. *American Economic Review* 91(1):,1–32.

Jorgenson, D. W., and K. Vu. 2005. Information Technology and the World Economy. *Scandinavian Journal of Economics* 107(4): 631–50.

Kahn, J. G., J. Yang, and J. S. Kahn. 2010. "Mobile" Health Needs and Opportunities in Developing Countries. *Health Affairs* 29(2): 252–58.

Kaplan, W. A. 2006. Can the Ubiquitous Power of Mobile Phones Be Used to Improve Health Outcomes in Developing Countries? *Globalization and Health 2006* 2(9).

Karlan, D., M. McConnell, S. Mullainathan, and J. Zinman. 2010. "Getting to the Top of the Mind: How Reminders Increase Savings." Unpublished document. Yale University, New Haven, CT.

Karlan D. and J. Zinman. 2010. Internet-based Commitment Contracts for the Environment in Latin America. Forthcoming Working Paper. New Haven, CT: Innovations for Poverty Action.

Kazdin, A. E. 2009. "Psychological Science's Contributions to a Sustainable Environment: Extending Our Reach to a Grand Challenge of Society." *American Psychologist* 64(5): 339–56.

Kenny, Charles. 2006. *Overselling the Web? Development and the Internet.* Boulder, CO: Lynne Rienner Publishers.

Kinsella, W. P. 1982. *Shoeless Joe*. New York: Houghton Mifflin.

Kirby, D., 2001. *Emerging Answers: Research Findings on Programs to Reduce Teen Pregnancy*. National Campaign to Prevent Teen Pregnancy, Washington, DC.

Kirby, D., B. Laris, and L. Rolleri. 2006. Sex and HIV Education Programs for Youth: Their Impact and Important Characteristics. *Journal of Adolescent Health* 40(3): 206–17.

Klonner, S., and P. Nolen. 2010. Does ICT Benefit the Poor? Evidence from South Africa. Proceedings of the German Development Economics Conference. Hannover, Germany. June 18–19, 2010.

Koshy, E., J. Car, and A. Majeed. 2008. Effectiveness of Mobile-Phone Short Message Service (SMS) Reminders for Ophthalmology Outpatient Appointments: Observational Study. *BMC Ophthalmology 2008* 8(9): 1471–2415.

Kumar, A., A. Nair, A. Parsons, and E. Urdapilleta. 2006. "Expanding Bank Outreach through Retail Partnerships: Correspondent Banking in Brazil." World Bank Working Paper 85. World Bank, Washington, DC.

Labelle, R., R. Rodschat, and T. Vetter. 2008. ICTs for e-Environment: Guidelines for Developing Countries with a Focus on Climate Change. International Telecommunication Union (ITU), Geneva.

La Ferrara, E., A. Chong A, and S. Duryea. 2008. "Soap Operas and Fertility: Evidence from Brazil." Working paper WP-633. Washington, DC.

Lasida, J., C. Peirano, and E. Severín. 2009. Antecedentes e Indicadores del Plan Ceibal. Unpublished document. Washington, DC: Education Unit of the Social Sector Department, Inter-American Development Bank.

Leff, N. H. 1984. Externalities, Information Costs, and Social Benefit-Cost Analysis for Economic Development: An Example from Telecomm. *Economic Development and Cultural Change* 32(2): 255–76.

Leuven, E., M. Lindahl, H. Oosterbeek, and D. Webbink. 2004. The Effect of Extra Funding for Disadvantaged Pupils on Achievement. IZA Discussion Papers Series 1122. Bonn, Germany: IZA.

Li, S., M. Lipscomb, and A. M. Mobarak. 2010. "Does the Expansion of ICT Carry an Environmental Cost? Evidence from Brazil." Forthcoming working paper, Yale University.

Lin, S., and C. Hsieh. 1997. Health Information and the Demand for Preventive Health Care among Elderly in Taiwan. *Journal of Human Resources* 32(2): 303–33.

Linden, L. 2008. Complement or Substitute? The Effect of Technology on Student Achievement in India. Unpublished document. New York, NY: Columbia University.

LLECE (Laboratorio Latinoamericano de Evaluación de la Calidad de la Educación). 2008. SERCE: Segundo Estudio Regional Comparativo y Explicativo. Santiago, Chile: Regional Education Office, UNESCO.

Lopez-Boo, F., and M. Blanco. 2010. ICT Skills and Employment: a Randomized Experiment. Unpublished document. Inter-American Development Bank, Washington, DC.

Machin, S., S. McNally, and O. Silvatitle. 2007. New Technology in Schools: Is There a Payoff? The Economic Journal 117(522): 1145–67.

Madden, G, G. Coble-Neal, and S. Savage. 2004. United States Internet Penetration. Applied Economics Letter 11: 529–32.

Madden, P., and I. Weissbrod. 2008. Connected: ICT and Sustainable Development. London: Forum for the Future: Action for Sustainable World.

Malamud, O., and C. Pop-Eleches. 2010. Home Computer Use and the Development of Human Capital. Working Paper 15814. Cambridge, MA: National Bureau of Economic Research.

Marsch, L. A., W. K. Bickel, and G. J. Badger. 2007. Applying Computer Technology to Substance Abuse Prevention Science: Results of a Preliminary Examination. Journal of Child and Adolescent Substance Abuse 16(2): 69–94.

Martínez, A., V. Villarroel, J. Puig-Junoy, J. Seoane, and F. del Pozo. 2007. An Economic Analysis of the EHAS Telemedicine System in Alto Amazonas. Journal of Telemedicine and Telecare 13(1): 7–14.

Mas, I. 2008a. "Being Able to Make (Small) Deposits and Payments, Anywhere." Focus Note No. 45. Consultative Group to Assist the Poor (CGAP), Washington, DC: CGAP.

———. 2008b. "An Analysis of Peru's 'Cajeros Corresponsales.'" Focus Note No. 46. Consultative Group to Assist the Poor (CGAP), Washington, DC: CGAP.

Meigs, J. B., et al. 2003. A Controlled Trial of Web-Based Diabetes Disease Management. The MGH Diabetes Primary Care Improvement Project. Diabetes Care 26(3): 750–57.

Microsoft. 2009. National Police Force Improves Efficiency, Cuts Costs with Unified Communications. Microsoft Office System, Customer Solution Case

Study. Available at: www.microsoft.com/casestudies/ServeFileResource. aspx?4000012870. Last accessed August 2010.

(MINEC) Ministerio de Educación y Cultura: República Oriental de Uruguay, Instituto Nacional de Estadística (INE) y Dirección de Innovación, Ciencia y Tecnología para Desarrollo (DICyT) y Programa de Desarrollo Tecnológico (PDT), 2006. La Innovación en la Industria Uruguaya. 2001–3. Montevideo, Uruguay.

Ministerio de Economía, Chile. 2006. Acceso y Uso de Tecnologías de Información y Comunicación en las Empresas Chilenas. Santiago de Chile, Chile.

Ministry of Communications, International Communication Unit, Republic of Colombia. 2004. Compratel Programme of Social Telecommunications: Case Study. Bogota, Colombia.

Ministry of Communications, Republic of Colombia. 2007. Resumen de la evaluación del impacto y análisis de viabilidad de los programas Compartel – Internet Social. Bogota, Colombia.

Mitra, S. 2003. Minimally Invasive Education: A Progress Report on the "Hole-in-the-Wall" Experiments. *British Journal of Educational Technology* 34(3): 367–71.

Morandé, F. 2010. "Resultados Mesa de Trabajo Comunicaciones para Emergencias." Presentation by the Chilean Ministry of Transport and Telecommunications, Santiago, Chile.

Morawczynski, O., and M. Pickens. 2009. "Poor People Using Mobile Financial Services: Observations on Customer Usage and Impact from M-PESA." Brief. Consultative Group to Assist the Poor (CGAP)/The World Bank, Washington, DC: CGAP.

Mortensen, D. 1986. Job Search and Labor Market Analysis. In O. Ashenfelter and R. Layard, eds., *Handbook of Labor Economics*, Vol. 2. Amsterdam: North-Holland.

Multilateral Investment Fund. 2010. Conectando a mi País: A Low-Cost Connectivity Project in Marginalized Neighborhoods of the Metropolitan Region in Chile. Funding proposal. Inter-American Development Bank, Washington, DC.

Mungai, W. 2005. "Using ICTs for Poverty Reduction and Environmental Protection in Kenya: The 'M-vironment' Approach." In: Willard, T., and M. Andjelkovic eds. *A Developing Connection: Bridging the Policy Gap between the Information Society and Sustainable Development.* Winnipeg,

Manitoba, Canada. International Institute for Sustainable Development (IISD).

Murray C. J., and A. D. López, eds. 1996. *The Global Burden of Disease: A Comprehensive Assessment of Mortality and Disability from Disease, Injuries and Risk Factors in 1990 and Projected to 2020*. Cambridge, MA: Harvard School of Health.

Muto, M. and T. Yamano. 2009. The Impact of Mobile Phone Coverage Expansion on Market Participation: Panel Data Evidence from Uganda. *World Development* 37(12): 1887–96.

Nickerson, D. 2007. Does E-mail Boost Turnout? *Quarterly Journal of Political Science* 2(4): 369–79.

Nolan ITU, Centre for Design RMIT, and Eunomia Research and Consulting Ltd. 2002. Plastic Shopping Bags—Analysis of Levies and Environmental Impacts. Report submitted to the Department of the Environment and Heritage, Commonwealth Government of Australia, Canberra.

Oaxaca, R. 1973. Male-Female Wage Differentials in Urban Labor Markets. *International Economic Review* 14(3): 693–709.

Ocampo, J. A., and J. Martin, editors. 2003. *Globalization and Development: A Latin American and Caribbean Perspective*. Palo Alto, California: Stanford University Press and United Nations Economic Commission for Latin America and the Caribbean.

O'Donoghue, T., and M. Rabin. 2001. "Choice and Procrastination." *The Quarterly Journal of Economics* 116(1): 121–60.

OECD (Organization for Economic Co-operation and Development). 2001. *Understanding the Digital Divide*. Paris: Organization for Economic Co-operation and Development.

———. *OECD e-Government Studies: Mexico*. Paris: OECD Publishing. doi: 10.1787/9789264010727-en. August, 2010

———. 2006. Programme for International Student Assessment (PISA) Database. Paris: OECD. Available at: http://pisa2006.acer.edu.au/. Last accessed June 2010.

———. 2007. Statistical Glossary of Terms. Available at: http://stats.oecd.org/glossary/detail.asp?ID=6805. Last accessed August, 2010.

———. 2009. Guide to Measure the Information Society. Paris: OECD. Available at: www.oecd.org/dataoecd/25/52/43281062.pdf. Last accessed May 2010.

Oliner, S. D., and D. Sichel. 1994. Computers and Output Growth: How Big Is the Puzzle? *Brookings Papers in Economic Activity* 25(2): 273–334.

———. 2002. Information Technology and Productivity: Where Are We Now and Where Are We Going? *Federal Reserve Bank of Atlanta Review* 87(3): 15–44.

OLPC (One Laptop Per Child) Deployment Workbook. 2010. Available at: http://wiki.laptop.org/go/Deployment_Guide/Workbook. Last accessed August 2010.

Orleans, C. T. 2007. Increasing the Demand for and Use of Effective Smoking Cessation Treatments. *American Journal of Preventive Medicine* 33(6S): S340–48.

OSILAC (Observatory for the Information Society in Latin America and the Caribbean). 2010. Estadísticas e indicadores sobre TIC. Available at: http://www.eclac.org/cgi-bin/getprod.asp?xml=/socinfo/noticias/paginas/6/34206/P34206.xml&xsl=/socinfo/tpl/p18f-st.xsl&base=/socinfo/tpl/top-bottom.xsl. Last accessed March and June 2010.

Ospina, A. V., and R. Heeks. 2010. Unveiling the Links between ICTs & Climate Change in Developing Countries: A Scoping Study. Centre for Development Informatics, Institute for Development Policy and Management, University of Manchester. Available at: www.niccd.org/ScopingStudy.pdf. Last accessed May 2010.

Overå, R. 2006. Networks, Distance, and Trust: Telecommunications Development and Changing Trading Practices in Ghana. *World Development* 34(7): 1301–15.

Pagés, C., ed. 2010. *The Age of Productivity: Transforming Economies from the Bottom Up*. Inter-American Development Bank. New York: Palgrave Macmillan.

PAHO (Pan-American Health Organization). 2007. *Health in the Americas 2007.* Washington, DC: Pan-American Health Organization.

Pahwa, B., and D. Schoech. 2008. Issues in the Evaluation of an Online Prevention Exercise. *Journal of Technology in Human Services* 26(22): 259–81.

Paperny, D. M. N. 1997. Computerized Health Assessment and Education for Adolescent HIV and STD Prevention in Health Care Settings and Schools. *Health Education and Behavior* 24(1): 54–70.

Patrick, K., et al. 2009. A Text Message-based Intervention for Weight Loss: Randomized Controlled Trial. *Journal of Medical Inter Research* 11(1): e1.

Pearlstein, S. 2010. "In Studying Behavior, Scientific Testing Has Advantages—and Limits." *The Washington Post*, August 4, p A12.

Pedraza, A. and M. Montenegro. 2010. "The Impact of Mobile Phones in the Colombian Kidnapping Industry." Manuscript, Inter-American Development Bank, Washington, DC.

Peres, W., and M. Hilbert, editors. 2009. *La sociedad de la información en América Latina y el Caribe: Desarrollo de las tecnologias y tecnologias para el desarrollo.* Santiago: CEPAL.

Perlin, J. B., D. A. Collins, and L. G. Kaplowitz. 1999. State of the Art: Telemedicine. *Hospital Physician* 35(11): 26–34.

Piette, J. D., et al. 2006. Use of Telephone Care in a Cardiovascular Disease Management Programme for Type II Diabetes Patients in Santiago, Chile. *Chronic Illness* 2: 87–96.

Pineda Burgos, A., M. Aguero Rodriguez, and S. Espinoza. 2010. Impact of Information and Communication Technologies on Vegetable Farmers in Honduras. Unpublished document. Inter-American Development Bank, Washington, DC.

Pissarides, C. 2000. *Equilibrium Unemployment Theory.* Second edition. Cambridge MA: MIT Press.

Political Risk Service Group. 2005. *International Country Risk Guide.* Available at: www.prsgroup.com/ICRG.aspx. Last accessed August 2010.

Popkin, B. M. 1998. Worldwide Trends in Obesity. *Nutritional Biochemistry* 9(9):487–88.

———. 2001. The Nutrition Transition and Obesity in the Developing World. *Journal of Nutrition 2001* 131(3): 871S–73S.

Pritchett, L., M. Woolcock, and M. Andrews. 2010. Capability Traps? The Mechanisms of Persistent Implementation Failure. Unpublished manuscript.

Ramírez, J. 2006. Las Tecnologías de la Información y de la Comunicación en la Educación en Cuatro Países Latinoamericanos. *Revista Mexicana de Investigación Educativa* 11(28): 61–90.

Ravallion, M. 2008. Evaluation in the Practice of Development. Policy Research Working Paper 4547. The World Bank. Washington, DC.

Rheingold, H. 2008. Mobile Media and Political Collective Action. In J. Katz, editor. *Handbook of Mobile Communication Studies.* The MIT Press, Cambridge, MA and London, England.

Riggins, Frederick J., and S. Dewan. 2005. The Digital Divide: Current and Future Research Directions. *Journal of the Association for Information Systems* 6(12): Article 13 p. 298–336.

Roglieri, J. L., et al. 1997. Disease Management Interventions to Improve Outcomes in Congestive Heart Failure. *Journal of American Managed Care* 3(12): 1831–39.

Roller, L-H, and L. Waverman. 2001. Telecommunications Infrastructure and Economic Development. *American Economic Review* 91(4): 909–23.

Rouse, C. and A. Krueger. 2004. Putting Computerized Instruction to the Test: Randomized Evaluation of a Scientifically Based Reading Program. Economics of Education Review 23(4): 323–38.

Santiago, A., et al. 2010. Evaluación Experimental del Programa "Una Laptop por Niño" en Perú. Washington, DC: Inter-American Development Bank. Available at: www.iadb.org/document.cfm?id=35370099. Last accessed July 2010.

Sawin C. T., D. J. Walder, D. S. Bross, and L. M. Pogach. 2004. Diabetes Process and Outcome Measures in the Department of Veterans Affairs. *Diabetes Care 2004* 27(Suppl 2): b90–b94.

Scartaccini, C. 2008. The People's Choice? The Role of Opinions in the Policymaking Process. In: Inter-American Development Bank (IDB). *Beyond Facts: Understanding Quality of Life.* Cambridge, MA: Harvard University Press.

Schultz, P. W. 1998. "Changing Behavior with Normative Feedback Interventions: A Field Experiment on Curbside Recycling." *Basic and Applied Social Psychology* 21(1): 25–36.

Seira, E. 2010. "Electronic Payments of Cash Transfer Programs and Financial Inclusion." Unpublished document. Instituto Tecnológico Autonómo de México (ITAM).

Sen, A. 1981. *Poverty and Famines: An Essay on Entitlement and Deprivation.* New York: Oxford University Press.

———. 1984. Food Battles: Conflicts in the Access to Food. *Food and Nutrition* l0(1): 81–89.

Shogren, J. F., and L. O. Taylor. 2008. "On Behavioral-Environmental Economics." *Review of Environmental Economics and Policy* 2(1): 26–44.

Skinner, B. 1954. The Science of Learning and the Art of Teaching. Harvard Educational Review 24(2): 86–97.

Stead, L. F., R. Perera, C. Bullen, D. Mant, and T. Lancaster. 2008. Nicotine Replacement Therapy for Smoking Cessation. *Cochrane Database of Systematic Reviews 2008* Issue 1. No.: CD000146. DOI: 10.1002/14651858. CD000146.pub3. Last accessed July, 2010.

Stern, Paul C. 1999. "Information, Incentives, and Proenvironmental Consumer Behavior". *Journal of Consumer Policy* 22(4): 461–78.

Stoneman, P., G. Battisti, and S. Girma. 2010. Measuring Innovation as the Successful Exploitation of New Ideas: An International Firm Level Panel Data Analysis. Paper presented at the Summer Conference at Imperial College London Business School, June 16–18.

Strömberg, D. 2001. Mass Media and Public Policy. *European Economic Review* 45(4–6): 652–63.

———. 2004. Radio's Impact on Public Spending. *The Quarterly Journal of Economics* 119(1): 189–221.

Suhrcke. M., R. A. Nugent, D. Stuckler, and L. Rocco. 2006. *Chronic Disease: An Economic Perspective*. Oxford Health Alliance, London.

Sunkel, G. 2006. Las Tecnologías de la Información y la Comunicación (TIC) en la Educación en América Latina. Una Exploración de Indicadores. Serie de Políticas Sociales 126, Social Development Division. Santiago, Chile: ECLAC (Economic Commission for Latin America and the Caribbean). Available at: www.educarchile.cl/UserFiles/P0001/File/CR_Articulos/docuemnto_cepal.pdf. August 2010

Syme, G. J., B. E. Nancarrow, and C. Seligman. 2000. "The Evaluation of Information Campaigns to Promote Voluntary Household Water Conservation." *Evaluation Review* 24(6): 539–78.

Tipones, R., and L. Fernández. 2006. Predictors of Smoking Cessation 1 Year after Enrollment in a Smoking Cessation Program in a Tertiary Hospital. *Philippine Journal of Internal Medicine* 44(January–February): 7–12.

Tomasi, E, L. A. Facchini, E. Thumé, M. F. S. Maia, and A. Osorio. 2009. Information Technology for Primary Health Care in Brazil. In: Richard, Nivritti G. Patil, Richard E. Scott, and Kendall Ho, editors. *Tele-health in the Developing World* Royal Society of Medicine Press/IDRC. Available at: www.idrc.ca/en/ev-137419–201–1-DO_TOPIC.html. Last accessed May 2010.

Torero, M., and J. von Braun. 2006. Impacts of ICT on Low-Income Rural Households. In: M. Torero and J. von Braun, eds., *Information and Communication Technologies for Development and Poverty Reduction. The Potential of Telecommunications*. Baltimore, MD: The John Hopkins University Press.

Transparency International 2009. *Corruption Perceptions Survey*, Berlin: Transparency International.

Tschang, T., M. Chuladul, and T. Thu Le. 2002. Scaling-up Information Services for Development. *Journal of International Development* 14(1): 129–41.

UNCTAD (United Nations Conference on Trade and Development). 2007. Science and Technology for Development: The New Paradigm of ICT. Information Economy Report 2007–2008. United Nations, New York and Geneva.

UNEP (United Nations Environment Programme Environment for Development). 2009. "Report Brings to the Surface the Growing Problem of Marine Litter." Washington, DC, United States and Nairobi, Kenya. UNEP Press Release June 8, 2008. Available at: www.grida.no/news/press/3712. aspx. Last accessed May 2010.

———. 2010. *Global Environmental Outlook: Latin America and the Caribbean.* Panama City, Panama: United Nations Environmental Programme.

UNESCO (United Nations Educational, Scientific and Cultural Organization). 2008. A View Inside Primary Schools: A World Education Indicators (WEI) Cross-National Study. Montreal, Canada: UNESCO.

———. 2010. Institute for Statistics Database. Montreal, Canada: UNESCO. Available at: http://stats.uis.unesco.org/unesco/TableViewer/document. aspx?ReportId=143&IF_Language=eng. Last accessed August 2010.

United Nations. 2010. E-government Survey 2010: Leveraging E-government at a Time of Financial and Economic Crisis. United Nations, New York.

———. 2010. The Global Partnership for Development at a Critical Juncture. Millennium Development Goal Gap Task Force Report 2010. United Nations, New York.

Valdivia, M., D. Karlan, and A. Chong. 2010. "Evaluating the Effectiveness of Radio and Video as a Means for Financial Education among Low-income households in Peru." Unpublished document. Inter-American Development Bank. Washington, DC.

Vicente, M. R., and A. J. López. 2006. "Patterns of ICT Diffusion across the European Union" *Economics Letters* 93(1): 45–51.

Vicente, M. R., and F. Gil-de-Bernabé. 2010. Assessing the Broadband Gap: From the Penetration Divide to the Quality Divide. *Technological Forecasting & Social Change* 77(5): 816–22.

Vigdor, J. and H. Ladd. 2010. Scaling the Digital Divide: Home Computer Technology and Student Achievement. Working Paper 16078. Cambridge, MA: National Bureau of Economic Research.

Vital Wave Consulting. 2008. Affordable Computing for Schools in Developing Countries: A Total Cost of Ownership (TCO) Model for Education Officials. Available at: www.vitalwaveconsulting.com/insights/articles/affordable-computing.htm. Last accessed June 2010.

Viteri Díaz, G. 2006. Situación de la Educación en el Ecuador. Observatorio de la Economía Latinoamericana 70. Available at: www.eumed.net/cursecon/ecolat/ec/2006/gvd.htm. Last accessed June 2010.

Wang, T. H., and R. D. Katzev. 2006. "Group Commitment and Resource Conservation: Two Field Experiments on Promoting Recycling." *Journal of Applied Social Psychology* 20(4): 265–75.

Wattegama, C. 2007. *ICT for Disaster Management.* UNDP-Asia-Pacific Development Information Program e-Primer for the Information Economy, Society and Polity. Available at: www.apdip.net/ publications/iespprimers/eprimer-dm.pdf. Last accessed May 2010.

Waverman, L., M. Meschi, and M. Fuss. 2005. The Impact of Telecoms on Economic Growth in Developing Countries. In: *Africa: The Impact of Mobile Phones*, Vodafone Policy Paper Series, Number 3, March: 10–23.

WEF (World Economic Forum). 2010. World Economic Forum Global Information Technology Report (2009–2010). Available at: www3.weforum.org/docs/WEF_GITR_Report_2010.pdf. Last accessed April 2010.

Williams, M. 2004. "Think Upgrade before Buying a New PC." *Infoworld* (IDG News Service). March 7, 2004. Available at: www.infoworld.com/t/hardware/un-study-think-upgrade-buying-new-pc-601. Last accessed August 25, 2010.

Wishart, N. 2006. "Micro-Payment Systems and Their Application to Mobile Networks." Washington, DC: infoDev/World Bank. Available at: www.infodev.org/en/Publication.43.html. Last accessed April 2010.

World Bank. 1998. Latin America and the Caribbean: Education and Technology at the Crossroads. Discussion Paper 19645. Washington, DC: World Bank.

———. 2001. *Making Sustainable Commitments: An Environment Strategy for the World Bank,* Annex A-Regional Strategies, Latin America and the Caribbean. Washington, DC: World Bank.

———. 2005, World Development Report. 2006. Equity and Development. World Bank. Washington, DC. Oxford University Press.

———. 2006. Worldwide Governance Indicators. Washington, DC: World Bank.

———. 2008. LAC Electricity Benchmarking Database 1995–2005. Washington, DC: World Bank. Available at: http://info.worldbank.org/etools/lacelectricity/home.htm. Last accessed October 2010.

———. 2010. World Development Indicators. Washington, DC: World Bank. Available at: http://databank.worldbank.org/ddp/home.do?Step=12&id=4&CNO=2#. Last accessed August 2010.

———. 2010a. *World Development Indicators.* Washington, DC: World Bank. Available at: http://data.worldbank.org. Last accessed April 2010.

———. 2010b. *World Development Report 2010: Development and Climate Change.* Washington, DC: World Bank. Available at: http://econ.worldbank.org/. Last accessed March 2010.

———. 2010. *World Development Indicators Online.* http://data.worldbank.org/data-catalog/world-development-indicators. Last accessed August 2010.

———. 2010a. Enterprise Surveys (ES). Washington, DC: World Bank. Available at: www.enterprisesurveys.org/. Last accessed August 2010.

———. 2010b. World Development Indicators. Washington, DC: World Bank. Available at: http://databank.worldbank.org/ddp/home.do?Step=12&id=4&CNO=2. Last accessed August 2010.

———. 2010a. World Development Indicators. Available at: http://ddp-ext.worldbank.org/ext/DDPQQ/member.do?method=getMembers&userid=1&queryId=135. Last accessed April 2010.

———. 2010b. World Governance Indicators. Available at: http://info.worldbank.org/governance/wgi/inde2.asp. Last accessed May 2010.

———. 2010b. Enterprise Surveys (ES). Available at: www.enterprisesurveys.org/. Last accessed May 2010.

Yáñez-Pagans and Machicado Salas. 2010. "Public Service Delivery, Accountability, and Local-level Monitoring: Evidence from a Field Experiment in Bolivia." Unpublished document. Washington, DC: Inter-American Development Bank.

Yang, D. 2008. "International migration, remittances, and household investment: evidence from Philippine migrants' exchange rate shocks." *Economic Journal* 118(528): 591–630.

Yang, D., D. Aycinena, and E. C. Martinez. 2009. "The Impact of Remittance Fees on Remittance Flows: Evidence from a Field Experiment among Salvadoran Migrants." Unpublished document. University of Michigan.

Yang, D., N. Ashraf, D. Aycinena, and A. C. Martinez. 2010. "Remittances and the Problem of Control: A Field Experiment among Migrants from El Salvador." Unpublished document. University of Michigan.

Yang, D. and C. Martinez. 2005. "Remittances and Poverty in Migrants' Home Areas: Evidence from the Philippines." In: Caglar Ozden and Maurice Schiff, editors., International Migration, Remittances, and the Brain Drain, World Bank. Washington, DC.

Yang, D. and H. Choi. 2007. "Are Remittances Insurance? Evidence from Rainfall Shocks in the Philippines. *World Bank Economic Review* 21(2): 219–48.

Index

Page numbers in *italics* refer to boxes, figures, and tables.